WOMEN KEY TO SUCCESSFUL DEMOCRACY

WOMEN KEY TO SUCCESSFUL DEMOCRACY

Varalakshmi Janapathy

KALPAZ

Women Key to Successful Democracy

Rs. 750

ISBN: 978-81-7835-736-2

Published in 2009 in India by
Kalpaz Publications
C-30, Satyawati Nagar,
Delhi-110052
E-mail: kalpaz@hotmail.com
Phone : 9212729499

Laser Type Setting by: Quick Media, Delhi
Printed at : **Young Art Press,** Delhi - 92

DEDICATED TO

Dr. Sri M.S. Rajalingam Garu

A close associate of Gandhiji in Sevagram Ashram, Freedom Fighter, Former Minister of Labour in Burugula Rama Krishna Rao Ministry, present president of Association of Freedom Fighters and well known and respected figure in the political circles of Hyderabad and my well-Wisher and a close companion of my brother, Sri Madala Veerbhadra Rao, also a freedom fighter and an eminent journalist.

CONTENTS

Swatantra Bharat Panorama—Dr. (Mrs.) K. Lakshmi Raghuramaiah—Golden Jubilee of our Freedom 15.08.1997—Gandhi On Woman and Society—Freedom Struggle and its beginnings—The Flouting of the Basis of Partition—About Subhas—Freedom or Myth—Dr. Muthulaksmi Reddy—Raj Kumari Amrit Kaur—Ms. Vijayalakshmi Pandit—Ms. Kamla Devi Chattopadhyaya—Ms Hansa Mehta—Ms Dhanvanthi Rama Rau—Indira Gandhi—Ms Lata Mangeshkar—M.S. Subbulakshmi—Ms Sitara Devi—Mother Teresa – A Legand—Quotes From Mother Teresa—On a Woman she Found on a Calcutta Street—On happiness—On Forgiveness—On the Poor—On Service to God—On her Order—On the Family—On Sacrifice—A Prayer she Composed—Arundhati Roy Could Become First Indian Citizen to Win Booker—Princess of Prose Arundhati Roy—Dr. Ms. Kalpana Chawla - First Indian Woman Astronaut—Wing Commander (Mrs.) P. Bandopadhyay—Mahasweta Devi Wins Magsaysay Award—Indian Women Still Await Independence Women and Freedom Movement—World Religions and Equality - Hindu Tradition -Copenhagen – UN Forum—Newspaper Clippings Courtsey MCM Library (Post — Beijing)—Chinese Women Fall Prey to Western Ways—The Beijing Carnival—Women Divided Over 'Family Values'—Delegates differ, but not on 'Gender'—No more violence please, say women—Indians urge comprehensive Health Care for Women—NGOs Meet Closes with call for Equality—China Profits by Meet—The Chinese made the most of the Opportunity by Selling their Handicrafts, says—Tough Battle Ahead for Women—In Beijing - a Cry from the Heart—Beijing and Beyond—Beijing Meet Adopts Documents—Shyamala Shiveshwakar adds—Alternative Declaration—Differences may Weaken Beijing Document—Time to Speak out—Women's Meet Hailed.

Ph./Fax : 040-23212119

BHAVANA

JUSTICE Y. BHASKAR RAO

Former Member of
National Human Rights Commission
of India at New Delhi
Former Chief Justice of Karnataka
Chairman : Bharatiya Vidya Bhavan,
Hyderabad & Secunderabad

H.No. 5-9-22/63/3
Adarsh Nagar
Hyderabad-500 063

FOREWORD

The author is a scholar and well versed in problems relating to women. She is also an authority on questions of gender equality in various countries, being familiar with the speeches and views of eminent leaders, scholars and UN. Conventions etc. The present book is the outcome of her indepth research on emerging policies relating to national and international situations concerning women. The Indian Constitution envisages social, economic and political justice to all including women, as women representing nearly half the population of the country have been most illiterate, poor and backward. Seventy Third Constitution Amendment provides for the reservation for women from Gram Panchayat level to the Zila Parishad and the women are therefore participating in the governance of the Panchayat and effectively competing even as Chairperson of the Panchayat, Mandal Panchayat and Zila Parishad. There is considerable development and progress of women but not equally with other gender. The author correctly opined that unless equal participation is given to women in the governance and law making process by giving proper representation in legislatures and Parliament, the gender equality visioned by our constitution framers will not be achieved and full justice is not possible to them. The book is very useful for all to know the problems of women and the measures to be taken. The author further says that progress of the society cannot be achieved to meet the global competition unless gender equality is ensured in all fields.

(Justice Y. Bhaskar Rao)

PREFACE

The Indian constitutions has guaranted, in the preamble itself, "Justice", "social, economic and political, liberty of thought, expression, belief, faith and worship and also of equality of status and opportunity. Some fundamental rights also have been guaranted. Freedom of speech, protection of life and personal liberty are positive rights. Negative eights are prohibition of discrimination", on the basis of race, caste, religion, sex or denial of equal protection. Indian women are the beneficiaries of these rights in the same manner as men.

Article 14 ensures "equality before Law, and Article 15 prohibits any discrimination inter alia of sex. All these provisions ensure equal opportunity of political participation by women along with men".

Committee on the Status of Women in India revealed certain shocking data (as per 1971 census). "This was a watershed year which raised concern among lawyers, thinkers, planners regarding the servitude position of Women in India. Since then, demand for improvement and political empowerment of Women started at the global level."

Why reservation? Women were victims of age-old repression and exploitation. Reservation is a means of protecting weaker sections of society who have, for centuries, been socially, historically and politically exploited, thus giving them a chance to come on par with the stronger sections. Women come under this category, a historically victimised group. We know women are no where in the planning process even after 5 decades of democratic politics. It is also a well-known fact that power at political level only would change the status quo of any section of society.

In 1985, Rajiv Gandhi's Govt. took up women's issue on priority basis. In the sector of social welfare, a separate women's department was formed. But this had no impact of any sort. First craft of National Perspective Plan (NPP) recommended 30 per cent quote in all elective bodies — from Panchayats to Parliament. Between 1993-1996, women's organisations, began to demand for reservation in assemblies and Parliament. Demand was accepted and featured in the manifestoes of all major parties.

Janta Dal (JD)	:	"The reservation on 30% elective posts in local bodies for women has to be extended to Union and state legislatures."
Congress	:	It proposed to provide reservation for women in state assemblies and parliament.
CPI	:	Having made a beginning with Panchayats, the next step should be to reserve 1/3 seats for women.
CPI (M)	:	1/3 of the seats in legislature and Parliament be reserved for women.
BJP	:	In state assemblies and Parliament all elected Positions, 33% reservation will ensure that at the dawn of the 21st century, Indian women will have true participation.
Samata Party	:	The party will initiate legislation for the reservation of constituencies for women candidates in rotation for 1/3 of the seats in both the Lok Sabha and State Assemblies.

But against these Theoretical assurances, all major political parties are taking vogue position on the issue of caste-based and religion-based women's reservations regarding four sub-categories within women's quota—BCs, Muslims, Christians, and Sikhs. In 1996, when reservation bill was brought before the House, the first obstacle was about the fixed quota from the OBCs. The main Votaries were, Sharad Yadav, Ram Vilas Paswan, Mulayam Singh Yadav, and other OBC MPs. Main argument advanced by them was that within a blanket reservation, upper caste women would corner all the party tickets and get supremacy in the Parliament.

Both the houses witnessed clamorous scenes, cutting across party lines.

In 1997, once again the Government failed to put the bill before Parliament due to strong objections to the bill in its present form. It was deliberately attempted to keep the bill in cold storage by stating that "consensus" is needed to be evolved.

In 1998, although Bajpayee assured representatives of women's organisations that he would not only introduce the bill in the budget session but also put to vote and the Union Cabinet also approved the introduction of the bill. But it was again put under the lid on the issue that the quota should be slashed to 15% to OBC women.

The present bill is debated upon from many angles opponents state that, it requires analysis and discussion.

Senior advocate of Supreme Court, Sri Abhishek M. Singhvi says "The constitutional mandate for rotation of constituencies reserved for women is impracticable and harmful.

Madhu Kishore, Women's a activist comes out with suggestive measure. Instead of 33% rotating lottery system of reservation, we provide for 50% reservation by having double member constituencies. That is to say each constituency should be represented by 2 members thus doubling the figure of MPs will also lighten in load of work and remove possibility "Bivi-Beti" brigade.

Caste and communal card is confusing the whole issue. What is essential today is "general involvement" of women at all levels of power structure, to evolve a society, without any quota within quota for political leverage. As Brinda Karat puts it, "OBC made any demand. It is only a pretext to shelve the bill".

Abraham Lincoln's concept of democracy is ansideal one achieved in the world. Democracy falls short when women of whatever colour or ethnic group cannot vote or cast an effective Vote, cannot expect success in electing representatives of their choice or being elected to the legislative bodies and have little hope for enactment of Laws they believe are critically needed.

The integrations of women in political process at all levels of political life is essential for democratisation of politics. It is not the demand of a few when elite. It reflects the will of the people, especially women folk. For the betterment of society, reservation for women is needed, because she is the maker of the coming generation as mother and pivot in the family.

History of Freedom Movement Linked Women's Movement

Many of the aspirations of the freedom movement had to be relegated to the background, in order to meet the exigencies of practical politics. This was quota obvious in the deliberations of the Constituent. Assembly, which was inaugurated in December,

1947 and worked until the end of 1949. The new constitution was then introduced on January 26, 1950; the 20th anniversary of the resolation of the National Congress, which had first specified as an independent Republic as the aim of the freedom movement.

One subject that deeply interested Pandit Nehru, the 1st Prime Minister of India, was the reform of Hindu Law, particularly with regards to the rights of Hindu womens and he found a supporter in Dr. B.R. Ambedkar in this work.

However, Sardar Patel and others supported the conservative of position to the reform of Hindu Law and Dr. Ambedkar was finally so frustrated that he resigned for his post on 12th October, 1951, within months of the adoptions of the constitution, Dr. Ambedkar expressed his frustration by walking out of Parliament.

Nehru himself did not give up his attempt to reform Hindu society though he could not do so by means of a single reform code. A bill to codify law relating to marriage and divorce was introduced in December 1952. Nehru stated that he considered this as his greatest achievement in Indian politics. After a short spell by Sri Lal Bahadur Sastry, Indira ji came to power, as the third Prime Minister of India; she also even being a woman Prime Minister could not bring about drastic changes in Indian society.

Indira Gandhi was left with a brittle political system after the elections of 1967. She then adopted a bold and risky course of actions, which turned out to be ultimately successful and assured her of a position of unchallenged leadership. But she could not feel the necessity of an amendment to the constitution as regards rights of women. After her assassinations, no drastic action was taken.

Her Son Sri Rajiv Gandhi won the elections in 1984, by the largest mandate ever given to an Indian Prime Minister. It was during his time that the Panchayat Raj system was introduced and $33\frac{1}{3}$ of the seats were allotted to women members. This turned out to be a landmark in the history of the nation. It brought out revolutionary changes in the rural community, as well as Indian society and women could get a good opportunity to speak out boldly and preside over village matters. They became very bold and vocal and could rule the village community, though with the help of their brothers or husbands.

I wanted to study the whole issue of that women's reservation bill, not from a politician's point of view or not even a women's activist but from the point of view of an intellectual, who can look at things, not with a biased mind but very objectively and dispassionately; from the welfare point of view to the Indian society and to womens folk at large.

To quota Allama Iqbal, the eminent poet-philosopher

"Old Greece has varnished; so have Egypt and Rome
Little of their civilisations now remain
But there is something about India
which refuses to die
Though for centuries the world has been
Conspiring to wife out her every race.

To quote Pandit Nehru's daughter, Indira Gandhi "The Discovery of India" delves deep into the sources of India's national personality. The layers increased but nothing was erased or obliterated, leaving for future generations the sum total of an experience, of a civilisation which managed to survive, come winter or come rains.

"India, a bundle of contradictions held together by strong, invisible threads ... her spirit was never conquered" says Nehru. She is a myth, and an idea, a dream and a vision and yet very real, present and pervasive. From age to age, she has produced great men and women, carrying on the old tradition and yet everadopting it to changing times.

The mind-set of the people of India is also alike in spite of various castes, creeds and religions. There is no uniform civil code that applies to all sections. But people feel they are one and Indians only, though there are some upheavels and struggles now and then. Women also have come to a matured stage, to make demands for their rights and for participation in social activities. This is an appreciable phenomenon.

ACKNOWLEDGEMENTS

Because of my interest in women's issues, and the interest in studying provisions made by the Indian Constitution, I studied the Women's Reservation Bill and its contents from the beginning and followed the developments from time to time as recorded in newspapers and the reasons for the delay in passing the Bill.

I cherish with happy memories the spirit of dedication from Dr. Durga Bai Deshmukh, Smt. Lakshmi Menon, who were responsible in inculclating in me, a sense of allegiance towards women's problems and putting them on paper after serious study.

Several articles published in Roshni by eminent people a Magazine published by the All India Women's Conference, I could include in their original form and heartly thank the president, AIWC and Asstt. librarian Mrs. Saroj Chabra for having given me their fullest cooperation. I hereby acknowledge Kalpaz Publication, for having completed publication of this book within a short time, with a good get-up and cover page.

I also acknowledge with thanks several organisations, individuals and politicians who were helpful to me in this effort. When I offered to dedicate the book to Sri M.S. Rajalingams Garu a veteran freedom fighter, a former minister and the Chairman of the Freedom Fighters Association, Hyderabad and a close associate of my father, also a freedom fighter he readily accepted and gave me his encouragement in my efforts to write this book.

INTRODUCTION

Women have established themselves as actors in the movement of humanity for peace and solidarity.

At its founding 50 years ago, United Nations held the promise of securing justice, human rights, social progress and maintaining international peace and security.

Growing confidence of women in their abilities is evident in the successful functioning of self-help groups (SHGs). To build this determination into an organized strategy women would have to come forward to build coaliations with other issues and construct strategic alliances.

Governments have to come forward to give them opportunities for equal participation in all endeavours of humanity to develop.

In addition to our aims and ideals, we have to work harmoniously for development of women through trust, love and in a sense of oneness. Now, I would like to quote a few lines of Dr. S. Radhakrishnan, our philosopher and multifaceted personality and our ambassador in Russia and our President "Women arc human beings and have as much right to full development as men have. In regard to opportunities, for intellectual and spiritual development, we should not emphasise, sex of men. The fact that we are human beings, is infinitely more important, than the psychological peculiarities which distinguish us from one another. Men and women are born equally free and independent members of the human race, equally endowed with intelligence and ability and equally entitled to the free exercise of their individual rights and liberty."

So, Government of India's decision to formulate a national policy is most welcome and the Reservation Bill is something which the women's organisations have been demanding from several years.

In the words of UN Secretary–General Boutras, Boutras-Ghali, in his concluding message to the 4th women's conference (1995), "The movement for Gender equality the world over has been one of the defining developments of our time. I am proud and honoured that the United Nations has been part of this movement", says.

I wish and hope that this booklet would be helpful to the Government and International organisations, women friendly technical know-how and training for developing income generation and gives information relating to all the fields concerning NGOs, especially women.

It is important to see woman as the equal of man, and as deserving of respect and dignity. This is a concept which we have to recognise and share among ourselves and also men. It is a well-known fact that women in our society still continue to be socially excluded from mainstream. As we move into a new millennium, we have to work for women's empowerment.

In poverty alleviation programmes, there are special reservations for women extending upto 40 percent in schemes like the massive Integrated Rural Development Programme.

Rapid economic growth without economic empowerment only leads to negative effects. Our basic governing block of our political and economic system is the panchayat. Government has amended the constitution to ensure that 1/3 of all seats are reserved for women. This constitutional amendment has enabled one million women to occupy elected positions of decision-making at the grass root level.

Violence against Women

Women in India are experiencing enormous unacceptable levels of violence in the family, within the community, work place, public places and custodial institutions. Govternment must take a serious view of all human rights violations against, Dalit, minority, and tribal women and stringent action must be taken.

Landownership, Housing and Settlements

Women in flagile economic zones, displaced and refugee women, tribal and Dalit women and those living in shum areas are worst effected.

So, it is mandatory that the state plays a supportive role in helping women as they are the real victims.

Employment

Productive role of women in building up the national economy is not recognised and under remunerated. They also suffer from underemployment. Today 90% of the women work in the informal sector as cultivators, agriculture labourers, hawkers, domestic servants and in some home-based industries.

Political Participation

Women are under represented in all policy making bodies throughout the country. So, the state must ensure that women are provided with proper environment for political participation of women in all bodies, with child care and supportive services. Accordingly, women should be trained for their effective participation in politics.

Challenges of Feminism

We know that tradition, culture and family have great influence on women.

Women have their own sense of responsibility and can run the homes with maximum care and efficiency. Modern woman is still more careful in playing her role in discharge of her duties, her career and home.

Asian women have gone to Nairodbi seeking an understanding of political solutions. Religious identity and conservation are two factors that confront progress. Cynicism as regards-politics and political considerations and policies also add to the age-old tendencies.

The word 'woman' is replaced by 'gender'. World agencies like World Bank etc. have coopted 'gender'.

Can women achieve ? Can they communicate? It is an important dream for women from ideological perspective. But what about constraints and lack of facilities?

Gender discrimination down the centuries has kept the women folk a backward social force and so, representative mechanisms like representation of women in legislative bodies like the Parliament and the Assemblies are worked out. Introduction of the Womens Reservation Bill in Parliament created much heat and dust. But, the very fact that the bill has been introduced is itself an indication of success and we must proudly say that women's organisations have achieved a great deal in a patriarchal country like India.

In the early days of our freedom struggle, we don't find women working along with Gokhale, Tilak, Surendranath Baneree. Only Annie Besant, a foreigner could play a political role. Visible role of women started with Sarojini Naidu in a later stage i.e. the Gandhian era.

In the post-Independent India, emergence of Indira Gandhi as the Prime Minister of India, and some Chief Ministers like Mrs. Nandini Satpathi; Ms Jayalalitha, Mrs. Sushma Swaraj, and Mrs Shiela Dixit, and a host of other political leaders can be traced. It is because of their education and family background. An unlettered Rabri Devi also emerged as Chief

Minister of Bihar on account of some political reasons and family background. Only two important exceptions are Mamata Banerjee and Mayavati. They become leaders, perhaps by their struggle and determination.

Anyway, we can summarise that our civil society came to a level of maturity to recognise women as capable leaders and personalities to handle responsible positions and institutions. This is a happy trend.

Our planners, politicians and functionaries also have realised the importance of the fifty per cent women's participation in the development of the country. So, the need for reservation of women arose and the government also have taken steps to introduce the 108th Constitution Amendment Bill. Agitation by women's activists and women's organisations also was responsible to a great extent for bringing out this change.

1

GENDER EQUALITY STILL A DISTANT DREAM

The survey, published by the Geneva-based World Economic Forum–shows that full economic and political empowerment remains a distant dream for millions of women in much of the western world, leaving apart the developing countries. Of the 58 countries covered by the survey, only a handful of European nations seem to have real progress in lowering the glass ceiling.

The report says "no country has yet managed to eliminate the gender gap" but the Nordic states–Sweden, Norway, Iceland, Denmark and Finland have "succeeded best" in narrowing it.

They are seen to provide a "workable model" for the rest of the world to follow. Other "female friendly" countries include Britain, Germany, New Zealand, Australia and significantly, several East European countries where women benefit from the support system built during the Communist era.

USA—Poor Record

America, with its restrictive maternity rights and poor state child welfare system, does not even figure in the Top 10, woman-friendly countries. Even Britain fares badly in a range of areas, lagging behind even India, in terms of economic opportunity.

The most glaring gender inequality in Britain relates to wages where women still earn less than men for the same work — and this despite an Equal Pay Act passed 30 years ago. This is confirmed by official figures.

How does India rank in the WEF survey? Despite scoring high in economic opportunity, India is at the bottom of the heap by most criteria – above only Pakistan, Korea, Jordon, Turkey and Egypt.

India is placed at the 53rd position—embarrassingly behind economically less developed countries such a Bangla- desh and a host of Latin American and African Nations which have done much better in narrowing the gender gap.

"The Indian rhetoric is clearly not matched by the achievement on the ground" commented an Indian women rights activist.

Although WEF chief economist **Ango Lopez-claros** has said, the survey is "not intended as a tool for embarrassing nations but as a bench mark for improvement." It has already provoked calls for a review of strategies to close gender gap.

Cherri Blair, wife of the British Prime Minister, Tony Blair, has expressed concern over the continuing inequalities faced by women and called for positive discrimination.

She further said "she supported unequivocally" quotas for women in parliamentary elections as a means of political empowerment.

Saadia Zahidi, a co-author of WEF survey says there is a link between how a country treated its women and that country's ability to compete globally. The report underlines the "clear economic incentive" behind empowering women. "Countries that do not fully take advantage of one half of the talent in their population are misallocating their human resources and undermining their competitive potential" she said in an interview to mark the launch of the report.

Its findings are based on "hard data" from leading International organisations and the countries have been ranked on the basis of five main criteria laid down by the United Nations Development Fund for Women (UNIFEM)—economic participation, economic opportunity, political empowerment, educational, attainment and health and well-being.

"Measuring the magnitude of the problem is a first step—we hope that governments and NGOs alike can use the ranking in our study to identify issue–areas and to learn from the experiences of nations that have been more successful in narrowing the gender-gap" Ms Zahidi said.

The WEF stressed that inproving educational prospects for women should be the main priority for countries around the world, especially in developing countries.

This is the first time the WEF has attempted such a survey and commentators said, it reflected a recognition by the International business community that women's status was an area of critical importance for development.

2

WOMEN'S EMPOWERMENT IN THE TRUE SENSE

We have reached some crucial crossroads in the long history of humanity. These were many transisitions in the past, such as Journey from caves to forest, and then to agricultural, the-industrial, industrial post-industrial civilisations. We are now involved in the most crucial and difficult of all transitions, the transition to a global society. Under the influence of the development of science and technology, all aspects of life are undergoing a process of globalisation.

A new consciousness that would enlighten every individual is emerging and is transforming tremendously the human soul and dignity.

Today, we are in a new-era-the information era. Indian society, once a feudal and traditional society is changing into a modern society, in changing access to media and education.

Of course, it is not an easyjob to bring about social development in a traditional society because of the strong relationship between economic, cultural and several of the social aspects.

Several conflicts and tensions are evident between various sections of society, on the basis of religion, region or caste and also gender and social stigmas and sentiments.

Worst victims are women, because of the socially contructed power relationships between men and women, in which women occupy a subordinate position.

Of course, planners policy makers, scholars have started thinking for new strategies, new development concepts and models.

We need to evolve an agenda, which will address not only gender-based subordination but also the relationship of people to natural resources and issues of sustainable future. So, we have to think and rethink about our strategies; we must have a vision, a clear vision. For achieving the vision, we must find out ways and means to bring about an ethos and thrust that will enable women to come out of their isolation and subjugation. For that, we have to chalk out a time-bound action plan to enable women to play an active role.

What is Empowerment ?

Creating confidence among women and bringing awareness to fight for their rights is empowerment.

Of course 73rd amendment to our Constitution has succeeded in drawing women out of their hearths and making them join the mainstream of village life. A Berth in the Panchayat Raj system for women, has, no doubt empowered women to a great extent.

Purdah is lifted in villages and this is a manifestation of empowerment of women. Women are walking with their heads held high and are able to interact with men of their village and others and their self-confidence has increased. This journey from "chulha to chaupal"—from the kitchen to panchayat—is a major achievement.

Contrary to popular notion, that it was the family which prevented a woman from shedding the traditional mould, a survey conducted by PRIA- a voluntary organisation, showed that 95 of the politically empowered women enjoyed the support of the family. So, it is the society that is not encouraging.

Actual participation of women in decision-making process is needed and this can be made possible only by reservation of seats to Women in Indian Parliament as well as in State Assemblies. Of course, a sizable number of women are illiterate. But leadership needs some skills other than literacy. With firm resolve and integrity, all the hurdles posed by illiteracy, can be over come.

Development for Whom and for What?

Benefits of our planned development over the past years have gone to those who are well off. Even the projects meant for the deprived sections of our society, have not benefited them in India.

4th world conference on women in Beijing, for the first time, identified the legal rights of a girl child as follows:

- The right to life
- The right to health and food
- The right to education

All these basic rights are denied or ignored in every country in the world.

During the last seven years of this century, it has been established that the number of children aged 6 to 11, who are not attending any school, will rise from 129 to 144 millions. Female illiteracy will worsen in southern Asia and the African countries. When we examine female literacy rate from 1961-81, the situation is very alarming. Out of 212 million females, in 1961, only 27.6 millions were illiterate. In 1971, the literates are 49.4 million out of 264 millions of female population. In 1981, there are only 79.2 million out of 318 female population

In the report released by Government of India, Ministry of Education, during 1978-79, it is stated that wastage and stagnation is 42-85% between classes 1 and 2, 12.12% between classes 2 and 3, 8.5% between 3 and 4, and 8% between classes 4 and 5. This is really a staggering rate of drop-outs. The divide between rural and urban India is age-old and still persisting. Thus, there are two Indias as William Digby put it in 1901. The problem of the rural masses is non-accessibility and non-affordability.

What for Education for all Women?

Education is essential to change the situation and to build a better world for future generations.

We have to give education to poor and under-privileged women. How is it possible? In their work places in the fields where they work. During leisure time or as per their convenience, not insisting on their presence in schools.

It need not be necessarily literal education simply book reading or writing on slates. It can be simple literacy, which is nearer to their day-to-day life. That knowledge, which can be useful in their routine work.

This can be one way of awakening among millions and millions of women, who are still living far away from civilization, who live in either ignorance or complete isolation in forests. So programmes based on moral values, built on equality, where there is no discrimination and which promote harmony, peace and human dignity should be evolved.

For achieving this, our enthusiasm should be our strength.

Access to what is needed?

(a) access to build a barrier-free environment

(b) access to knowledge

(c) access to communication

(d) access to information, and

(e) right to services

Awareness should be generated among women about their rights and privileges. Of course some good work is being done through DWCRA groups in villages. In Andhra Pradesh, I am proud to say, that lakhs of groups are working and women are saving crores of rupees and are involved in economy building measures. I am also glad to say that I have worked in this DWCRA programme in Srikakulam district, the first district selected and was winner of an award for forming highest number of groups–more than 500 in 1986.

Budgets are increased but there are no performance indicators, placement services are in adequate. Sector of non-governmental organisations as neglected. So, policy reformation and improvement of the systems already working is needed.

Now, let us think of some possible employment opportunities for women.

(a) Firstly, identification of jobs, exclusively for women and reservation of posts, should be there in employment.

(b) There should be special employment exchanges, vocational training in institutes in every corner of the country.

(c) Wages should be fixed according to production.

(d) Human engineering should attract the attention of our planners. A new cadre of professionals, who can guide and encourage the functionaries working in the field from time to time.

(e) State Governments, local authorities, should take up some new long term and short-term courses for empowerment of women.

(f) Equal opportunities in jobs and other promotional avenues should be created for encouraging women to take up careers of benefit.

(g) All kinds of discrimination should be eliminated and some positive, affirmative action should be evolved for achieving quick results.

(h) Incentives to the employers who appoint women candidates in the industrial field should be provided.

(i) Among a cluster of villages, in a central place, small-scale industries should be started

(j) Full time and part-time jobs should be provided to married women for providing livelihood and for improving their quality of life.

(k) Media should make very useful propaganda about the importance of literacy among women.

(l) Registration of NGOs and professionals is essential.

(m) Government should help and encourage NGOs to start hostels, VTCs and to develop self-help groups.

(n) A campaign approach is needed to make literacy programmes a success.

(o) Networking of the efforts of NGOs and their activities is also needed.

(p) A campaign approach is essential to achieve good results.

(q) A time-bound action plan to enable women to play an active role in society.

(r) A strategy to take the action plan to the grass root level is needed and a movement is to be built up.

Finally, to empower women, enforcement machinery such as special Boards should be constituted with experts.

Gandhian Concepts of Development and Women's Equality

When I was participating in a conference at Hongkong, its organiser introduced me to the audience that I am from the country, where Gandhiji was born. I felt proud for a moment and spoke about Gandhiji's Philosophy and sentiments and his concern to the cause of women.

Though I had no occasion to see him in person or participate in his freedom struggle, I had the proud privilege to stay at Wardha for a fortnight, while writing a chapter on Gandhian age and listened to stories about him from his daughter-in-low Smt. Nirmala Gandhi and from two stalwarts, who worked with Gandhiji very closely.

I felt he was a rare human being and a "Saka-purusha". He created a new chapter in the annals of history of India. With "Truth" and "nonviolence" as his main instruments, he could lead a great movement and win independence to India. The great Gandhi, whom Sir Winston Churchill described as a "Naked fakir" could kindle the spirit of freedom in the minds of people and many sacrificed their lives in the struggle.

Gandhiji needs no memorial. Story of his life would be told and retold. India after independence, "Nav-Bharat" is indeed a memorial to him. He lives in the hearts of the millions of people as a burning light in the words of Albert Einstein, future generations may not believe that such a man lived and worked in blood and flesh. It was a Mahatma.

Gandhiji gave an ideal to India, with so many, religions, cultures and castes. He has left a great and noble heritage, which lives for all times to come. The ideals and the principles he liked and tried to realise in his life time are pious. His love for humanity, world peace, liberty, justice, social, economic, political values will live forever. He instilled courage and confidence into the structure of a nation, during its difficult days, and made a silent revolution, a great success by his noble path of Satyagraha and made the Britishers leave India.

Gandhiji was the greatest champion of the cause of women. He has shown a way to fight the evil. We give an honest and sincere trial to the path shown by him. This is the time when all right thinking men and women of the world should take up the issues in right earnest before it is too late to reconstruct or reform the age-old ills of our society. When we assess or evaluate the progress made or the achievements of the past decades, we find that we have not even touched the outer surface of the problems. On the contrary, we find that we are not moving on the right track with the ideals placed before us by Gandhiji and others.

Gandhiji once said, with all seriousness that if it was left to him, he would make a Harijan girl sit on the Presidential chair of India. Its men and women can put their heads together and take up the threads where Gandhiji has left for the emancipation of women in particular and reconstruction of society. They can pave the way to save the whole world from being destroyed because of violence, materialistic and sensual values of life.

The problem of growth and development of woman is as old as probably the woman herself. It is also not less true to say that the history and account of the attempts made to solve this problem are equally old. In all ages and in all countries, wisemen and women have been projecting this problem and **emphasising** the need to lift women.

In spite of all good intentions, honest pursuits and most sincere desire of the reformers of all times, this problem seems to be **aggravated** in volume and intensity.

Gandhiji was the greatest champion of the cause of women and completely identified himself with the problem of women. He understood woman and her problems more clearly and exactly than woman herself. In fact it was he and the Congress organisation that brought out woman from the four walls of the house into the wider world initially. He conducted a special session for women in every AICC meeting and tried to change the age old mental, moral or physical barriers for women. If we remember correctly he sent women volunteers to picket near the toddy shops during the salt Satyagraha movement. In his peace mission, all the women were sent to different places in Noakhali district as messengers, and ambassadors of peace. He never accepted the superiority of man over woman and maintained that for all projects of development, and peace, men and women are the equally integrated.

Let me quotehere a little from Gandhiji's writings to show how intensely he felt about women. It said "woman is the companion of man gifted with *equal* mental capacities. She has the right to participate in the minutest details of the activities of man and she has the same right of freedom and liberty as he".

Speaking about the status of woman, he said "men and women are equal in status, but are not identical. They are a peerless pair being complimentary to one another; each helps the other so that without the one the existence of the other cannot be conceived and therefore, it follows as a corollary from these facts, that anything that will impair the status of either of them will involve the equal ruin of both". He further said "I am uncompromising in the matter of woman's rights. In my opinion, she should labour under no legal disability not suffered by man. I should treat the daughters and sons on a footing of perfect equality". In fact he felt very sad when women expressed their unhappiness at the birth of a daughter.

Gandhiji often said woman is the image of peace. "She is the personification of self-sacrifice, unfortunately, she does not realise what a tremendous advantage she has over man because, as Leo Tolstoy" said "they are labouring under the *hyqnotic influence* of man".

Gandhiji in the final analysis of things, found and got convinced that the problem of all problems is man himself. He has lost sight of the direction of the final goal of his life. He is moving like a rudderless ship and down by the winds of sea of life, and has forgotten that he is not the body' body is only a means to take him to his ultimate destination and self realisation."

Gandhiji was a very shrewd social scientist. He took lessons from past history and discovered for himself a way out to replace the old social older by reconstruction of her human society on new values. He said physical right is not right. Man is not what he *appears to be* in his material, physical form."

The second point he discovered is "that salvation of man is in and through work. This work should be economically productive, socially useful, and done in the spirit of worship. He should work not only for his dignity and salvation but also to enhance the prestige and weave equality with other workers—male or female.

"Without the *fetters* of the body," he said any woman like any man should be allowed all facilities to grow to the highest possible height of growth. In fact, in his scheme of non-violent or Sarvodaya order of society, woman the incarnation of ahimsa as she is world no more be called the weaker sex.

She will wield more power and *authority* of land when she transfers that *love* that she has for her children to the whole of humanity and *forget* that she *ever* has or can be the object of man's lust. She would then occupy her proud *position* by the side of man as his mother, maker and silent leader"

In the path of non-violence, education is the only way to social change. Education of course, does not mean passing of information as is in the present system. It has to be more on the line of positive and constructive teaching. We want the education *by which* character is formed, strength of mind is increased, the intellect is expanded and all the will and *skill* to work and shines by which one can stand free from all fear on one's own feet."

In a nut shell Gandhiji said "It is *wrong* to divide and discriminate people on grounds of sex. Men and women are equal as the same Brahman or spirit *dwells* in both. In Gods scheme of work, there are no privileges and no monopolies. All and every one are equally born and entitled to grow."

Spirituality, sacrifice and self-control ingrained in *service* of humanity at large are the *bricks* required, said Gandhiji for all-round growth and development of the country. Gandhiji therefore directed all his constructive work and scheme of political and economic decentralizations and all his ideas of Gramarajya and Ramarajya towards this change of man and change of society.

We see now more stress on rural development. No sought, India is essentially a country with 80% of the masses living in villages and to improve their lot, only way is to build up rural economy. This idea is gaining more importance today and the norms laid down for implementation of various schemes are gaining popularity and progress is visible of course, these are some impediments but they can be eliminated in course of time, with the awakening of the masses. Bottlenecks like the middlemen are to be removed for achieving speedy results. As a person involved in implementation of some of the developmental schemes, I feel strongly that there is tremendous change in the very outlook of the people and this would pave the way for effective and *early* implementation of schemes.

People can feel self-reliant, when once they are educated on the facilities available and when once the sense of exploitation is not there. Lack of education among the masses in the *literal* sense is also another barrier standing in the way. The indifference of people to what is happening around them, is to be tackled first. There is a battle of ideas, a Kurukshetra going on and *currents* and cross-currents of thoughts are flowing and out of this *churning* of ideas, an amazing and rich ideology and an order of society might emerge. Economically, the passage of India from feudalism to democracy, and medievalism to modernism and the marvellous gains of science, have all been the results of the new magic of certain ideas gaining ground in the country.

Before the dawn of the next decade, India would be one among the powers of earth in invention and industry, in wealth and trade, in knowledge and wisdom to teach humanity of the world, the tolerance of a matured mind.

Certain enlightened classes are in the know of things but there are millions and millions of people who are still dumb. They are to be developed. In this context Gandhiji's outlook and broad vision are to be implemented with a sense of dedication.

Gandhiji dreamt of a world, which is free from anger, hunger and worry. He always felt that there was much to be done and much *to be* seen. The only salvation lay in removing unrest and trouble and is making life worth living.

With his dedication to higher and nobler ideals, he could discover India and the world, the people and their aspirations.

Pandit Jawaharlal Nehru, the architect of modern India, once said "Gandhiji has *put* an ideal before us, that we should *wipe* out every tear from every eye.. We must try to *alleviate* pain " True. Thus he endeared himself to the masses, as a leader, as a friend, guide and philosopher and also as the father of the nation and presented India to the world that *here* is a "wonder that is India."

The foundations laid down by him are strong enough to bear the burden of the reconstruction of society. The path which he lighted for us is *visible* and clear and miraculous mansions can be built on this basis.

3

WHY EMPOWERMENT OF WOMEN? NEEDED?

Indian constitution guaranteed certain rights to all in the preamable "justice", social, economic and political, liberty thought, expression, belief, faith and worship, equality of status and opportunity fundamental rights guarantees freedom of speech, protection of life, and personal liberty. The positive rights negative rights a sow" Prohibition of discrimination on the basis of race, caste, religion, sex, or denial of equal protection. Indian women are the beneficiaries of these rights in the same manner as men. Art 14 ensures "equality before law" and Art 15 prohibits any discrimination in terms of sex. All these provisions ensure equal opportunity of political participation by women, along with men.

Committee on the status of women in India revealed shocking data (after 1971 census). This was a watershed year which raised concern among lawyers, thinkers, planners, regarding the position of women in India. Since then the demand for improvement and empowerment of women started at the global level.

Why reservation? Women are victims of age-old repression and exploitation. Reservation is a means of protecting weaker section of society who have for centuries been socially, historically and politically exploited, giving them a chance to come on par with the stronger section. Women are in this category, a historically victims group. Women are nowhere in the planning process after 5 decades of democratic politics. Power at political level would only change the status.

NPP Demanded 30% Reservation

In 1985, Rajiv Gandhi Government took the women's issue on priority basis. No impact 1st draft of national perspective plan (NPP) demanded 30 per cent for women in all elective bodies—from Panchayats to Parliament. But 1993 -1996, women's organisations demanded for reservation in assembles or parliament demand was accepted featured in the manifestoes of all major parties.

Janata Dal (JD) "The reservation on 30% elective post in local bodies for women has to be extended to union and state legislature.

Congress: It proposed to provide reservation for women in state and parliament.

CPI: Having made a beginning with Panchayats, the next step should be to reserve 1/3 seats for women.

CPI(M): 1/3 of the seats in legislative parliament be reserved for women.

BJP: In state assemblies and parliament all elected position, 33% reservation will ensure that at the dawn of the 21st century, Indian women will have true participation.

Samata Party: The party will initiate legislation for the reservation of constituencies for women candidates in rotation for 1/3 of the seats in both the Lok Sabha and State Assemblies.

But, against these theoretical assurances, all major Political parties are taking vague position on the issue of caste-based and religion-based women's reservation required. 4 sub-categories within women's quota–OBCs, issue was Muslims, Xians and Sikhs. In 1996, when reservation brought before the house, the first obstacle was about the fixed quota from the OBCs. The main votaries were Sharad Yadav, Ram Vilas Paswan, Mulayam Singh Yadav and other OBC MPs. Main argument advanced by 'them' was that with a blanket reservation, upper caste women would corner all the party tickets and get supremacy in Parliament.

Both the Houses witnessed clamorous scenes with members cut across party lines.

1997—Once again the Govt failed to put the Bill before Parliament due to strong objection to the Bill in its present form. It was deliberately attempted to keep the Bill in cold storage bystating that "consensus is needed to be evolved".

1998—Although Bajpayee assured representatives of women organisations that he would not only introduce the Bill in the budget session, but also put to vote in the cabinet also approved the integration of women in political process at all levels of political life is essential for democratisation of politics. It is not demand of a few urban elite. It reflects the will of the people.

Introduction of the Bill

It was again put under the lid on the issue that the quota **should be slashed** to 15% to OBC women. The present bill was debated from many angles. It refires analysis and discussion.

Senior advocate of Supreme Court Abhishek M. Singhvi, says "The constitutional mandate for rotation of constituencies reserved for women is impracticable and harmful."

Madhu Kiswans women's activist comes out with a suggestive measure. Instead of 33% rotating lottery system of reservation, we provide for 50% reservation having double member constituencies. That is to say, each constituency should be represented by 2 members. Doubling the figure of MPs will also lighten the load of work and remove possibility of "bivi-beti" brigade.

Caste and communal card is confusing the whole issue. What is essential today is "general involvement of women at all levels of power structure to ensure a society without any quota. Within quota for political leverage. As Brinda Karat puts it, OBC made any demand. It is only a pretext to shelve the bill. Last Parliament had 200 OBC male MPs.

Abraham Lincoln's concept of democracy is an ideal achieved in the world. Democracy falls short, when women of whatever colour or ethnic group cannot vote or cast an effective vote, cannot expect success in electing representatives of their choice or being elected to the legislative bodies and have little hope for enactment flaws they believe are critically needed.

Women's Bill—An Analysis

Some people think that gender discrimination down the centuries has kept women folk in India a backward social force and so representative mechanisms like reservation are thought of women representing their own caste or class come forward and others would be denied this opportunity. This assumption cannot be correct.

Since caste and class have collapsed to a great extent in the modern context, it is not correct to argue that only upper caste women would get the benefits of reservation. No doubt, they have had some benefits in the post-independent India because of their earlier education and encouragement from their men folk. Some upper caste families, with there experience of handling political institutions like political parties, have passed in their knowledge and experience to their women also, especially their daughters.

When we look back to our days of freedom struggle, there was no single Indian woman who worked with stalwarts like Gokhale, Gandhi, Surendranath Banerjee, Tilak or others. It was only one Annie Besant, a foreigner and a theosophist, could play a political role along with the above leaders. The visible role of upper caste women.

Started with Sarojini Naidu that too in Gandhian era. In the entire period of nationalist political life, we don't find a Dalit-Bahujan woman, whose name can go down in the annals of history. This does not mean that they did not play any public role in the nationalist civil society at the village and town level. Of course Dalit-Bahujan women played important roles on Telangana, Mopla and Choury Choura movements. The historic role played by Chakali. Illamma, an illiterate washer woman, in the Telangana armed struggle is an illustrious example. So also, the role played by Rosamma of Nellore district in starting recent Arrac movement in Andhra Pradesh is worth mentioning, though the movement died down later on due to so many reasons.

Anyway in post-independent India as result of English Education and family background, Indira Gandhi emerged as the woman Prime Minister of India and chief minister like Sucheta Kripalani, Nandini Satpathy also emerged in states.

The significant point to be noted that alongwith caste/class, education played an important role in throwing away any male antagonism. Women belonging to OBC families still un lettered and are still backwand. It is a fact, no doubt. But, the oppressed women cannot remain indifferent to the more oppressed.

When once in parliament passes the bill and women get the opportunity to voice their the political parties that come to power with their "voters" cannot keep them in darkness. Planners, social scientists, philosophers of every country have realised that unless the skill, and intelligence of women is harnessed, it is not possible to develop the country, their talent cannot go wasted and un-represented. Gone are the days when women can sit as passive spectators. They are alert, more vocal, bold and sincere in their efforts.

If anyone tries to put obstacles on their path of development, it will not get any results.

Societal interaction is through women. Any civilised society prospers only when women are developed. One cannot underestimate the capacity or the role of a woman, in the name of class or caste or social structure.

So, we must dispassionately judge or examine the issue before us namely the passing of the Reservation bill grievances, other Socio-political problems may be settled.

There is an argument that when once the bill is passed, it becomes a "Fashion Parade". This may not also be correct. Of course, women with a sense of responsibility for society, only come to the forefront, to speak on behalf of some millions behind them and they will be certainly answerable to their sisters for all their deeds or misdeeds. Women, who were the worst sufferers till yesterday, cannot sit quiet when something against them is happening in parliament. Certainly they will protest in one voice. Women's movements cannot sit idle also.

There is also another argument that "Parliament" may be a "battle front" for quarreling factions of women. This is also a false assumption. We are witnessing scenes clearly how some uneducated and also educated men are behaving in the parliament and how they are creating noisy scenes and running to the "well" of the house. So, any decent woman member, who enters the house, cannot behave roughly with others.

Of course, women are coming to the forefront after so much of struggle and with determination. They are more than half of the population. They are mighty force.

Mr. Tobuy Horward and other religious scholars addressed the gathering. Mr. Aga Raja Eirw Consul-General of Iran at Hydrabad was present.

This will show how Muslim girls are being educated and how the elderly leaders ore encouraging. When it comes to Muslim girls being public life, there are well qualified women who can perform well.

For SCs and OBCs, more educational facilities are provided in the rural areas also and more and more girls are being educated.

Even among Muslim girls, many are getting educated the "Hindu" of 13th December '98 carries the following news item (Hydrabad)

"Educate" a women to educate the whole family". This was the resounding message delivered by several speakers at the 10th Allama. Imam Khomeini State Educational Awards Function, Organised by Imam Zamin Talemi Wakf at Hyderabad.

About 218 students of Shia community from school to postgraduate level were given certificates for their outstanding academic performance. Mr. K.M. Khan, M.P., Mr. Zaheed Ali Khan, Editor, Siasat, Mr. Aga Shaik Md. Hassan Akhtari, religious leader from Iron, Dr. M.D. Raza Baluri, cultural Consul of Iran, Syed Alamdar Hussain attended.

Public Opinion

Let us now know something about the public opinion about this controversial Bill. Heads of political parties, ministers, and responsible leaders expressed their ideas on several occasions.

The Rashtriya Lok Tantrik Morcha (RLM) convener and Samajwadi president, Mr. Mulayam Singh Yadav, said in Delhi on December 98, that his party would not allow the Government to introduce the Womens Reservation Bill in its present form and described it as a conspiracy by upper caste leadership of major parties and a revenge against the implementation of the Mandal Commission report.

Addressing a news conference, a visibly agitated "Mr. Yadav" accused leaders of Congress (I) and left parties of falling into a "political trap of the BJP and appealed to them to realise the "real game plan" behind the Bill. He said the "Bill in its present form is a question of life and death for us and we will take it up with the people".

He reiterated his party's stand on supporting the controversial Bill. He said in categoral words that "percentage of reservation to women should be limited to 10 per cent. There should be quota within quota with proportional reservation to women belonging to minorities OBCs, SCs and STs. He charged the BJP Government with catching a conspiracy to push through in five minutes. But he said, he alerted RLM MPs about it. To quote his actual words, he said," There parties want to deprive the women for the down trodden sections of their legitimate rights and we will not allow it happen".

Commenting on the incidents in the Lok Sabha he said, Mr. Yadav charged the Trinamul Congress leaders Ms Mamata Benerjee and a few other women MPs with attacking RLM MPs without any provocation and with the intention to divert the attention from the country wide opposition sponsored strike.

The Samajwadi party president said "a delegation of the RLM MPs met the Lok Sabha Speaker Mr. GMC Balayogi and apprised him of their version of the unruly incidents on the floor of the Lok Sabha. To quote his own words". We have asked the Speaker to take appropriate action against the guilty persons involvd in the incident. If no action in taken by December 14, we will not allow functioning of the House".

Mr. Yadav accused the PM, Mr. A.B. Vajpayee of adopting double standards and said while he condemned the incidents of July in the Lok Sabha when MPs of Samajwadi party snatched copies of the Reservation Bill from the hands of the Indian Law Minister, Mr. Thauli Durai and wondered why he had not uttered a single word about todays incidents.

Quota for Women : Law will be Enacted

Addressing a conference "Panchayat Raj and woman empowerment", the minister of state for rural areas and Employment, Mr. Babagooda Patil said 11th December 1998 at Devri that the Government was Committed to enacting a legislation "for providing 33 percent reservation for women in parliament and legislatures. The conference was jointly organised by the PHD Chamber of Commerce and Industry and Konnad Adenouer Foundation, one of the sponsors of rural development programmes.

Another Union Minister of State for Health, Mr. Delit Ezhilmalai pointed out to the danger of the principal party in the Govt, the BJP, and the principal opposition party, the Congress (I) are coming together on the Women's Reservation Bill to the west quotas for SCs, BCs and minorities. In the angurating first all India conference of the All India Telecommunication BC Employees Association, on 26th December 1998 at Chennai, he said the SCs and BCs should from hands in cornering reservation benefit. The Govt could not be expected to handout benefits to the weaker sections. Legislation or constitutional guarantees would have no meaning if a large section of the society did not recognise them, he further added. Sri Ezhilmalai underscored the importance of reservation within the private sector.

The TMC General Secretary, Mr. Peter Alphonse said the leadership of the Scheduled Castes and backwards classes were to blame for the present situation. All struggles ended, when once the leadership came to enjoy the fruits of power and privilege, he said. The president of the Association, Mr. V. Narayana Swamy demanded reservation for backward classes, in education also. The General Secretary, Mr. J. Prasad, wanted the removal of the concept "creamy layer" in apportioning reservation benefits.

Hindu of 24 December 98 carries this news item: There is no proposal before BJP to provide 33 per cent reservation for women or separate quotas for the weaker sections in the party structure and it will not be an issue before the national Executive meeting in Bangalore on January 2 and 3.

The party general secretary and spokesperson, Mr. Venkaiah Naidu, pointed out that the BJP had a rule that every party committee must have at east two women members and some representation from the socially weaker sections. The party did not feel the need to provide reservation Mr. Naidu said. He was answering questions on the BJP's response to the recent changes in the Congress (I) constitution, providing reservation for women.

There are murmurs in thin the BJP, especially from the MPs belonging to the backward classes, who want the party 'not to lag behind' the Congress (I) in giving reservation to the weaker sections in every community. And it will not be a surprise if this issue comes up at the meeting.

Hindu dated 18th December 98 writes as follows "The congress (I) today became the first political party to change its constitution to give 1/3rd posts to women at all levels of the party structure from the working committee down to the block level, signalling its intent to bring about a major change to empower women politically. This was expected to be a trend setter which other major political parties have to follow. It also meets the general criticism that though the Congress, the BJP and the Left parties have proposed legislation to give 33 per cent reservation for women in the Lok Sabha and Assemblies, they have done little to better women's representation in the Party structures. Recently, there were protests from CPI (M) against the male dominated party Structure (No woman has ever served as a Polit Buro member).

Some of the major changes suggested by the Congress (I) are inclusion of women in Pradesh Congress committees and the Working Committees.

The resolution seeking the amendments described as "historic" and fulfilling the dream of Rajiv Gandhi to empower women and the weaker sections of society, was moved by Mr. K. Karunakaran and put to vote after the debate by Pranab Mukherjee.

Sonia Gandhi expressed satisfaction of the changes made in the party constitution and the task ahead was to train women for their new responsibilities is in the party structure.

CM Writes to Prime Minister on Women's Bill

The Chief Minister of Andhra Pradesh, Sri Nara Chandra Babu Naidu wrote to the Prime Minister, Mr. A. B. Vajpayee urging him to get the Women Reservation Bill passed in the present session of Parliament.

In his letter dated 11th December 99, Mr. Naidu said, the AP legislative Assembly had already passed a resolution in 1996 for introducing reservation for women in the assembly and the parliament. He told the Prime Minister that the TDP leader, Mr. K. Yerran Naidu was advised to assist the Central Government in passing the bill during the current session. He added "it is high time for us to demonstrate our commitment and political will by passing the Women's Reservation Bill without any further delay during the current session of Parliament.

Activists and leaders of women's movement undertaking a journey for launching a mass contact programme "Rail Chetana Yatra" a week-long journey by Mangala Express from New Delhi to Kanya Kumari by members of the National Commission for Women, Central Social Welfare Board and Joint Action Front for Women to mobilise public opinion on women's issues, has flagsed off on 4th December from Nizamuddin Railway station.

Mridula Sinha speaking on the occasion–said that not only women and women organisations but the whole society needed to be committed to issues concerning women. The timing of the rally coincides with the winter session of parliament. The yatra also seeks to sensitise masses on gender equality and the need for gender justice in society. It will also provide an opportunity to the women's groups to interact with the people in order to create awareness among the masses on the issues concerning political empowerment of women. It also announced that 1998-99 would be the year of "Awareness on women's issues and their Rights"

A separate bogey was allotted in the train wherein women's groups put up their exhibits, pamphlets and posters depicting unity of women and efforts being made to empower them through various social, economic, political and legal programmes. A special poster printed and exhibited by the

Central Social Welfare Board which carried the slogan "make the world safe for women" has been displayed on the train prominently.

The awareness programme was addressed by the members travelling to the public who were invited to visit the exhibition and would interact with the activists and media persons. Since the train halted at Mathura, Agra, Gwalior, Jhansi, Bina, Bhopal, Itarsi, Nasik, Igatpuri, Ratnagiri, Mudgaon, Kozhikade and Ernakulam, it could afford an opportunity to the local women groups and residents to interact with yatra participants.

Let us now ponder a little on the Bill and gender equality. Is it enough if caste based quota is included in the bill? No ! definitely not the Bill alone cannot and will not do to achieve the goal of gender equity. It can only help for preparing a ground for equality.

Gender Equity is a larger issue. It goes beyond all caste considerations. The so called custodians of OBC women's interests can perpetuate caste conflicts, thus making women forget the real issues. After all, it is a patriarchal society predominantly, trying to keep women under subjugation for ever. The demand of the times is enabling women to rise above politics and caste distinction and work unitedly for woman should rise.

Quota within quota means women are allowing themselves to be exploited by vested interests. This will be exploitation of another kind. It must be remembered that the atrocities on OBC or BC women were brought into limelight by organized women's groups, irrespective of caste connotations.

What is needed is not an agitation over quota but a will among women of all categories to fight against atrocities on women in general.

The diversionary tactics of a few members of the Parliament should not be taken into consideration and the bill should be passed for the benefit of all women. Major political parties like the Congress (I) and BJP should not yield to the demands of a few on some pretext or other. Let us hope the saner elements in our political spectrum will take a right decision and pass the bill, thus giving women their due share in society.

4

EMPOWERMENT OF WOMEN

Women's empowerment is not a topic recently invented. It was found to be important for the development of society by Gandhiji and he expressed his opinions on several platforms.

Empowerment and autonomy of women and improvement in their social, economic, political and health status was recognised as highly important for achivement of sustainable development of society. Decision-makers have come to the conclusion that women's empowerment would contribute to the economic growth of the country by the powerful role of women which is needed to be promoted by society.

Economic Empowerment

Poorest of the poor are women. Economic disparities persist still. Much of the unpaid work is evident in families and communities, and women face discrimination in economic sphere.

Political Empowerment

Social and legal institutions still do not guarantee women in basic legal and human rights in access to or control of land or other resources, in employment, and earnings and social and political participation. Laws against domestic violence are often not enforced on behalf of women. Empowerment of women comes only from education, economic and emotional independence.

Educational Empowerment

About 2/3 of the adults in the world are females. Their levels of education are strongly associated with infant mortality, lower furtility as well as economic opportunities for their children. All have realised that education is the most important means of empowering women in the knowledge, skills and self-confidence, necessary to participate fully in the development process of the country. India has a record of highest number of women being harassed by men.

A critical aspect of promoting gender equality in empowerment by women with a focus on identifying and reducing power imbalances and giving women more autonomy to manage their own affairs.

When women are empowered, the whole family would benefit and these benefits will have effect on future generations also.

I would gather some good articles by some eminent people and included them in this chapter.

Gandhiji and Indian Women

Much has been written on the subject of Gandhiji and Indian Women and yet one feels that enough is not said on the subject as to how Gandhiji was able to rouse the dormant spirit of Indian women and how he cast his magic spell which like that of the pied piper brought women in hundreds out of their homes, women from all classes, castes and creeds to join his non-violent struggle for freedom. For centuries Indian women had suffered from social disabilities. Fifty years ago when Gandhiji started his first campaign of non-cooperation against the British Government, the position of woman was anything but satisfactory. She was illiterate, ignorant and bowed down by social customs, like child-marriage and purdah and her complete dependence on man for everything. Gandhiji had realised that India could never be free nor progress if half her population was shackled with chains of social customs and unable to participate in any national work. He wrote "The sooner it is recognized that many of our social evils impede our march towards Swaraj, the greater will be our progress towards our cherished goal. To postpone social reform till after the attainment of Swaraj is not to know the meaning of Swaraj". He took up cudgels against the social evils, and wrote strongly against child marriage, against purdah, in short against any social evil that kept woman back. He said "what we are doing to our women and what we are doing to untouchables recoil upon our heads with force thousand times multiplied. It partly accounts for our weakness, indecision, narrowness and helplessness. Let us then down the purdah with one mighty effort". Writing about purdah he said "chastity is not a hot-house growth. It cannot be superimposed. It cannot be protected by the surrounding wall of purdah. It must grow from within and to be worth anything it must be capable of withstanding every unsought temptation". He blamed men for this sorry state and told them: "men are undoubtedly to blame for their neglect, may their ill use of women and they have to do adequate penance. He exorted the progressive women "those women who have shed superstition and have become conscious of the wrong have to do the constructive work of reform". He wished that women would revolt against the injustice perpetrated on them by man made social laws and said "when woman freed from man's shares rises to the full height and rebels against man's legislation and institutions designed by him, her rebellion, no doubt, non-violent will be none the less effective". He appealed to women to realise their own strength and to learn self-respect. He said: "would that woman will realise the power she has latent in her for good, if she has also for mischief. It is in her power to make the world more livable both for her and her partner, whether as father, son or husband, if she would cease to think of herself as weak and fit only as a doll for man to play with" — It is not surprising that women rallied to Gandhiji's clarion call to join his non-violent army to fight for freedom. Their part in the struggle made them shed their weakness and gain back their self-confidence. The picture that the Indian woman presents today is so different from what it was fifty years ago. It is amazing what strides towards progress, Indian woman has taken during the last fifty years. Today under the constitution of Indian Republic she enjoys the same status as man. She has the same political rights; her economic rights are more or less on par with those of man; she can inherit and she can her own living without anyone pointing a finger at her. She can marry a man of her choice irrespective of his caste or creed. If a widow she can remarry if she wishes and under certain conditions she can divorce her husband if necessary. It was Gandhiji's championship for the emancipation of Indian woman that brought about this great change. Her participation in the struggle for India's freedom was thus rewarded and she has regained her lost position in Society.

It is difficult for the present generation of women to realise what deep debt of gratitude Indian woman owes to Gandhiji. The question is can we repay that debt? One way to show this gratitude is to try to live up to his ideal of Indian woman — Gandhiji described woman as "the noblest God's creation" His ideal of woman can be summed up in his own words "mother, maker and silent leader of man". He places woman as mother on a very high pedastal. He has said "the future of India lies on your knees for you will nurture the future generation. You can bring up children of India to become simple, God fearing and brave men and women or you coddle them to be weaklings unfit to brave the storms of life and used to foreign fancies which they would find it difficult in after life to discard." There is another way also to show one's gratitude and that is to follow Gandhiji's advice and take up the constructive work of reform particularly among women. Ignorance is a great obstacle in the way of women's progress. While the percentage of literacy among women has improved during the last fifty years it is still very very low. Less than fifteen percent of women are literate today. This is a great handicraft and efforts have to be made to remove it. If the young women of today launch a vigorous campaign against this ignorance and illiterate among women they will have rendered agreat national service."

—Hansa Mehta (Courtesy—Rashmi)

Gandhiji and the Part Played by Women in the Freedom Movement

Shri S. Radhakrishnan in his introduction to the Book, "all men are Brothers", has said, "A great teacher appears once in a while. Several Centuries may pass by without the advent of such a one. That by which he is known is his life, he first lives and then tells others how they may live likewise. Such a teacher was Gandhi."

In the struggle for India's independence Gandhiji insisted that we should adopt civilized method of non-violence and suffering. He was a great votary of Truth and (non-violence) ahimsa. The fact that India won her freedom entirely with non-violent methods will in itself show that women could join in the peaceful battle. Mahatma Gandhi had great faith in women. "Who but woman", he said "the mother of man, shows this capacity of suffering in the largest measure? What can beat the suffering caused by the pangs of about? But she forgets them in the joy of creation. He said, "I would love to find that my future army contained a vast preponderance of women over men. India's salvation depends on the sacrifice and enlightenment of women." He had paid special attention to the emancipation of women in India by drawing them into the freedom movement. A number of incidents during and after the first world war had provoked the people, and the feeling.of anger increased with the massacre of innocent Indians at Jallianwala Bag. The non-cooperation movement was now set in full swing. In 1920 the whole city of Bombay mourned the death of Shri Bal Gangadhar Tilak, and we all joined the memoth funeral procession led by Mahatmaji.

There was a big bon-fare arranged and Gandhiji asked women to give their foreign clothes for burning. Many women willingly gave away their rich sarees for the bon-fire. He preached that people should do away with the habit of possessing more than their wants. Gandhiji said one can serve society better if their wants are few. His personal life was a shining example of simple living and high thinking.

He had strongly pleaded for Khadi and Village Industries, mainly for providing productive work to millions of our people who suffer from enforced idleness-Swadeshi was a burning passion with him. He constantly wrote and spoke advocating Swadeshi in language, dress and thinking. Then there is another example how women can be persuaded to part with their superfluous jewelleries. At a place near Calicut, having made his speech at a largely attended public meeting, he made his usual appeal to women in the audience requesting them to donate their jewellery for the Harijan work. A girl of sixteen Kumudini, walked up to the platform. She had a gold bangle on each arm. Taking one bangle she asked Gandhiji, if she could have his autograph. As he was writing a line, she took off her other bangle too. Gandhiji in the autograph wrote, " Your renunciation is a truer ornament than jewellary that you have discarded."

He endeavoured to advance the cause of the downtrodden and Harijans in every manner possible. Shri G.A. Natesan in his reminiscenses, writes the following incidence about Gandhiji's visit to Madras; "While staying with me in my house in Tambu Chetty Street, he brought with him a panchama boy called Naiker-with Gandhiji action must correspond with aspiration and utterance. The inmates of my house, including my old mother-rigidly orthodox in their way of life were horified by the desecration. The boy fell ill and hour by hour Gandhiji was to be seen sitting by the side of the patient and nursing him. This quiet action was more eloquent than any amount of preaching and I discovered that my old mother was steadily reconciling herself to the new situation. This transformation was brought almost silently".

In 1929, Gandhiji gave a call to the country to observe January 26 as the Independence day and to take a solemn pledge to win Independence through self-sacrifice and self-suffering. The famous Dandi March in 1930 of Mahatma Gandhi was the prelude to a country wide mass civil disobedience.

Malayalam poet Vallathol in his poem, "Do You remember" writes "He, the Gentle-souled, walked over arrogant imperialism, which raised its angry Mane in sten guns. And stooped to fill his pot with brine to make a pinch of salt; and at that in stant India stood Erect".

Women old and young, city women and village women, rich and poor, literate and illiterate awoke from their stupor and marched forward to participate in the freedom movement. Women were anxious to follow him and suffer imprisonment, but he persuaded them to take up another important work, which he said women were more suited to do than men. Women were asked to take up the picketing of foreign cloth and liquar shops.

By now the old tradition of keeping women at home had been broken. They marched and courted lathi charges and imprisonment, suffering untold hardship. Women conducted peaceful " WAR Councils", and led groups in all parts of the country, until the Mahatma himself declared that " the part played by women will be written in letters of Gold". Once while addressing a meeting of women in Bombay he challenged those who called women weaker sex. He said, "to call women weaker sex is a lible, it is man's injustice on women. If by strength is meant brute strength, then indeed is woman less brute than man. If by strength is meant moral power, then woman is immeasurably man's superior".

On his return journey from England after attending the round table conference in 1931, he travelled through Europe. Women of those countries asked him for his message. He told them about the heroic sacrifice of Indian women in his non-violent movement, and asked them to take a lesson from the Indian women, and help in bringing peace in the world. He said "It is for American women to show what power women can be in the world. By aping men, you neither become mennor can you function as your real selves and develop your special talent that God has given you. Women are the natural messengers of the gospel of non-violence if only they will realize their high estate."

Gandhiji espoused the cause of women with great concern. It is mainly due to his untiring efforts in this direction that women in free India occupy high position in national life. — Jayashri Raiji *(Courtesy Roshni)*

The Empowerment of Women—An Assessment

Indian women have travelled a long way forward since the establishment of the colonial regime. The spread of education, the impact of new ideas, the freedom struggle, the attainment of independence and the steady working of democracy can be identified as the main causes of progress of the entire nation and of women and the backward classes in particular.

In this first decade of the twenty first century if we try to assess where Indian women stand, a very complex situation can be seen comprising success and failure, both these of many kinds and many degrees. Success, social, economic and political is obvious, encouraging, even inspiring. The problem areas naturally need more attention, and I am concentrating more on failures and problems rather than on the impressive success story of Indian women.

Women are now motivated mainly by three concepts—equality, human rights and power. Equality means not only equality with men, but with men and women the world over. Human rights is much more than equality because it envisages an ideal situation of rights pertaining to the highest values of humanism, and power can be defined as the ultimate assurance of rights. All the three are high enough to draw our efforts towards them for a very long time, but not too long, let us hope.

What is it that keeps us even now as rather second rate citizens eventhough our constitution has only one category of citizens? On a comparative scale the answer to this question is backwardness in education, scarcity of gainful employment and no adequate measure of decision making power from the governance of the home to that of the country. Reservation of seats for women from the Panchayats to the Parliament may help to accelerate progress and solve problems to a certain extent and that is something to strive for. But the problems are deeper, or so it seems to me.

The gap between information centred education and clear independent thinking is a major flaw in Indian education. This gap, evident in colonial education, has widened after independence because neither the infrastructure of education nor its methods could catch up with the huge increase in numbers. We are not yet aware that information by itself or information for technology is no substitute for information's transformation into ideas. Another serious flaw in education is that it has seldom encouraged initiative in the individual student or teacher or institution. Yet another and obvious flaw is that education is not related to Indian society. Add to all this that our students are not trained in handling responsibilities, and in team work for the community. There is also the inevitable presence of the past with all its good and bad. That we are Indians with a great civilization or civilizations at our back is our glory and our strength, at the same time the past is a sickness in our very blood.

All this is affecting us, especially as women. To give very evident examples—child marriage, dowry and the flourishing wedding industry. What power do we have, what equality can .we claim, when female foeticide and dowry deaths are so common? What self-respect can we boast of when the wedding industry, harvesting billions of rupees a year, glamourises the bride, the bridegroom and an obscenly lavish ceremony, bringing about poverty and despair to the not-so-rich, and reducing woman to a foolish fantasy, a burden, and a mere commodity?

Violence against women, especially sexual violence is on the increase. Child abuse is rampant. Violence in the home is frequently reported, but the number of incidents not reported may be staggering. Discrimination against women is not uncommon in the workplace, harassment seems to be on the increase even in schools and colleges, and sub-human working conditions prevail in some industries where women form the majority of the work force. Prostitution increases as poverty increases and there is a vicious campaign gaining ground to wrest for it rights and status, and very little is done to save the girls trapped in it or to rehabilitate the women in jobs not damaging to body and mind.

There is much to be done. And the question is whether the political empowerment of women would help to solve these problems, and how soon, how very soon? Political parties are huge patriarchal bodies, but the climate is in women's favour and it is not impossible for women to make their presence felt in the parties and in Parliament in spite of resistance and rivalry from the men. No doubt it would take some time. But more important than the factor is the organizational nature of political parties, and their political priorities. The ethics of conformism asks for human sacrifice. When both men and women turn conformists in the name of ideology, or party discipline or the immediate aims of power politics, does it matter much whether women are there in smaller numbers or larger numbers? Another question is whether it is possible for women to be full time public workers, or whether some new idiom of work would emerge where the woman can combine the roles of wife, mother, home-maker, an income-generating worker and a political worker? An old fashioned question, but I suppose not irrelevant. As a voter I do not expect a woman legislator or minister any more than a man legislator or minister to have gender based priorities, but I do expect her to do her best to bridge the gap between a society which goes in for female foeticide and a social leadership which swears by human rights. She may have to educate her party, fight her party on their values and priorities, flout her party discipline. I do not see her doing it if she desires a seat next time. But I see her doing it if she is sure of community support and women's support. Again tricky matters, if you take a short-term view. On anything important there cannot be or should not be men's politics and women's politics in different compartments. When you think of it, it seems to be a matter of ideas and values and long-term goals for the whole country.

Women's empowerment is on a wheel chair now. Somebody has to push it around. But soon it would get off the chair and walk about and take long strides forward. But let us not be too optimistic. We have learnt our lessons from the politics of our own country and the world. Empowerment for the under-privileged is as essential as life-breath, but empowerment to be wholesome and beneficial requires education, values, a sense of the past, and imagination enough to have a vision of the future. (*Courtesy–Roshni*)

> *"Subjugation and exploitation of woman was the product of man's interested teaching and women's acceptance of them."*
>
> **Mahatma Gandhi**

Gandhian Approach to Empowerment of Women

I feel extremely honoured to be invited by my former colleague and friend Prof. Aparna Basu and the President of the All India Women's Conference to give Smt. Lakshmi N. Menon Memorial Lecture for the year 2003. She was born on 27 March, 1899, and died on November 30, 1994.

Smt. Menon rose from a humble rural girl to a national and International leader. She occupied all the high positions lightly and not tightly as the case with the present politicians. She believed in the Gandhian dictum that to educate a girl, you educate the whole family, the neighborhood and the world community. She frowned on people who confined girls in the four walls of a house. She worked tirelessly to raise the status of women. People used to rush to her wise counsel and guidance.

She dealt with problems which are timeless and universal, because they spring from enduring weakness to human nature and human society. Since the solutions she found for them were based on eternal verities, her influence and her relevance are also timeless and universal.

On this day 30th November, we can have no better wish for India and the rest of the world than that the great spirit of Smt. Menon may always abide with our people in general and women in particular.

I should also like to congratulate—All India Women's Conference for continuing the torch lighted by Smt. Menon by developing excellent programmes, activities and services to shed their inferiority complex thrust upon them by men.

I have chosen the topic "Gandhian Approach to Empowerment of women" for my talk.

Introduction

"Empowerment" has become, a fashionable buzzword. It essentially means decentralization of authority and power. It aims at ensuring participation of the deprived sections of people in the decision-making process, in other, giving voice to the voiceless. Activists want government to empower poor people including other women by legislative measures and welfare programmes. Unless necessary capacity is built in these sections in reality, the power is used by others rather than by the sections for which it is meant. Empowerment may mean equal status to women and provide opportunity and freedom to develop themselves. Man should control the pleasure of senses and not to consider the women just a sex object. Sensual pleasures have no known bounds. Gandhi said "The mind is a restless bird, the more it gets the more it wants and still remains unsatisfied. The more we indulge in our passion the more unbridled they become." The goal of empowerment depends on a threefold revolution; Firstly, to change people's head and heart, secondly, to create a change in their mindset and lives; and thirdly, to change the social structure.

Much more work needs to be done at the grass-root levels, especially in the thousands of Indian villages. The village workers, through living and working alongside the villagers, act not merely as advises and technical assistants but also work to promote a sense of self-reliance and communal responsibility amongst the villagers that transcends divisions of family, caste, class, religion and gender. In working to encourage the participation of villagers in a collective decision-making process, particular attention is paid to the position of women whose domestic responsibilities, allied to the discouragement of men, have traditionally precluded them from participating in decision-making at the community level. In encouraging women to meet together for such purposes, a forum has to be created wherein they gain confidence in their own abilities and collective strength, confidence in their own abilities and thus begin to make their "voice heard" in community affairs and the Panchyat deliberations and the Gram Sabha [usually dominated by men].

The ultimate goal of empowerment of women, based on Gandhi's vision, is Sarvodaya [the welfare of all] through cooperation and trusteeship in the economic sphere, equal participation in the political sphere, and mutual-aid in the social sphere without regard to caste, creed, or class, or gender. Thus, empowerment of women in general and village women in particular cannot be imposed from above, it must grow from the bottom upwards.

In brief, empowering women socio-economically through increased awareness of their rights and duties as well as access to resources is a decisive step towards greater security for them. The 73rd and 74th Constitutional Amendments on Panchayati Raj and Nagar Palika with 33 percent reservation for women has created a political space for women. But in most cases they exercise "proxy" power on behalf of men. In reality women have never been able to get more than ten percent seats in

Parliament or other bodies of decision-making. It is hoped that the 81st Constitutional'Amendment when passed will give 33 percent reservation of seats in Parliament and State legislatures to women. This will go a long way to provide active involvement and participation of women in political bodies. We should be ashamed of ourselves that even after more than half a century of freedom, we have been able neither to clothe our women nor provide something as basic as secure and adequate number of toilets and shelter even in the capital city of Delhi.

Place of Women in Indian Society

There is an inherent discrimination against women in the Indian social structure. A woman is considered subordinate to a man. A boy is preferred to a girl. Motherhood is nailed but not mother. A woman is considered a reproductive machine to bear and rear man's children. She is not considered a person in her own right. She has always to stand in relation to a man as his daughter, wife or mother. This prejudice is widespread even among the educated and enlightened people. She is still largely dependent on her menfolk and legal and formal equality can become meaningful only when backed by everyday social equality. To achieve this status is an uphill task.

God and Divine mother are inseparable. According to the Hindu religious conception, Manu, the lawgiver, has said that wherever women are honoured God chooses it as his abode. A verse says that if God is the lamp, she is the radiance that it spreads. If he is the spoken word she represents the meaning. The scriptures have eulogized the place of women in Indian society. But the reality is very different.

Universal Preference for a Boy

To many to be girl is the worst curse and crime. For that you are punished your whole life. The parental preference for sons is, of course, nothing new, nor indeed a feature peculiar to Indian wives who produce male offsprings tend to be honoured. The daughter is considered a burden; primarily because of the low status that she is accorded both within home and in society. The women in the home personifies emotionally - the mother most of all, "she kills herself," people say of a good mother, in order to bring up her children.

Women's Influence on Gandhi

Woman is God's greatest gift to humanity. She has the power to create or destroy. Kalidas and Tulsidas became great poets because of their wives. There is a saying that behind every successful man there is a woman. Napolean had aptly said, "Give me good mothers and I would produce a great nation." Gandhi learnt much from Kasturba and perhaps even more from his mother. His spiritual bent of mind seems to have come from her. Richard L. Johnson says that Gandhi learnt the fundamental aspects of his life from his mother and his wife, but women's influence on him was not limited to his family. The *bhadra mahila* [respectable or new women, crested in the nineteenth century by Indian cultural reformers], became the model for Indian women of the nationalist era. Women in the late nineteenth and early twentieth century created organizations and founded educational institutions that transformed the conditions of women predominantly among the upper-middle class in urban centers. Gandhi believed that women could do much to transform India at all levels. He believed that equal rights for women and men were necessary but not sufficient to create a mere just social order. What good does it do us to have equal rights if we are divided within ourselves and unable to attend true unity with others?

Discrimination—Son and Daughter

Gandhi did not like Indian society's preference for a boy and general neglect of a girl child. In fact, in most cases a girl child is not allowed to be born. If born, her survival is not ensured. If somehow she survives, she is subjected to neglect. She does not get the respect and the status she deserves equal to that of a boy. Given the frantic preference for a male child in India every year about four million women risk their lives and get illegal abortion done. Many pregnant women die in the process but their deaths are never reported by their family members or by those who carry out those sex selective abortions. Gandhi was totally opposed to gender discrimination. According to him, the girl is the nobler sex. If she is weak in striking, she is strong in suffering. Gandhi described as "the embodiment of sacrifice and ahimsa." A daughter's share must be equal to that of a son.

The husband's earnings are the joint property of husband and wife as he makes money by her assistance. If a husband is unjust to his wife, she has the right to live separately. Both have equal rights to the children. Each would forfeit these rights after they have grown up, and even before that if he or she is unfit for them. In short there is no distinction between men and women except such as been made by nature and can be seen with human eyes. Fundamentally man and woman are one, and their problems must be one in essence. The soul in both is the same. Each is a complement of the other. The one cannot live without the other's active help.

Present Situation and Conclusions

One of the biggest illegal trades going on in the world is in the smuggling of human beings from poor to rich countries. Globally, about 1.2 million women and teenagers are trafficked for prostitution each year and many are trapped forever in the flesh trade in European countries. Even after 55 years on Independence, atrocities on women continue unabated. Seventy percent of the rape victims disappear from their homes, according to a recent study. They leave due to scornful attitude of their parents, relatives, threats and continued harassment from the offender. The offender is mostly a known person and only 4 percent of them are convicted. The greatest tragedy of the present-day situation is that even after almost 62 years of our development work, we have not been able to clothe our women. The conditions of women in some parts are pathetic and shocking. Their sub-human existence can be described, as solitary, poor, nasty, and brutish. These poor, helpless women have to live without food, clothes and shelter. Something needs to be done on a war footing to mitigate their suffering.

It is a "wake-up-call" for women activists to get into action to uplift their sisters. Empowerment without sharing is not possible. Sharing requires sacrifice. In short, this is the Gandhian formula [sharing and sacrifice]. Women have to be conscious and aware to feel and realize at every step of their life they are the builders of the nation and the peaceful world. Despite the fight for gender equality, there has been no perceptible change in our perception about women. A woman is still considered to be delicate. Her mild behaviour and nature is seen as a negative point. 62 years after our constitution gave women 'complete' equality their participation in politics on an equal footing with man remains a distant dream. Let the pursuit of power be not the only aim of women empowerment. It should be their "total emancipation". His insistence on women's education is the first step in the right direction. We still have miles to go to achieve our cherished goal to empower women. In one sentence, we can hazard to say that if women cease to consider themselves inferiors, men cannot be their superiors.

The National Family Health Survey in the second round investigated 90,000 women in the age group 15 to 49 years, reported that 58 to 65 percent women had been beaten by their husbands, fathers, brothers, or sons for reasons ranging from neglecting the home, being disrespectful to their in-laws, and going out without informing their husbands. Of the domestic violence, women said; they had experienced physical abuse at the hands of their husbands. Even more shocking, women widowed, simply move from one male domination to the next. In the absence of husbands, sons step in to continue the mistreatment. On 1 January 2001, Prime Minister Atal Bihari Vajpayee in his New Year Message to Indian women said: "Ensuring gender equality by removing gender discrimination is the key to real empowerment....Let us actively promote women's access to equality, education, credit, health care, employment and social security." The Union Government had declared the year 2001 as Women's Empowerment year. It was flagged off in January 2001 when the stree Shakti Puruskar was awarded to deserving women.

It is hoped that women's empowerment policy will be finally put into practice. The policy unveiled talks about a multi-faceted approach to removing various imbalances in the socio-economic environment which works against women. There is a plan to ensure that all laws deemed discriminatory to women would be reviewed and suitably amended by the year 2003. The facts are not encouraging.

Grim Facts

The United Nations Population Fund [UNFPA] stated that the national average in India dropped, to 927 girls per 1000 boys in 2001 from 945 per 1000 in 1992. And Punjab, Haryana, Gujarat and Himachal Pradesh had a child sex ratio less than 800 girls for every 1000 boys. The reasons for decline have been attributed to the determination of sex of the unborn child or foetus eliminating when found to be female. The ratio stands at a mere 770 in Kurukshetra district of Haryana, 814 in Ahmedabad and 845 the South West district in Delhi which are the most prosperous regions in the country. The average in the state of Punjab is 793, no district has more than 850 girls per 1000 boys. Ten of the 17 districts recorded as low as of less than 800 per 1000 boys, with the lowest 754 per 1000 in Fatehgarh Saheb. Haryana is the next with five district recording less than 800 girls per 1000 boys in 2001. In Gujarat the situation worsened in Mehsana where the ratio declined to 798 per 1000. The Gujarat average too has dropped from 928 in 1991 to 878 in 2001. Rajkot has shown a sudden decline from 914 in 1991 to 844 in 2001. Delhi is no. 4 the ratio declined to 865 from 915 in 1991. The worst affected is Delhi's South West district with the ratio dropping from 904 in 1991 to 845 in 2001. Himachal Pradesh, Rajasthan, Maharashtra and Tamil Nadu follow with a state average of 897, 909, 917 and 939 respectively. Ideally the CSR {Child Sex Ratio} for every 1000 boys the number of girls should be between 940-950 girls.

Rape committed on women is a heinous and shameful crime which reflects badly on the reputation of Indian society. What is more worrying is that this heinous crime is occurring frequently. It is not only the Law and Order machinery but society as a whole should gear upto prevent this. Rape, a harsh reality which, unfortunately, has always been a part of Delhi's life. The recent rape of a Swiss diplomat has-once again-brought back to the limelight the alarming incidence of crime against women. Because rape is an emotional, psychological and physical truth which refuses to go away. It is a crime which is repeated on the streets of Delhi every day. The figures are chilling. This year [2003] alone, Delhi has silently witnessed 380 cases of rape and 360 of molestation. Seventy-five percent of such crimes are committed by persons known to the victim. More than 60 percent of the victims are below 18 years of age and, in 60 to 70 percent of the cases, the accused goes free. Shocking as it sounds, what the proverbial long arm of the law is doing to check this crime is a matter of conjecture.

Women's rights activists insist that the situation could not be worse. When the definition of the rape itself is flawed, how can the implication be right? According to the law, rape occurs only when there is penile penetration. If this is not proved, the accused gets females was $1, 195 as compared with that of males to be $3,236 in 1999. This implies that female income just was 37 percent of male income. Obviously, it cannot be derived that female suffered gender bias both in education and employment.

Atrocities on Women

Women have been subjected to dowry deaths and battering by their husbands. The steps taken by the Rabri Devi Government [Bihar] is worth emulating by other governments. The women of Assam and other adjoining states have taken to broom formula when their persuasion failed to restrict men folk from drinks and drugs.

Forget Dowry

The Rabri Devi government {Bihar} has made it mandatory for its employees who get married to give a declaration in writing that they did not take any dowry. But self-declaration alone will not do. The statement has to be vetted and signed not only by the spouse but also the father and father-in-law of the candidate. The state Cabinet took a decision to this effect on 4th Nov, 2003 when it approved the Bihar State Prohibition of Dowry Rules, 2003, in a bid to curb the dowry menace. Employed government employees are in great demand in Bihar's flourishing marriage bazaar, when even a lower division clerk demands more than Rs. 5 lakh in cash and other "essentials" as dowry. According to the new law, the bridegroom's father has to submit a list of all gift items including ornaments, received to the districts prohibition officer within a month of the wedding ceremony. District welfare officers have been given additional designation of dowry related cases in the districts.

Broom Formula for Prohibition

When persuasion failed, the women of Assam decided to let the brooms do the talking. Armed wit brooms made of bamboo strips, members of the Bishnu Nagar Jana Kalyan Samiti vigilants against drunkards. They would get together after dusk, chase them out and wallop some sense into them. They claim the "broom formula" has dissuaded a few men from frequenting the liquor dens in the area. Since, the 1970s the Meira Paibis {torch bearers}, social-body of women in Manipur, has been both vocal and physical against drinking and drug abuse. Across the Nagaland and the hill district of Manipur, The Naga Mothers Association has also been active against the drinking menace, but its methods have been mild.

The process of empowerment lay in persuasion and education, and peaceful means as well as laws will all help us to reach our goal to bring women at par with man. The Gandhian method of changing the negative mind-set of both woman and man will bring gender equality, always free," says Kalindi Deshpande of the All India Democratic Women's Association. Worse still, the 'victim's trauma does not end there. The long process that is Indian Jurisdiction that prolongs the suffering. 'The victim is questioned by the police and has to face prosecution in court. The case drags on with the end result being an extremely low conviction rate. The maximum punishment for this heinous crime is 10 years," says Deshpande.

The trauma is most severe when the victim is a minor-and minors are the victims of a high percentage of the total rape cases. "Victims are unable to handle the police, media and social attention, says psychiatrist Sanjay Chugh, MD, "Sometimes, they can't comprehend the implications of rape and post-traumatic stress is extreme. Moreover, because the accused is known to the victim in 75 percent of rape cases, she is unable to trust anyone again in her life."

The need of the hour is to amend the laws, says additional solicitor general Abhishek Singhvi, "Existing rape laws need to be interpreted purposively." He elaborates, "Why should penile penetration be so important when it is stipulated nowhere in the statute? More than the letter of law, what is required is effective policing, education, confidence and reassurance for the complainant to come forward." The official initiatives notwithstanding, safety still eludes women in this capital city of India. And it is not someone, somewhere-but everyone is responsible for this state of affairs.

A society that practices positive discriminations towards women and the girl child hope to advance. Education is the key to enlightened citizenry.

Gender Equality Countries

It may be noted Gender equality exists in Norway, Canada, United States, United Kingdom, Japan, Mexico, Russian Federation, Malaysia, Venezuela, Philippines, Sri Lanka, China, Vietnam and Indonesia. Gender inequality countries are: Saudi Arabia, Pakistan, Iran, India, Egypt and Nigeria.

UNESCO's latest Education For All [EFA] Global Monitoring Report says Bangladesh has achieved gender-parity-equal enrolment of boys and girls at school-at the primary level. India scrapes the bottom of the list, just a little above Pakistan. In fact, it may not be able to meet the gender parity target even by 2015.

Education: Gender Parity Still Distant. Reasons: Men dominate decision making, early marriage and work load, number of women teachers low, even when girl outshines boys, it does not reflect later in life.

Wayout

— NGOs and social groups can help

— Need for benefits and incentives

— Changing Laws and attitudes in Empowering women

India's literacy rate was 52 percent in 1990 had gone up to 65.4 in 2001. Change in girls education is reflected in the percentage of the girls in the total enrolment in the country which is 47 percent as against 44 percent in the year 2000. Gender parity index has risen from 41 percent in 1995 to 83 percent in 2001. It is expected to achieve Gender Parity and Gender Equality by the year 2010.

Human Development Index

There are three types of indices of human development in India: 1. The index of life expectancy, 2. The index of per capita income, and 3. The index of education considering literacy rate and school enrolment ratio.

Gender related Development Indicators

Life expectancy at birth of females in 1999 was 63.3 years but for males, it was 62.4 years. Although gap between life expectancy of females and males is very small, but in other gender related development indicators, this gap is very wide. For instance, adult literacy of females was barely 44.5 percent against 67.8 percent of males in 1999.

Education: An Agent of Women's Empowerment

Development and Empowerment are related terms. For development of any society, it is essential that its people, both men and women are educated. 'Empowerment' in the context of female literacy implies the right to attainment of knowledge at any age and every field, whether it be latest computer technology or traditional home-making. An 'enlightened' and educated women gains respect, is self dependent and is an asset to the society in which she lives.

The argument herein revolves around Indian Women and how far education has empowered them. Has education really helped them in realising and raising their status in a patriarchal society as India?

To evaluate achievements and failures in the field of women's education it is essential to make comparisons. Unfortunately, the rate of literacy even at the verge of the 21st century is not to the mark when compared to other countries of the world. India is much behind even when compared to South Africa. This is one of the main reasons why India's position in the Human Development Index remains low. India ranks 132 among HDI prepared for 174 countries. In Gender Development which measures female literacy, its position is 122, although there has been substantial improvement in the female literacy since last two decades i.e. it was 0.69 percent in 1901 which increased to 8.86 percent in 1951 and thereafter to 39.29% and 54.1 % subsequently. Despite achievement in the field of female literacy since 1991 it is essential to note that wide gap in percentage between male and female education and among rural and urban literacy rates remains.

These, thus has been the gross neglect of women particularly in rural areas where illiteracy prevails. Interestingly Southern states especially in Kerala the rate of female literacy is much higher when compared to the North. In Rajasthan, Madhya Pradesh, Bihar and Uttar Pradesh female literacy rate is even lower than the others. This proves lack of fulfillment of even the constitutional guarantee provided as part of Article 14 or Fundamental Rights and Directive Principles (Article 46).

The question herein arises why despite the efforts for uplifting of female education made by missionaries, reformers, freedom fighters and government bodies, the status of women's education in India remains bleak. The reasons are many.

(a) Female education is considered waste of energy, time and money as many traditional minded parents do not see their value for any economic or social purpose.

(b) Women have to do domestic work which does not require any higher skills or learning.

(c) More educated the girl is there would be more problems in finding a better match or bridegroom of the same level.

Among the poor, the causes of illiteracy are different. Education has no meaning when the stomach is empty. Poor girls, (despite the labour laws and prohibition of child labour) often go out to work either in the factories, fields or are sent, to work as housemaids. In case they do not do so they sit at home to either cook or take care of their younger siblings when both the parents go out to work, thus the daughters remain illiterate.

Despite drawbacks it is pertinent to mention that women's literacy has gone a long way. Increase in female literacy from

39 percent to 54 percent is not an easy job. The emergence of distance education as a popular mode of learning; the establishment of the Open University System started by Indira Gandhi National Open University wherein education is imparted through printed material, electronic media as TV, computers, audio-visual aids, contact courses etc. is no mean achievement. The scheme of coordinated course of Education for Women funded by the Social Welfare Board; Mahila Samakhya and the Adult Education programmes conducted both by the NGO's and government is no less an achievement which will show positive consequences in the near future. However, what is needed is awareness to various free education schemes as Navodaya Vidyalayas and Kendriya Vidyalayas. More incentives, both on the part of the Government and public schools, for the education of the girl child require special attention.

Requirement in fact is for gender sensitive curriculum, both at the school and college level—an educational curriculum that would promote a scientific and rational temper.

Overall, education although an important agent of change cannot alone promote women's empowerment and equality. It has to be gender sensitive. There is need for a change of attitudes towards the upbringing and education of girl child. There is need to discard the dowry system completely. Education of course, among Indian Women to an extent has led to change in Indian society but there is much to be achieved. Education, Employment, Health, Inheritance, Legislative Rights are all indicators of 'Empowerment' or 'Development' and so must be seen in totality. Education, no doubt gives woman greater awareness of her rights, makes her self-confident, articulate and able to take decisions. But mere literacy is not enough, the content of education, the curriculum is extremely important in making them gender sensitive.

The power to ensure that teachers perform their duties, besides taking proper action, and utilization of funds. At present all these powers are vested with either the education department or local bodies. Responsibilities of the government towards education will increase due to the Right to Education Act.

In a way the provisions of this Act will make the teachers accountable to their stakeholders.

Constraints of the Act

There are some constraints, which can hinder the implementation of the Right to Education Act.

- The State governments need to allocate more funds to education. It may become a challenging job for the governments.
- Nowadays quantity is not a problem. Quality in teacher training is a problem. The State must take initiatives for quality in teacher training and innovation.
- Does the liberal admission policy hamper the process of achieving equitable quality?
- The Act bans teachers from undertaking private jobs to get financial benefit. It bans private tuitions by teachers. There is already a similar ban in States like Andhra Pradesh and Maharashtra. But still some teachers indulge in this malpractice. To implement this provision, it needs attitudinal changes and mechanism.
- The data on school-age population available at present is not totally reliable. Figures are changing from survey to survey, day-to-day and agency-to-agency. The government has to think about this seriously. It is a big challenge before the authorities. Without reliable data on children, this Act cannot be implemented properly.
- Banning public examination up to the end of elementary education helps in reducing the number of dropouts. Now the States have to dispense with the public examinations for 5th or 6th or 7th or 8th classes. But there is a talk of deterioration in quality because of non-detention system in Andhra Pradesh. The problem has to be tackled intelligently.
- The teachers associations need to be consulted about the provisions of this Act.

Conclusion

- All-out effort is necessary to implement the Right to Education Bill, 2006 by the States, and local authorities. It is essential to spend on this programme. Money should not become a constraint in this context.
- A nation's progress largely depends on its literate people. Accordingly all steps should be taken to implement the Bill in letter and spirit.

Role of Women in India's Development

The year 2001 was observed as the Year of Women Empowerment throughout the world. In 2002 India celebrated the 50th anniversary of the Republic.

India, after independence, opted for a mixed economy and economic planning for development with a democratic political system. It cannot be gain said that there has been economic development since 1952 when the First Five Year Plan was launched as some macro economic indicators reveal. There has been phenomenal rise in national income, rapid industrial growth and tremendous improvement in agricultural production described as Green Revolution. Considerable fall in death rate together with rise in life expectancy, increase in literacy percentage, fall in the percentage of people living below the "poverty line" so on and so forth. But one of the main objectives of planning remains dismally unfulfilled—social justice for the people of India because of poverty, hunger, unemployment, disease, malnutrition, economic inequalities, neglect of women's progress glaringly stare at us even today in the seventh year of the 21st century. Special mention/must be made of the relative backwardness of women in general, keeping in mind the slogan during the struggle for independence: "India shall not awake until and unless Indian women be awake." Women have not been enabled to play their due role in the making of New Independent India. The importance, relevance and urgency of the fulfillment of the twin objectives of the development of women and positive, proper utilisation of women's power can hardly be over emphasized in the context of the ground realities as are today.

In our male-dominated society the women are victims of oppression, suppression, deprivation - bride burning, exhorbitant demand for dowry by groom parties even amongst the so-called educated families, unilateral right of the husband to divorce the wife amongst a sizeable section of the society, sale and infanticide of the female child, poor progress in the female literacy percentage, continuous fall in the percentage of females in the total population, lower expectancy of life of females compared to that of the males-all these lead to the inevitable conclusion that women's development remains will-o-the-wisp and we must remind ourselves that the points stated above are illustrative only and not exhaustive. Even affluent educated people, blame the wife for having no child. One of the main reasons of the unabated population explosion albeit population planning is the indomitable desire to have male children. Many so called modern husbands try to know the gender of the child in the mother's womb through ultrasonic test for reasons too obvious to be elaborated. As a woman I feel ashamed when I find in many cases of bride oppression the villains are the female in-laws themselves. We were 36 crore in 1951 and now we have crossed the 100 crore mark and it is apprehended that in another decade, we shall earn the dubious distinction of the most populous country in the world. In the demographic transition graph India continues to be languishing in the second stage as while the death rate has sharply fallen, the birth rate does not show any pari passu similar downward movement. It is to be mentioned in this context that in the states like Kerala where the literacy percentage of women is high enough, the birth rate is significantly lower than the all India figure. High rate of female illiteracy must be diagonised as the main factor for high birth rate and continuing population explosion which is the main bane in regard to India's development. But alas, the women remain neglected in our polity—it is a little consolation that after the recent 2004 Assembly elections in four states three have women Chief Ministers.

Goddess Durga was empowered by the gods with all kinds of weapons to demolish the Demon but there has been little evidence of such empowerment of women in the country even after 60 years of Independence. Women played a glorious role in India's struggle for freedom - the list of women martyrs is too long to be stated here. But in Indian Republic women are mostly treated as untouchables by the political parties for Assembly and Lok Sabha elections. There has been a steady decline in the percentage of women MLA's and MP's. The reservation of 1/3 seats for women in Assemblies and Parliament remains a proposal almost cold shelved and the Bill for necessary Constitution Amendment has not been even introduced in the Parliament. It is the general public opinion that female Panchayat and Municipal members elected under 33% quota system have performed quite satisfactorily and hence non-extension of the system to Assemblies and Lok Sabha can only be explained as male arrogance and malice.

In the first War of Indian Independence Lakshmi Bai, Rani of Jhansi fought heroically and embraced death at the hands of the Imperialist British Army. Netaji Subhas Chandra Bose honored her memory by naming the women's Brigade in the Indian National Army as Jhansi Brigade. In independent India there is no Jhansi Brigade nor any women's Brigade though girl cadets of NCC have done quite well.

The female workers whether in fields or factories are to work no less harder than their male counterparts. Yet they are often under paid vis-a-vis the males. At the school going age, female child instead of being sent to school by the parents is subjected to serve as a domestic help either at home or outside. Women are suffering deprivation in many ways and the deprivation is large writ over the entire society and not limited only amongst the poor.

In the socio-economic milieu of India to-day the importance and necessity of a crash programme for the spread of literacy amongst women obviously suggests itself. An educated mother will naturally do everything to get her children - male or female—educated. An educated woman will definitely refuse to be a mere procreating machine. In order to enable the women occupying a position commensurate with human dignity of the mother in the society, the entire planning process is to be so oriented as to give top priority to such a crash programme. The various women's social service organizations in the country should come forward unitedly to fight for women's empowerment, constitute a nodal co-ordinating agency to carry on the movement unitedly and stead fastly. AIWC as the premier women's social service organization may take the initiative and take active steps for constituting such a co-ordination body with a nation-wide network upto the grassroot level.

Corruption is becoming almost a way of life in Indian society. Its cancerous growth must be resisted at all cost. Women can play a positive fruit bearing role in this urgent matter. If the wife tells the husband, "I am satisfied with whatever you can earn through honest means. I shall not touch any black money." That will have a far-reaching salutary effect. Let us remind ourselves of Maitriyee, the wife of Rishi Yagnavalkya who told him "Yanehang Namrita Syang Kimaham tena Kuryam" i.e. what shall I do with those things which will not make me "Amrita". Let every girl take a vow that she will refuse to marry where the groom's party demands dowry. Let her be trained in Karate like things to defend herself against sex abuse, let her have vocational training to enable her to have some economic independence. Let us remind the young generation of Indian girls of the life and teachings of Sri Sri Maa Sarada wife of Param purus Shri Rama Krishna who was the prime-mover in the establishment of Ramakrishna Mission by Swami Vivekananda. Rabindranath Tagore in his famous poem "Sabala" gave a clarion call to women to win over their own destiny. Let't inspire Indian womanhood.

Let me conclude by quoting what Chitrangada said to Arjuna in Tagore's dance drama of that title.

"I am not a goddess nor a mere woman

I am not to be worshipped, installed on a pedestal.

Nor I am to be pushed backward in negligence,

If you keep me beside you in weal or woe.

If you give consent to associate myself with your life's mission,

Then and then only, you will truly recognise me."

Let this be the attitude and objective of the 21st century's Indian womanhood.

Women Empowerment History of Women's Rights Peace the Ultimate Aim

Women enjoyed a status of equality and partnership with the menfolk during the ancient period of our history. Their participation in the creative and literary activities and in philosophical discussions helped the society to grow. The period is regarded as representing highly civilized, progressive and socially, culturally and spiritually developed society. Whenever distortion in their status crept in, society witnessed a decline and experienced disharmony, violence and suffering.

Reforms introduced in the last century contributed to a realization of the importance of Women's participation in the socio-political life of the country. A lot was done to restore their ancient status. The freedom movement in every colonial country gave impetus to the endeavours of social reforms leading to a genuine transformation in the attitude of the society towards women. Philosophers and Reformers have advocated larger involvement of women in the national movement and provided opportunities of freedom and dignity.

The history of women has been a history of "SILENCE" but now it is time to tell the world loudly that abuses have continued for long. In the new millennium, let us take a pledge to break our silence here, and to raise our voices in favour of women for equality under the law, education, justice and access to the full range of opportunities for development which enshrined in the Constitution of almost every country but not implemented in practice. We want gender justice, gender equality not on paper but in actual reality.

Today the words of our Nobel Laureate Rabindranath Tagore about the women come to our mind "I would neither like to walk ahead of you, nor behind you, but BESIDE you". This should be our goal, we have to empower women so that they can work alongside men to build a better world for everyone - men and women.

Women's rights are Human Rights, literally a burning issue today. The parameters of Women's Rights are all encompassing, including within its ambit, issues that are critical and cognent, and which need our undivided attention and action.

The world has just celebrated the 50th anniversary of the Universal Declaration of Human Rights in 1998. Yet half a century after the international community committed itself to protecting and promoting the human rights of all, millions of women continue to experience violations of their most fundamental rights. Since the 1985 Nairobi Conference on Women, the world has experienced profound changes, with both positive and negative effects on women and it is a fact that the last decade has seen human rights moving center-stage of the global development debate.

The recognition of violence against women as a human rights violation, and the implementation of legal and policy measures to further enforce this recognition, have been pivotal goals of the international movement for women community. The World Conference on Human Rights in Vienna in 1993 was the first global review of human rights and the work of the UN in this area since 1968. The representatives from 171 nations adopted by consensus the Vienna Declaration and Programme of Action, which for the first time declared that "women's rights are human rights". It outlines a common plan for strengthening the implementation of human rights and highlights the crucial links between development democracy and the promotion of human rights. By underscoring the universality, indivisibility, and interdependence of civil rights, cultural, economic, political and social, the Vienna Conference confirmed that the protection and promotion of human rights, as the birthrights of all human beings, is the first responsibility of Governments. Since the Vienna Conference women have used the International Conference on population and development in Cairo (1994) the World Summit for Social Development in Copenhagen (1995), and the Fourth World Conference on Women in Beijing (1995), as areas to gain visibility for abuses of women's human rights. All these conferences have emphasized that the protection of human rights is a fundamental imperative of civilized society and that development cannot be sustained without human rights.

Looking at the history of UN work for women, the Beijing Conference was a milestone. The Beijing Declaration and the platform for Action were a call to commitment and action, representing the culmination of a chain of global conferences, embracing all the issues covered by them and more. In its wide canvas were included all development and human rights issues within the control of our socialization process, relationships and mind-sets, which empower some and for others which build barriers and create demeaning stereotypes, and negate everything that development stands for.

Women still constitute 70 percent of the world's poor and two-thirds of the world's illiterates. They occupy 14 percent of managerial and administrative jobs, 10 percent of parliamentary seats and 6 percent of cabinet posts...In many legal systems, they are still unequal. They often work longer hours than men, but much of their work remains undervalued, unrecognized and unappreciated. $ 11 trillion is missing from the global economy-each year because of unpaid housework, child care, agricultural and other labour performed by women. Wages for women lag behind men for similar work in all countries, with women performing an estimated 60% of the world's work, but owning only 1% of the world's land and earning just 10% of the world's income. And the threat of violence stalks their lives from cradle to grave.

These facts, figures and statistics all reveal the level of infringement of women's human rights even today. Other statistics of this nature confirm this, and it is an undisputed fact that with poverty spreading like a cancer, the South Asia region is home to the largest number of poor in the world wearing an increasingly feminine face. Further, the declining sex ratio in South Asia (94 to 100), is a complete reversal of global biological trends.

History of Women's Rights

It may be a very long time since A.D. 865 when a conference was held in France to consider whether women were human beings. However, it is very difficult to point out any significant departure even today, from the resolution of that conference that women are human beings but created purposely to worship men. Before then and since then, women have, on the basis of sex differentiation been treated differently by men. "Differently" however from the perspective of patriarchal means, "Inferior" or "Sub human" and this justified discrimination. For a very long time, the biological difference in the women was evidence of her inferiority. With time, social roles which were to a 'large extent defined by biological factors were differently valued on hierarchical scale. Thus, the valued goods—wealth, power and prestige were and still are, unequally distributed on the basis of this hierarchical stratification with the consequence that women have become completely dis-empowered against their opposites. Even after some struggles (by individuals and groups) though it has been possible for some women to push against and break the barriers, women as a group remain marginalised from access to the valued goods.

The first documents which enshrine some kind of bill of rights were the English Magna Carta of 1215 and the English Bill of rights (1688). These documents however, had severely restricted scope in terms of the objects covered and subjects protected. The French Declaration on the Rights of Man (1789) is describable as the first real bill of rights, in which individual rights were generally and clearly postulated. The declaration reflected the nature of human rights as an inherent part of man and so inalienable.

U.N. and International Women's Year

In 1975, following the International Women's Year Conference held in Mexico City, the United Nations declared 1975-1985 as the United Nations Decade for Women in recognition of the fact that women, comprising approximately 50% of the world's population have been marginalised and have not participated in social and economic development to an optimal level. The Decade was to be used to remedy the wrongs of the past as concrete steps were to be undertaken to bring women into the mainstream of social development. The 1975 International Women's Conference in Mexico adopted a World plan of Action and Declaration on the equality of women and their contribution to development and peace.

UNESCO in 1975 observed that the key to any decisive change in any society lies to awaken, participation not only in increased numbers but also in a more active role in all social-economic and political spheres.

Present Scenario in India

The Indian experience in improving the quality of life of the people and promoting equity provides a wealth of ideas and practices for new directions for the future. The achievements are significant and reflect the efforts made in all directions, the thrust towards poverty eradication, investment in social and economic infrastructure, spread of extension services, information, dissemination and strengthening of institutions—social economic and political - both Governmental and Non-Governmental. This political administrative framework has also ensured space for reflection and accommodation of the diversity and heterogeneity of India.

A deep concern about the rights and status of women has marked Indian political thinking. A striking feature in Indian society has been the symbolic and mutually complementary relationship that has developed over the years between Governments, women's movement and non-Government organizations. The women's movement in India continuously interacts with and influences public opinion and Government action. This is a tribute both to the maturity of thinking within Government and the movement and to the deep-rooted democratic tradition of this nation. Today all political parties in India have decided to ensure a definite percentage of women in the legislatures. It is thought to give 33% seats to women which is of course under dispute. But it is certain a definite quota is in the offing. Example of Scandinavian countries are being quoted where women are around 40% in the Parliament and also in the Cabinet.

In Norway the last women Prime Minister ruled for a decade, Mrs. Indira Gandhi had a track record of one and a half decade, Golda Meir in Israel was a name to reckon with, Margarette Thatcher was an effective world leader, Turkey had a woman to rule, so also Canada. Given opportunity women can excel men in all spheres.

Support for Women's Empowerment from the Top

It is heartening that Bangladesh Prime Minister Sheikh Hasina announced a national policy to promote "equality between men and women in all spheres of life" at a gathering recently of 14000 women local officials. She urged the women to insist on equal treatment, saying "Nobody will give you your rights, you have to achieve it through struggle and fight". Empowerment of women is dependent on their economic self-reliance. She added-outlining "nation-building tasks" for women, such as supporting family planning, expanding girls' education and engaging in economic endeavours such as raising poultry and livestock. Women should also speak out against illiteracy, prejudice and poverty.

The World Women Parliamentarians for peace declared, in 1986, at Delhi conference that women claim their right to be heard primarily because they have so far been left out when vital decisions affecting the future and fate of all human kind as regards war and peace and disarmament have been taken. They claim their right to participate in the decision making process. They refuse to be victims of the violent state of affairs in the world today - violence overt, subtle and silent. They believe that women have a decisive role in saving this planet and silent. They believe that women have a decisive role in saving their plant from total destruction, and preserving it for the present and future generations.

Peace and non-violence are two sides of a medal. Non-violence Gandhiji said, is not merely a personal virtue. It is also a social virtue to be cultivated like the other virtues. Society is largely regulated by the expression of non-violence in its mutual dealings. What is needed is an extension of it on a larger national and international scale, through education.

At no time in human history has there been a greater need for understanding peace and considering the use of non-violent means towards achieving it than now. At no time in human civilization has the imperative of drawing together the races, the castes, the regions and the nations of the world been more compelling, so that their creative energies may be channalised towards cooperation for human progress instead of being frittered away in conflict and violence. At no time in human history has it been more urgent to rethink and direct activities of the young generation into uplifting and life affirmative channels.

So far, violent means have been considered inevitable for resolving disagreement. It is time that non-violent means were considered not only as ANOTHER way, but perhaps, the only viable way for resolving conflict and disagreement in any civilized society.

Study of peace is not the study of pacification, or suppressing dissent, or maintaining the status-quo however unjust and immoral. The study of peace, in essence, is understanding peace not as just the absence of war and overt violence, but also removing subtle forms of violence perpetrated through the ages due to lack of creative thinking. The state of world as we see it today, calls for an "UNDERSTANDING". Of peace and non-violence urgently. It will not be enough just to talk about peace. The women have a big role to play women should be used as catalyst.

The Universal Declaration of Human Rights and the Women's Liberation Movement: The Social Aspects

An ancient prophet, diagnosing the expanding civilization of his time with its perils and possible disasters, said: "The powers havc brought us into great waters."

It is no longer an ancient situation in a seldom read book, but a vivid picture of our own time and the world in which we live. We have indeed been carried out of safe and comfortable harbours into great and stormy waters. This age of ours which puts artificial satellites into orbit around the earth, reaches the moon in a rocket, wipes out half a million people in a city in one blinding moment of an atomic flash, has made each one of us, in a new and terrifying sense, "our brother's keeper". Technology has annihilated the space and brought peoples, religions, races and cultures within point blank range of each other. The world has become a neighbourhood with men and nations living in one another's backyards; physically neighbours, but psychologically strangers still.

Self-contained societies belonged to yesterday: this is the day of the mass society. In this kind of a shrunken world, ignorance or indifference about our neighbours, across the seas or across the street, can no longer be tolerated. Indeed, it is dangerous to do so when politics has become planetary, economic a global concept, and the fate of humanity rests on a push button! We all know how the decisions of one country—its trade and aid policies, its immigration laws, its defence programmes—impinge on the lives and livelihoods of people in the farthest corners of the earth. A narrow 'nationalistic approach to freedom, justice, security, is both morally and practically obsolete.

There is ample evidence in recent history that what happens in one part of the world can bless or torment people in places far removed from it. If there is a flood or famine in India, or an earthquake in Iran, that fact is bound to affect others. Conflict between tribes in the Congo could rock the United Nations to its foundations, the fate of a child in Africa with that of a child in Australia is linked together as surely as the tides are linked with the moon. We can ignore each other at our deepest peril.

It is a small world, too small for violence, too small even for the intolerance that breeds violence. With this nearness, paradoxically, has come deeper distrust, sharper conflicts. There is no escape from the rapidly mounting pressures engendered by unsettled disputes, overriding ambitions—territorial, economic, political and racial. It is a world of injustice and exploitation in new and subtle forms. It is also a world in conflict—democracy versus totalitarianism, coloured versus white, new nations versus old empires—though happily we have witnessed in our own life time the dissolution of the latter.

New nations have been born with a passionate, often fractitious nationalism, with the realization that poverty, ignorance, disease, and the other tragic components of a submarginal existence are not the necessary conditions of life for anyone. With freedom, have come problems. People are asking: Have we, perhaps, defined freedom in too narrow a sense? Is there something empty in our advocacy of the free way of life? What is freedom to the person who doesn't know where his next meal is coming from? What is freedom in a society where illiteracy, malnutrition, unemployment bar most people from its benefits? What above all, can freedom mean those who talk most incessantly of it seem to have so little awareness of its wider, moral dimensions? The question can be reduced to the simple one: Am I free if my brother is bound?

We see every where the spectacle of governments sagging under the weight of reactionary forces, corruptions from within, or becoming taut through opposite pulls of totalitarian and democratic trends where the bare necessities of food, shelter, work are denied, there is a penetrating truth in the remark made by penetrating truth in the remark made by Gandhiji. "To the hungry man, even God dare not appear except in the form of BREAD."

The restlessness of repressed people will continue till their status as the children of the same Father is acknowledged. Throughout the world, the voices of people of colour under oppressive rule, people in lowly circumstance, are raised against economic domination. They have gained political independence—a piece of paper, a flag, a national anthem. But this is not enough. For social progress requires a more equitable distribution of wealth to close the gap between the rich who are getting richer, and the poor whose numbers are increasing alarmingly.

Ours has been called the century of the homeless man: people have been uprooted because of war, religious persecution, political reprisals, racial hatred. What do they seek? They want quite simple things—a home, a job, a new start in life. The problem is colossal, for it involves not merely physical resettlement, but the healing of sick minds and the refashioning of broken lives.

This is the world we live in: a small, divided world, a world in revolt against exploitation and injustice, a world where human life is constantly being sacrificed on the "altar of abstract nouns." But this is not the total picture and new perils must not be allowed to obscure new promise. This divided world is coming together in new ways of cooperation and mutual aid.

Scientific and technological developments bring the hope of new possibilities for a better life. The process of secularisation is breaking open the traditional limitations of race, nationality, class and occupation. There is widespread interest in realising a true sense of world community, so that the basic unity of the human family may not be jeopardised. The process of nation building is shaking us out of the isolation of our communal shells and making us aware of our common humanity across religious, linguistic, ethnic and other barriers.

The transition from the traditional to the new community is not without tears, but the new is emerging. It is rooted in the discovery that a person is at the centre of society and the necessity for a framework of political, social, economic and cultural life which is common to all men.

This age has also seen the birth of the UNITED NATIONS, the best that mankind has been able to achieve in recorded history and a star of major magnitude has arisen on the international horizon, THE UNIVERSAL DECLARATION OF HUMAN RIGHTS. It is the most comprehensive document of all the historic declarations on the rights of man, and defines from a truly universal standpoint, the basic rights and fundamental freedoms to which all men, everywhere, are entiled: rights which belong to men as men, and as members of the human race.

Declarations, however lofty, are not worth the paper they are written on unless they are fulfilled in the lives of people rather than enshrined in documents. How are these to be given flesh and blood? What safeguards are to be provided? How are they to be enforced?

The Universal Declaration of Human Rights is not a law. In its own words, it is "a common standard of achievement for all peoples and nations, to the end that every individual and every organ of society keeping the Declaration in mind, shall strive, by teaching and education, to promote respect for these rights and freedoms and by progressive measures, national and international, to secure their universal and effective recognition and observance."

The Declaration is short. It reads the way people speak, and describes the way people have a right to live. It sets forth four kinds of rights: Personal rights, economic rights, political and social rights.

Finally, the all embracing Rights which are the right:—

— to equal opportunity in all areas of life, "without distinction of any kind;"

— freedom of opinion and expression;

— to education directed to the full development of the personality.

In the 25 years since its adoption, the Universal Declaration of Human Rights has exercised a profound influence. Though it is as declaration of intent, and not a legally binding document, yet so strong has been its influence, and so expressive is it of the needs and aspirations of mankind, that it has come to have increasing force and has been described as a a source of law.

It has set standards for the application of United Nations resolutions. The constitutions of many countries reflect its influence. National legislatures have been influenced by it, and it has shaped the legal system of many countries. It has inspired many International Conventions in the United Nations and its Specialised Agencies.

Although much has been accomplished, much more remains to be done. What about women and Human Rights? Faith in the equal rights of men and women is affirmed in the United Nations Charter, and in the mandate to the Commission on the Status of Women to promote equal rights for women in the political, educational, economic, cultural and social fields.

Great changes have taken place in the status of women. For centuries women lived in a state of subordination: business was none of her business: the workings and organisations of society did not concern her: except for the care of her home, she had no responsibility outside it: her power was restricted: she was valued, but not esteemed.

Today, she has achieved, or is struggling to achieve, a new place in society. Many doors are opening to her: she can work in many spheres: her vote can sway elections. Education is expanding her universe, and this expansion has thrust upon her the burden of choice after centuries of no choice at all. She is exhilerated by her new freedom, but is not yet quite secure in it. Political enfranchisement has widened her horizon, but opportunities are still limited by social customs and traditional beliefs, and above all, by the 'ignorance and apathy of women themselves. For millions the day has not dawned, and there is still a long way to go before the majority of them can be economically independent, socially secure and politically effective. Our protest against the disabilities under which women suffer must be strong and insistent, and our labour for their removal must be vigorous and steady.

To safeguard our human rights, what we have to do may seem so simple and obvious that many of us neglect it. It is to understand what our rights are, so that when they are violated, we can recognise the act as a violation.

Once we understand our rights, our next step is to promote them for others and for ourselves. And that responsibility begins with people around us, the local community, where we have the most influence. Acting through non-governmental organisations we can be effective in our efforts.

Let us ask ourselves some fundamental questions:

(1) How do individuals in our country suffer as a result of various social distinctions?

(2) Which of these distinctions are upheld by law?

(3) What more than the law is needed to ensure the rights of persons?

(4) How far do the laws of our country compare with the standards set forth in the articles of the Universal Declaration of Human Rights?

(5) Which should have greater weight in relations to marriage; equality of rights or shared responsibilities?

(6) Should the rights of the community be put above the rights of the individual?

(7) What obligations are imposed by the right to leisure?

Duties and obligations of the individual are commensurate with his rights. Society rests upon a balance of rights and duties.

The law has to be constantly revised if society is to grow. In our country the conditions for the implementation of the law and social reforms rarely exist. Illiteracy is our biggest problem. Even after more than 25 years of independence 79% of our people are still illiterate. We must combine our efforts to fight this greatest of all handicaps.

I would like to close with a quotation from the Peace Statement of the YWCA of India:

"This is a war we are fighting for peace. A war involves some killing but no loss of life. The things to be killed are ignorance, prejudice and superstition, hatred, egoism, narrow-mindedness, and cultural obsessions that are separatist. This war can be won, this peace can be established by the peoples of the world, without defeating anyone."

> *"We of to-day must conceive our relations to the rest of the universe as best as we can; and even if our images must seem fantastic to future men, they may none the less serve their purpose to-day."* —W. Olaf Stapledon

Ence favouring boys with regard to access to milk, eggs and butter in the family diet though there was no such difference between children of the two sexes with regard to cereals and vegetables. In the Registrar General's countrywide survey on infant and child mortality 1979, the percentage of children sick was higher in females. Estimates of infant mortality between the male and the female for 1982 suggest that the gap in mortality rate is being bridged at least in the urban areas. In the rural areas, female mortality is still higher in most states while in the urban areas it is higher only in Assam and Orissa. For 1983, the overall rate is the same for both males and females. An examination of child mortality in rural India in 1978 reveals a high male-female differential. In nine out of the 15 states of India from where data was available, the ratio of female to male mortality rates in the 0-4 years age-group is greater than 1. Most of the high diferential states are in the northern and western belt as compared to the southern states. The overall pattern rated is of poorer child care with respect to the female child.

Therefore, the number of invisible toilers around us is increasing. It is time to focus the spotlights on them, to identify the plans and the policies that will determine the space that they and their offspring will inhabit tomorrow.

On paper the rights of the girl are protected in the constitution and in the various laws of the land. Four decades after independence and more than a decade after a National Policy for Children and a National Plan for the Development of Women was adopted the girl child who embodies both youth and womanhood is still a barely discernible shadow on the periphery of national policy and public awareness. Today we deprive her of her rightful share of food, schooling, health care and employment, then marvel that she does not come running to get her children immunised or when she refuses to send them to school or practice good nutrition, hygiene and birth control. The glaring disparity between male and female infant mortality rates if plotted on a map, shows a clear belt running across the north-western part of the country with a few pockets elsewhere and this is where immediate health and nutrition interventions must now be focussed.

An integrated and holistic approach to the girl-child's development is essential for the creation of a new environment in which she can be valued and nurtured. This involves a process of social mobilisation that will make her everyone's concern: *The media, the family and the community as well as government and voluntary agencies.* Only this kind of a massive mobilisation can help her to walk out of the maze of neglect in which she has been lost for centuries.

Gandhi on Women

This book offers a collection of Gandhiji's writings and speeches, especially those related to women. Anand T. Hingorani had once published *Gandhi on Women,* putting together many of Gandhiji's writings and speeches for the benefit of readers. But that was quite a few years ago. Hence this compilation is timely and fulfils a need when interest in, and studies on, the women's movement and women's development are noticeably growing.

A contemplative man of action, Gandhi was unambiguous in his recognition of the fact that women were destined to play a positive role in the reconstruction of society. He was uncompromising in the matter of women's rights and repeatedly underscored the fact that for social justice, equal rights for men and women are imperative. He believed that many of the movements in his time stopped short of being successful because of the condition of 'our women', and much of the work did not yield appropriate results because women-power had not been utilized. In his understanding of the essence of the dilemma of women, Gandhi was far in advance of his lime. This attitude is well expressed in a primer, *Balpothi,* that he wrote for children. It is said that his colleagues, some of them at least, took exception to his 'non-sexist' approach to the subject, expressed in a dialogue between the mother and the child. Gandhi's rejoinder was, "I am building a new society', where, he envisioned, all children, girls and boys, would learn to pray, to play, to keep healthy, to enjoy work, to till the fields, to work with their hands, and also to do housework. Ela Bhatt beautifully illustrates this point in the Foreword.

Regrettably, Gandhi's understanding of women's rights and their role in the process of social evolution and political revolution in India are little known because no serious attep-tion has been paid to his views and actions in this area. Often, Gandhi has been quoted out of context with a very superficial reading of his words in secondary books and newspaper articles. Consequently, no in-depth examination of his thoughts on women and his sensitive awareness of the potentiality of woman as a 'person' in her own right has been undertaken in a systematic way.

The compilation under review is invaluable in as much as it offers the basic primary materials to help anyone interested in undertaking such an examination. Anyone, that is, who is genuinely interested and concerned with stimulating and in-depth and critical research of Gandhi's contribution to the understanding and assessment of women's potential role, not only in home-making, but in the reconstruction of society and in the political and economic revolutions in our country.

As these writings and speeches are presented in chronological order, they facilitate a historical survey of the different phases of Gandhi's life and work, bringing to the fore the evolution of his ideas, underscoring his sensitivity to the social, political and economic happenings of his time which affected his thoughts and actions, revealing a process of self-involvement from the contemporary perspective of the times in which he lived and acted. This is important when we reflect that today, four decades after his passing away, not enough advance has been made as far as women are concerned, despite our Constitution and the enactments that have taken place from time to time since 1950. That realization clearly provides a disturbing perspective and makes it imperative that we go back to his words and actions and study them. For, his words were not theories and his actions were not ineffective. Consider the invaluable contribution that women made to the freedom struggle, the unique resistance he offered to alien domination, to social injustice and inequality, and to economic deprivation. He ushered in a method of enquiry and a technique of action 'intended to replace methods of violence', an endeavour for engagement with 'the others', always directed towards conflict resolution—conflict resolution by means of what he called *satyagraha*.

As he said in his speech in 1931 (p. 257), "at the very beginning we had made it clear neither sex nor age would be any bar to one's participation in the movement! In fact, the women in India tore down the purdah and came forward to work for the nation. They saw that the country demanded something more than their looking after their homes....They marched to jails and they sustained lathi blows as few men did" (p. 238, speech made in 1932), and again, in 1939 (p. 312). "The salt campaign brought out tens of thousands (of women) from their seclusion and should that they could serve the country on equal terms with men". In an article in *Harijan* (24 February 1940) he wrote,"....ultimately women will have to determine with authority what she needs. My own opinion is that just as fundamental man and woman are one, their problem must be one in essence....But somehow or other man has dominated woman from ages past, and so woman has developed an inferiority complex. She has believed in the truth of man's interested teaching that she is inferior to him. But the seers among men have recognized her equal status" (pp. 313-16).

Barely six months before he passed away, on 18 July, 1947 (pp. 359-60) he upheld that "Women's marvellous power is lying dormant. If the women of Asia wake up, they will dazzle the world. My experiment in non-violence would be instantly successful if I could secure women's help".

If women are still under overt or subtle bondage, perhaps it is so because 'reforms came first by the force of public opinion' (p. 302). The confusion, the compromises and reaction in India, seen even among Gandhiji's followers in later years, occurred perhaps due to the lack of understanding of his ideas and views and the resultant absence of the force of enlightened public opinion. It is utterly important then that Gandhian study become a part of the core curricula in acade-mia at all levels today, that Gandhian thought and perceptions on women be included in all women's development studies. Only then will the realization of women's equality and development in all its dimensions become a reality. The goals of national policy which support fuller and equal participation of women in all spheres of national life and development can be reinforced if Gandhian thoughts and action are studied in-depth and understood in a disciplined way, whether through formal or informal and non-formal education, so that, as Ela Bhatt says in the Foreword, one could find 'substance for his (Gandhiji's) ideas in one's own life and work'.

> *It would not be an exaggeration to say that it is because an overwhelming majority of men and women in our country today are unfamiliar with Gandhian thought and perceptions on women (although he was in our midst for 79 years), that women's status and role have suffered so tragically. That because of this lacuna, Gandhiji's words and*

actions have not been given an opportunity to provide a positive support to the women's movement in India. This should offer some food for thought, I believe, in our time and day.

This book under review provides an excellent opportunity to every concerned person, the academic and the lay person, to understand theGandhian point of view, his perceptions and his thought, especially those related to women. The 416 documents, complete with dates and sources, covering the period from 24 November 1906 to 31 December 1947 serve as invaluable primary material for research. This compilation is enhanced by the addition of five appendices that include, among other things, a brief sketch of Gandhiji's life, his thoughts on brahmacharya, and an interesting conversation between Kasturba and Gandhiji in South Africa over the invalidation of Indian Marriages Law of 1913. The thematic index at the end of the compilation is useful for a systematic study of subject. The compiler has earned the reader's gratitude for this exhaustive collection of Gandhiji's writings executed so meticulously.

This publication has certainly opened up new possibilities in Gandhian study. One hopes that there will now be the possibility of a greater intellectual collaboration between those who are interested in the Indian revolution and others who accept the question of women's issues as basically political. While the production is impressive, the price would take the book out of the reach of many, especially scholars and researchers, who would benefit by reading this book.

Women Health Development and Administration Principles and Practices

This outstanding text in two volumes is easy-to-grasp language and with illustrations and charts, deals with various aspects of women's health development and administration its principles and practices.

If a nation has to develop, then half of its population (women and girls) must also develop, be educated, become healthy and develop positive self-image. If the so-called 'better half' continues to be neglected, discriminated and exploited in the matter of nutrition, education, health and legal rights, how can she be expected to give her 'Best' for the health and development of her child, family, society and Nation. In India and other S A ARC nations, she is the beast of burden.

Contents Include

Volume I : Women and health development, the girl child, the female youth, benefits of breast-feeding, health of working women, aspects of common ailments in women, etc.

Volume II: Situation of women, Sex differentials and demographic trends, Country rankings of the status of women: Poor, Powerless and Pregnant, New dimensions, Law and women's health etc.

This important book will go a long way to provide source material to professionals of health, medicine, women and social welfare; planners, administrators of hospitals and health centres; scholars and students of medicine, public administration and public health; all women colleges and other institutions; and all others interested in the welfare and development of women.

Women's Economic Development Related to Sustainable Developmet

Dr. Manorama Bawa (Former President AIWC)

Introduction

There are approximately 1.3 billion people in the world who are living on one to two dollars a day, out of them 70% are women. In a population of approximately 300 million in India 70% women are below poverty level. According to a World Bank report 60% of work force is provided by women working 60-70 hrs a week and still own only 1 % of the world property. They provide 70% of agriculture labour and grow food but do not own any land.

Because of their traditional responsibilities for collecting fuel and water, the time and physical effort expended by women, seriously limits their ability to engage in education and income generating activities. Literacy rates and school enrolment are dramatically different for men and women. In India the literacy percentage among *women is only 52% and in somestates it is* as low as 20%.

Discrimination against women from, or even before birth guarantees them a marginal role in developing societies and ensures that they are poorer, less educated and facing more unemployment and health risks than men. The cumulative effects of inequalities worsen deprivation. According to a report by Women's Empowerment and Development Organization (WEDO) "growing poverty, is a powerful trend.....harming millions worldwide......"

Dimensions of Poverty

Poverty indicators have expanded as the concept of poverty has broadened along with consumption in capabilities and entitlements. The concept of poverty refers to deprivation and vulnerability and can be interpreted in different ways. The key indicators of poverty include the inability to meet certain basic needs such as food, health, shelter, clothing and sanitation. Certain intangible needs that effect the poor form a broader definition of poverty such as powerlessness, dependence, isolation, leading to lack of self confidence. Poverty may be due to lack of resources or non-utilization of resources, inadequate levels of economic development, international trade terms, weak infrastructure and inefficient administrative system. Poverty may also be due to gender based difference in access to resources, employment of gender discrimination in labour market, increasing feminization of poverty due to lack of education among women and other socio-cultural factors.

Academic approach to understand the dimensions of poverty and below poverty line is not necessary, but there is need to focus on estimating poverty ratio and target poverty as a whole. The chronic poverty, seasonal poverty and structural poverty increase the gaps between the rich and the poor because of inequality in resources, availability of access to resources and production.

Today the world is moving towards unsustainable consumption lifestyles created for the consumer. This has given rise to an entirely different type of culture and ethics, affecting not only the economy but also the value system resulting in different kinds of poverty, giving rise to an adverse growth such as "jobless growth, ruthless growth, voiceless, futureless and rootless growth". The urban-rural divide is threatening to erode the social and cultural patterns, disturbing the means of livelihood of people, their economic security and replacing their craft skills with mass produced goods.

Globalization has presented new challenges for the fulfillment of commitments and realization of goals of social development. Despite impressive growth in some areas, globalization has resulted in a sense of insecurity, especially in developing countries, and marginalized them from global economy. Globalization on one hand offers opportunity for social and economic development promoting full and productive employment, fosters social integration providing an enabling environment for social development. But on the other hand it presents serious challenges including financial crises, insecurity, poverty by marginalizing certain sectors of society, especially women, and inequality within and among societies.

The issues of poverty alleviation has to be understood in the context of holistic and multidimensional development especially in developing countries. The term "social exclusion" has been coined to reflect the multidimensionality of the poor and detachment from the benefits of mainstreaming economic growth and development. The new economic approach to poverty alleviation takes into account the multidimensional aspects of social exclusion and attempts to build an alternative development strategy. This strategy goes beyond the conventional critique of economic management and income distribution but is based on "Bottom up" approach. This approach, while focusing on community level initiatives, cannot be thought of as a strategy unless there is a planned macro policy framework. Poverty eradication has to be understood as more equitable distribution of wealth, more opportunities, guarantee of social justice and re-enforcing linkages between economic and social justice.

While poverty is not the cause of gender bias, the link between gender and poverty is visible among the poor and women are the poorest of the poor.

Economic Development and Susceptibility

Development tends to have a male bias and in the process women get affected in different ways than men. The pattern of discrimination and gender bias is universal (depending on social and cultural norms) and these gender-based differences are visible in access to resources, employment and gender discrimination in labour market.

There is a close relationship between the sexual division of labour and the reliance of the poor on traditional energy sources. Women's work involves productive activities as well as tasks associated with child rearing, food processing and other household chores. The absence of basic labour saving devices and clean technologies such as fuel-efficient stoves etc., not only burden the poor women but also prevents their involvement in other productive activities. Women and girl children also work as unpaid family labour in physically arduous and time consuming agricultural activities of food production and processing for local markets. A similar pattern is found in income generating activities; women have less access to activities for economic self-sufficiency, credit facilities, information or skill improvement.

Till recently development planning was based on macro planning, which has been replaced by a policy for holistic approach to rebuilding impoverished communities and re-valuing low productivity work or unpaid work by marginal groups. Any development programme that ignores the life chances of half the population cannot address the problems of poverty and crisis of susceptibility.

The women's movement, all over the world drew the attention of the national governments and the UN on the poor status of women and the poverty that affected women especially in rural areas. The World Conferences of Women focused on these issues, so that women could become equal and active participants in the development process of societies.

At this juncture it is necessary that the development process incorporate an agenda for women's empowerment by understanding and including women's realities. New approaches to economic planning are needed based on the realistic understanding of the dynamics of new poverty i.e. exclusion from economic, social and political activities.

Development that enhances the welfare of all citizens especially women, poor and disadvantaged involves innovation and change. It requires new thinking, new activities and new approaches that involve perspectives from several disciplines. A comprehensive approach to development involves participation not only of the governments but also of NGOs, Industry, Corporations and Financial institutions. These stakeholders should be involved as partners at all stages and also the research process.

This approach does not challenge the structural or cyclic nature of economic growth, nor the critique of mal- distribution or the gains arising from local and state incomes.

Energy and Gender

Energy is one of the most essential inputs for sustaining people's livelihood. Nearly two billion people in the developing countries have no access to modern forms of energy such as electricity, gas etc., but depend on biomass fuel for heat and light and their own metabolic energy for mechanical tasks.

In India 86% of rural and 24% of urban households rely on biomass of their primary cooking fuel. Burning biomass in traditional stoves emits smoke containing harmful pollutants with serious health consequences for the exposed women population. This exposure to indoor pollution is estimated to cause 500,000 deaths, 550 million incidences of illness and 16 million years of healthy life loss among women in India. On a global scale India accounts for 30% of the disease burden from this risk factor in the developing world.

The traditional approach to energy in development policy and planning has assumed gender neutrality. It has assumed that a good energy policy, programme or project will benefit both male and female equally in meeting practical needs. In attempts to redress the issue, in more recent decades, attention is increasingly being paid to women in energy policies, and this attention is confined to household energy, as women are the main procurers of household fuels and within the household energy, the focus is confined to traditional biomass energy concerns. But women have other needs in energy as well, the productive activities for livelihood and income generation in which women engage, also use human and biomass energy. Current approaches in the planning of energy projects in developing countries, such as needs-based approaches, though achieving better results than earlier technology, push and supply driven approaches very rarely mainstream gender. In many societies, households are often taken as homogeneous units, without any recognition that men and women have different roles and areas of decision-making within the household whereas men and women have different energy needs as a result of their roles in society and within the household. For example, women use water for cooking or for other household purposes whereas for men, water is needed for irrigation. Many of agricultural activities like weeding, sowing and harvesting are done by women whereas men do the ploughing, may be with powered agriculture equipment. The energy sector is slow to acknowledge the links between gender equality, energy and development. Changes in the availability of energy, due to policy intervention have different impacts on men and women. The new development effort is to use energy as a part of the deliberate strategy to help raise production and the income of women.

Bringing a gender perspective to energy policy is important as energy has a key role to play in gender and poverty. At present women are being trained to use the non-conventional renewable energy technologies not only as time saving devices but also to improve the health of the women and the family.

The different sources of energy are Biomass, Solar Energy, Wind Energy and Water Energy as alternative to conventional energy. Energy plays a very important role in sustainable development. Gender issues have come to the forefront in many development sectors including agriculture, forestry, and water. Integrated energy based technologies help in sustaining development in the areas of environment, prevent pollution and improve the health of the community at large. At the same time these technologies are providing new opportunities for women's participation and leadership.

All India Women's Conference's experience shows that in implementation of various renewable energy technology's projects (RET) once women are given training and understand the advantages of using these improved devices, they are keen to adopt not only the technology to overcome the drudgery of household tasks but also to use them for income generation. Many valuable studies on gender and energy have been done at the micro and household level, descriptive of women's problems and the obstacles that women face, linking with critical and current policy concerns for the governments. Gender analysis approach helped to analyze the women's access and control over resources and benefits. The sustainable livelihoods framework helped to focus attention on energy for women's productive work and their control over assets.

There are no independent Millennium Development Goals (MDG) on Energy, the independent UN Millennium Project report has identified energy, including electricity, and safe cooking fuels, as an essential infrastructure service and part of the "means to a productive life". The linkages among gender, energy and individual MDGs on poverty, education, gender equality, child mortality, maternal health etc. is a very important element for empowering women by giving them more choices for organizing their priorities.

The year 2006 was a review of the Commission on Sustainable Development, air pollution and climate change. Sustainable Development is all about development of energy, environment and equity. Without economic growth there is no sustainable development. The Integrated Energy Policies are a process to expand its advocacy, lobbying and outreach efforts by facilitating increased productive participation of women in energy, and focus on issues of health, education, electricity and fuel. In developing countries, traditionally, biomass energy is used as fuel etc. and has a great potential as a very important energy source. Women can be trained to use the non-conventional renewable sources of energy for income generation.

Concern for global warming due to green house emissions has led to less polluting alternatives. The recent sustained increase in international prices and diminishing reservoirs of petroleum and coal have diverted attention to alternative sources.

Biofuels and Biodiesel

Biofuels as renewable liquid fuels coming from biological raw material have been proved good substitutes for oil in the transportation sectors. Oil provides energy for 95% of transportation and demand of transport fuel continues to rise. The domestic supply of crude can only satisfy only about 22% of the demand and rest has to be met from imported crude. The crude prices in the international market are very volatile and as bio-fuels have been accepted as an alternative, biofuels like ethanol and biodiesel are gaining worldwide acceptance as a solution to environmental problems, energy security, reducing imports, rural employment and improving agriculture economy. Biodiesel is made from virgin or used vegetable oils and animal fats through trans esterification and is a diesel substitute and requires very little or no engine modifications upto 20% blend and minor modification for higher percentage blends. The use of biodiesel results in reduced emited pollutants and its higher cetane number improves combustion. Raw material for producing ethanol varies from sugar, cereals, beetroot, etc. In Brazil ethanol is used as 100% fuel in 20% of vehicles and 25% blend with gasoline in rest of the vehicles. For biodiesel Thailand uses palm oil, Ireland uses frying oil and animal fats.

The rationale for encouraging production and use of biofuels in India and the developing countries is suitable in the following context:

Is Environment Friendly

Provides energy security especially for rural areas; for creating employment; provides nutrients to the soil checking, soil erosion and land degradation; addresses global concerns relating to carbon emissions and helps to reduce dependence on crude oil imports.

India has large tracts of wastelands which can be put to productive use by raising tree borne oilseed plantations such as Jatropha and Pongamia Pinrate. The future of biofuels depends on accelerated diffusion of new technologies especially in developing countries in rural areas. Biofuels have enough external benefits such as generating employment and income in rural areas and emitting less green house gases. All trees bearing oil seeds, both edible and non-edible, have the potential to be a source of biodiesel. India requires to focus on non-edible oils like Jatropha Curcas, Pongornia Pinnata, Neem etc. Jatropha has been identified as the most suitable Tree Borne Oilseed (TBO) for production of Biodiesel. Farmers in rural areas of India are already extracting oil from cultivation of Jatropha. After settling and decanting it, they are mixing the filtered oil with diesel fuel without any damage to their machinery. With research, improved technology and energy policies, the Jatropha product can provide desirable goals.

All India Women's Conference is a national women's organization established in 1927 by women leaders of those times, committed to create an enabling environment for women in the areas of education, health and economic self sufficiency etc. Since then AIWC with its network of 500 branches and one million women membership is involved in programmes for skill development and capacity building for improving their status through economic empowerment.

AIWC, nodal agency identified by the Ministry of Non-Conventional Energy sources, Govt. of India, is successfully conducting programmes for propagating improved stoves, biogas technology as well as solar technology for training in income generation in rural areas at the grass root level. Bangladesh experimented by launching the microfinance and microcredit programme for poverty elimination among women. This programme proved to be successful and was accepted by the poor as an answer to their problems due to poverty.

In India various microfinance initiatives have gained momentum providing funds as credit for entrepreneurial activities to poor women. The National Government through its

Five Year Plan initiated welfare programmes for improving the quality of life for women in all spheres of life, but the impact was not dramatic. The Reserve Bank of India, which is the Central Bank of India and acts as advisor to the Government of India in matters of economic policies, advised NABARD (National Bank for Agriculture and Rural Development) in 1991-92 for launching the pilot project of Self Help Groups in the country with a view of combining flexibility, sensitivity, responsiveness of technical and administrative capabilities and financial resources for formal credit institutions. NABARD framed the micro-credit module functioning through SHGs and took adequate steps for strengthening the programme by providing 100% refinance facility to banks, training facilities etc.

The Rashtriya Mahila Kosh initially worked in collaboration with NGOs working among women providing training and financial assistance for improving the condition of poor women in rural and urban areas. The unique feature in the SHG system is that there is no component of subsidy in credit given to poor women and it encourages them to become entrepreneurs with their own efforts without grant assistance. The SHG system has become popular among women as these women are now in a position to take up income generating activities and meeting their own consumption needs with the available financial help.

In Andhra Pradesh microfinance institutions as Thrift Societies or Mutually Aided Co-operatives, have been set up whereas in Gujarat SEWA the Self Employed Women's Association is helping women towards financial independence.

AIWC has at present nearly 5000 Self Help Groups all over the country successfully involved in achieving economic self sufficiency to support improved quality of life for their families through various initiatives including non-conventional energy technologies.

AIWC in collaboration with the Ujjain University took up this programme for 100 SHGs of 10 members each in rural areas around Ujjain. The group started with a small capital from their own savings. Through skill development training programmes in indigenous products combined with market training, today they have a capital of Rs. 20 lakhs revolving funds, improving their quality of life, with their children in schools. A project for growing nutritional vegetables among leprosy patients in Tamil Nadu has given them self confidence and sustaining income. In Pondicherry 100 Self Help Groups with a membership of 1000 are aiming for economic self sufficiency through various projects varying from marketing, masala grinding, handicrafts, food preserves, renewable energy technologies etc.

AIWC has SHGs in areas dominated by women-headed households owning agriculture land who can be involved in income generation for growing biomass, operating conversion technologies such as oil extraction and marketing of biofuels.

There is certainly speed for women employment in this areas of biofuels if women members of the SHGs can be trained to run the processing units and for marketing. A definite and aggressive motivational and capacity building programme has to be planned out to reach the women in villages where there is potential for Jatropha plantation.

The SHGs in one of the AIWC branches in Kerala gave training in the use of Solar Dryer Technology, as an income generating programme, for drying products, packaging and marketing of local products of pepper, tapioca, coconut powder, arrowroot etc.

In Sadrana, a village in Haryana, AIWC runs an integrated rural development project and the Panchayat has given agriculture land rights to three Self Help Groups for horticulture and vegetables growing, and these are marketed fresh or solar dried, generating self confidence among women.

Integrated approach to development initiatives will empower women and make them effective partners to sustainable development for tackling poverty, improved environment, energy security and positive growth.

Women, Know Your Law !

The landmark Domestic Violence Act of 2005 will provide protection to wives, mothers, sisters, daughters and live-in partners who suffer physical violence at the hands of male relatives.

The Act defines Physical Violence as:

* Any kind of bodily harm or injury.
* A threat of bodily harm.
* Beating, slapping and hitting.

But violence against women is not always physical. For the first time, the law has expanded the definition to include sexual, verbal and economic violence.

Sexual Violence

Under the law, Sexual Violence will include:

* Forced sexual encounter.
* Forcing a woman to look at pornography or any obscene pictures.
* Any act of sexual nature to abuse, humiliate or degrade a woman's integrity.

Verbal Violence

The Act defines Verbal Violence as :

* Name calling.
* Any kind of accusation on a woman's character or conduct.
* Insults for not bringing dowry.
* Preventing a woman from marrying a person of her choice.
* Any form of threat or insults for not producing a male child.

Economic Violence

Under the Act, Economic Violence is :

* Not providing money, food, clothes, medicines.
* Causing hindrance to employment opportunities.
* Forcing a woman to vacate her house.
* Not paying rent.

Women———Are You Incomplete?

By: Shevata Rai Talwar

She survived and was born,

a cherubic, bouncing girl child,

Their happiness was 'incomplete',

She became a toddler,
sweet, gentle, flaxen curls,
her mundan ceremony had it been a boy-a feast missed!
Society's happiness was incomplete.

She blossomed into a lissome girl,
pink ribbons, doll house forgotten, now a 'beauty peagent,
She is too short, timid and shy-so very incomplete.

Time flew by, horrors of
discrimination, rape, incest, marriage, dowry,
It was a Man's world- she became harsh and brusque,
She was still incomplete.

Old age dawned, beauty faded, body wasted,
Withered, weak. Will her offspring take care of her?
Oh-for once she really felt Herself- yet so incomplete.

References

1. The author is former Principal of H.H. the Maharaja's College for Women, Trivandrum. This is the paper presented at a Seminar on the occassion of the South Zonal Conference in Trivandrum in December, 2005.
2. Miss Ivy Khan is national general secretary, Y.W.C.A. of India.
3. Extracts from A Report published in NFIW Bulletin, Vol. II, No. 1 March 1990.

5

WINTER SESSION OF PARLIAMENT STARTS (1999)

The "Hindu" dated 21st December 1999, carries the news that Sonia Gandhi, the leader of the opposition, tells Govt. to "come clean". The Congress (I) president and the leaders of opposition found herself at the centre of a row in the Lok Sabha today over her demand that the Women's Reservation Bill be passed in the current session itself. With only three days left for the Parliament session to end, she wanted the Govt. to clarify its intentions".

Later on, she walked out of the House with her party members, protesting against the Governments' refusal to give a firm commitment on passing the Bill before the end of the session. The left parties and the AIDMK joined the walkout.

The Parliamentary Affairs Minister, Mr. Pramod Mahajan, took the stand that while the Government had every intention to introduce the Bill in "this session", passing of the Bill was in "the hands of the House". He said "we can only introduce the Bill" neglecting the queries on when exactly the Bill would be introduced.

Mr. Madhava Rao Scindia, the deputy leader of Congress (I) was apprehensive that the Government would bring it on the last day of the session simply as a formality. "They must introduce it tomorrow" he insisted.

Mr. K. Yerram Naidu, the leader of the Telugu Desam supported the demand saying that both the national Democratic Alliance and his party were committed to the Bill "why not introduce it tomorrow" he questioned the Government.

Earlier, unruly scenes followed Mrs. Gandhi's demand, with the Samajwadi Party (SP) and the Rashtriya Janata Dal (RJD) strongly objecting to introduction of the Bill saying that they would not allow the Bill to be passed in the present form which discriminates Dalits and minorities. They were even more enraged by Mr. Mahajan's assurance to Mrs. Gandhi that the Govt intended to introduce the Bill, in the present session itself.

His statement was greeted with shouts of "No", No" from the opponents of the Bill. They insisted that it should be amended to provide for sub quotas for OBCs and Muslim women.

Amidst Pandemonium, one SP member entered bare foot into the well Protesting Mr. Mahajan's announcement even as his party chief, Mr. Mulayam Singh Yadav charged that there a Congress (i), BJP "Conspiracy" aganist the PCs and Muslim women. He termed the supporters of the Bill as anti-Dalits and anti-minorities, thus provoking a strong reaction from the Congress (I) and the Left parties. Mr. Yadav said that his party was not opposed to women's reservation but to the Bill as it stood now in the present form. The Prime Minister, Mr. Atal Bihari Vajpayee promised to evolve a consensus on the issue but there was no consensus yet, he continued unless a broad agreement was reached, his party would not allow the Bill to be introduced. He was supported by Sri Raghuvansh Prasad Singh belonging to RJD and as the commotion continued, Mr. Chandra Sekhar, the former Prime Minister intervened on behalf of the Bill's critics.

Mr. Chandra Sekhar said some parties had "invalid" objections to the Bill and the Government should try to "meet" them instead of dividing the House on the issue. "If there is no unanimity, what is the urgency" he wondered pointing out there were more pressing issues than women's reservation before the Parliament. He also had a dig at the JD (U) leader, Mr. Sharad Yadav saying that he was not minister, he was one among the most vehement opponents of the Bill.

Mr Ajit Jogi spokesman of AICC said, though the Congress (I) was in favour of a 33 per cent quota, the party would go along with a "rational consensus" if the Government succeeded in evolving one. When he was questioned whether Congress (I) was in favour of a quota within a quota for OBC women, he replied that it was for the Government to take initative to evolve an acceptable formula and spell out its stand.

Vajpayee to Meet Opposition Leaders on Women's Bill

The Hindu dt 22nd December 1999 reports as follows:

Opponents of Women's Reservation Bill forced the Govt today to think again before pushing it through in the current session of Parliament. As the Lok Sabha witnessed noisy scenes for the second consecutive day also, the prime Minister, Mr. A. B. Vajpayee, agreed to have a discussion with the opposition leaders on 22nd December to break the deadlock.

He met them several times, but with little success. When the uncompromising tendency of the opposition leaders is taken into consideration, a consensus may not be possible. The leaders made it very clear on 21st December that they will not modify to provide sub-quotas for OBCs and Muslims, reservation planned for women in the Lok Sabha and State Assemblies.

Announcing the prime minister's move, the parliamentary affairs minister, Mr. Pramod Mahajan told the Lok Sabha that though the Government was committed to reservation for women legislators, it favoured maximum possible consensus. Consensus, of course, according of him, did not mean unanimity. There was no firm indication whether the Government still stood by its "commitment," given by Mr. Mahajan in the house last weak and reiterated yesterday to introduce the Bill in the current session itself.

Mr. Mahajan's statement followed a determined attempt by the Samajwadi Party and the Rashtriya Janata Dal to disrupt the business of the House they insisted on an assurance from the government that it would not introduce the Bill unless there was a consensus. Proceedings were reduced to a farce as the SP and RJD members occupied the "well" and raised the slogans against the Bill and its supporters, dared the chair to take action against them and shouted down anyone who did not support them.

Mr. Mulayam Singh Yadav refused to restrain his members in spite of repeated and strong warning from the Dy. Speaker, Mr. P.M. Sayeed. He threatened to "name" the SP/RJD members if they did not behave properly. But they continued to raise slogans and disrupt the house. Mr. Yadav watched with amusement and told Mr. Sayeed that he could expel them if he liked.

Trouble began soon after the house met in the morning. Though the Bill was not listed in the Agenda of the day, SP/RJD members were on their feet demanding that introduction of the Bill should be put off. Soon they were in the "well" which they occupied till the lunch time even though the chair went through the business of the House. Slogans calling the government "anti-Dalit" and "anti-minorities" drowned the minister's replies during question hour and "zero hour". Submissions by members. There were heated exchanges as the Congress (I) and the treasury benches protested the SP/RJD member's behaviour. Amidst very noisy interruption the Congress (I) Dy leader, Mr. Madhava Rao Scindhia opposed putting off the Bill under pressure.

The ruling alliance was divided, as the Janta Dal (U) opposed introduction of the Bill and Trinamul Congress favoured it. The JD (U) leader, Mr. D.P. Yadav had an angry argument with the chair, insisting that he should be allowed to speak. In his own words. I am the Dy. leader of JD (U) you cannot refuse me time", he shouted shaning with anger.

Later on, speaking on the bill, he said it violated the constitution which guaranteed equal sights to all citizens nobody was against reservation to women but there should be separate reservation for OBCs and Muslims. This point was also emphasised by Mr. G. M. Banatwala belonging to Muslim League and other critics of the Bill.

Continuing his theory of a "BJP- Congress (I) Conspiracy", Mr Mulayam Singh Yadav said the Government had agreed to the Congress (I) demand for introducing the Bill because it wanted the support of Congress (I) to push through some controversial Bills in the Rajya Sabha, where the BJP led alliance does not have a majority.

When the House resumed after lunch recess, noisy scenes continued until Mr. Mahajan's announcement that the Prime Minister would meet the opposition leaders tomorrow.

At last the doomsday dawned ! It has 23rd December 1999. The historical day on which the Women's Reservation Bill was to be introduced in *Parliament.* Hindu carried a beautiful cartoon by Surendra, about the Womens Bill. Mr. Vajpayee, the Prime Minister of India was trying to draw water from a well, his bucket the full of holes and women around were anxiously waiting for water with pots in their hands.

The Prime Minister held on all party meeting to arrive at a consensus on the Bill, the previous day. He categorically stated that Government was particular of introducing the bill in the present form in the Lok Sabha and effort would continue to arrive at consensus. Equally vehemently, the parties opposing the bill also made it clear that they will stop introduction of the Bill even at the beginning stage.

Representatives of 25 parties attended the one hour meeting. As was expected, major political parties restated their known positions once again.

The two major points on which there were differences among the parties culminated to (1) issue of sub quota for the BCs and (2) suggested rotation of reserved seats. It was pointed out by some, that though reserved seats are to be rotated, for SC seats, since 1978 there was no rotation as sitting MPs representing those constituencies constantly opposed the move. Similar fate could overcome rotation of seats for women also.

It was further pointed out that for a constitution Amendment Bill like this one voting would have to be done peacefully to enable head-count during division. Even if 100 MPs are determined to oppose passing of the legislation, it would be a problem.

The parties which expressed themselves in favour of introducing the bill, in the present form were, the BJP, the Congress (I), all four Left parties, the Nationalist Congress party, the AI ADMK, the Trinamul Congress, the Biju Janata Dal and the Telugu Desam.

Those who apposed the Bill in the present form and wanted sub quota within quota, were the Samaj Wadi Party, the Rashtriya Janata Dal, Bahujan Samaj Party, the Muslim League and the Rașhtriya Lok Dal.

The farce of the situation is there were dissident voices among the ruling alliance like the DMK, the Shiva Sena, the Janata Dal (United) the Akali Dal and the Indian National Lok Dal.

When the meeting started the Prime Minister asked the representatives of the parties to state their point of view, the Congress (I) President Mrs. Sonia Gandhi, was asked to speak first and she said that her party was in favour of introducing the bill in its present form.

Even those, who were against introduction of the Bill, did not oppose the idea of surviving a quota of the Lok Sabha assemblies for women one major point of difference was for a "Sub-Quota" for BC women. DMK stated clearly that it favoured reservation but not of the order of 33 percent as proposed. The suggestion was that a beginning should be made with 10 to 15 percent for women.

It was being suggested by some that even at the time of Gujral Government, the Bill could have been passed, if the 33 per cent share for women had been reduced to 15 percent there are some in the Government, who say that even after The introduction of the Bill, a serious and sincere effort should be made to identify a common ground for a complete consensus on the issue and lowering the percentage of the reserved quota should be considered.

The Government found its House divided. When the DMK favoured reducing the quota JD (U) and INLD vociferously supported the idea of Sub-Quota. Trinamul Congress and TDP favoured introduction of the Bill in its present form and passing of it. BJP did not favour a Sub-Quota for the BCs or any other community.

Finally, at 1.50 pm, the Bill was introduced in the Lok Sabha by the Law Minister, Sri Jethmalani and there were shouts from the SP, RSD members and there were counter shouts from the

TDP and Trinamul Congress S.P. Singh, Bagett, SP leader snatching and the Bill from Law Minister and tore the Bill into pieces. Pandemonium was there and chaos prevailed.

The Finance Minister, Mr. Yashwant Sinha and the Rly. Minister Mrs. Mamata Banerjee, put a protective "shield" around Mr. Jethmalani, when several SP and Rastriya Janata Dal (RJD) members around him, trying to prevent him from introducing the Bill. The protesting members raised slogans calling the Vajpayee Government, "anti-Dalit" and "anti-minorities".

The speaker, Mr. G.M.C. Balayogi took a quick voice vote, that the "A yes have it" and adjourned the House. When it resumed at 3 pm, the agitated SP and RJD members forced another adjournment into 5.30 pm. Normality returned afterwards towards the evening and after some legislative business, the House was adjourned sine die.

The Bill, which has sharply divided the political establishment, proposed 33 per cent reservation for women, in the Lok Sabha and in State Assemblies, its opponents insisted on a separate quota for women belonging to OBCs and Muslim women, within the 33 percent allocation.

Among those who opposed the Bill today was Mr. Prabhunath Singh, member of the Samata Party, a constituent of NDA. He protested the introduction of the Bill saying that it was "rushed".

At a hurriedly called Press Conference, the SP leader, Mr. Mulayam Singh Yadav, "claimed" that the Bill was not introduced" as there was too much confusion to make sense of the proceedings at that time. He was angry that the demand of the opponents of the Bill for a "division" had not been accepted, and condemned the manner in which the bill was sought to be pushed through despite wide spread opposition to it. Several ruling alliance members were also opposed to the Bill and the way, it was "imposed" on the House was against Parliamentary tradition and decorum he said.

In this context it is better to recall how the Bill was brought to the House for the 3rd time. First time, it was in 1996 during the United Front rule, 2nd time, it was in 1998, but it lapsed with the dissolution of the Lok Sabha. Now in 3rd time in 1999. Every time, its introduction was marred by unruly scenes. In 1998, a member snatehed Bill from the Law Minister's hands (Mr. Tambi Dwar at that time) and Ms. Mamata Banerjee had ended up catching an opposition member by the snuff of his neck.

Today on this historic day, 23rd Dec 1999, the Bill was introduced amidst pandemonium. Mr. Jethmalani, Ms. Banerjee and Mr. Yashwant Sinha were seen smiling and bantering with the SP and RJD members, who had crowded the "well". When the member tried to prevent Mr. Jethmalani introducing the Bill, he languid and raised his hands suggesting that he did not have it with him.

The whole atmosphere was surcharged with emotion and the SP and RJD members surrounded the secretary-general's table protesting against the Bill the Left parties and the Congress (I) watched from the sidelines, joining the proceedings only to say "Ages" when the speaker put the Bill to voice vote.

Mr. Mulayam Singh touched off a "gender" row, today saying that if a large member of "inexperienced" women were elected to the Lok Sabha and the state Assemblies, on the strength of special reservation, they could pose a "Thveat" to national interest in difficult situation.

Thveat

The remark made by him at the press conference provoked an angry reaction among media persons, particularly women. They took strong exception to Mr. Yadav's statement and wanted him to explain what he meant. Calling women a possible threat to national interest was a serious charge, they asked him to substantiate it. A woman Journalist-made a pointed reference to the unruly conduct of his party's "in experienced men" men members in parliament, and wanted to know if he thought national interest was safe in their hands. What about Phoolan Devi, his party' Lok Sabha member, who was as "raw" and "in experienced", was she a threat to national interest?

However, Mr. Yadav, Flanked by his party's general secretary, Mr. Amar Singh and particularly difficult Lok Sabha member Mr. Nagamani was infused and stick to his remark, without explaining it. When a journalist insisted that he should elaborate he mumbled and said "come to Uttar Pradesh and see". What did he mean by that ? No one knows the audience simply wondered........

Andhra Prabha a noted Telugu daily dated 24th December 1999, made some comments on the reservation Bill editorially. Commenting on the way the Bill was introduced and how it was torn into pieces, the paper remarked whether the Bill can see the light of the day and get the apparel of the Parliament this time also. But it sounded a caution that by giving 33 per cent reservation to women and thus giving a chance to women to sit in Parliament, without even giving place in the political parties, efficiency of Parliament may not be improved it is a total failure on the part of NDA Govt, no doubt, the paper added.

So people cannot be hoodwinked by mere slogans. The leaders should prove their sincerity through deeds not by simply words. The trend appears to be for diluting the Bill.

Spokesman of Telugu Desam, Dr. C. Ramachandran said in Delhi on 24th December, that his party was in the forefront among the other political parties, which have been seeking 33 per cent reservation for women and so, it cannot accept the suggestion for diluting the quota. He said "Andhra Assembly has adopted a resolution seeking 33 per cent reservation for women and would strive for adoption of the Constitution Amendment Bill on the subject. We can legitimately take credit for raising the demand for immediate introduction and eonsideration of the Bill in both the Houses of Parliament in the just concluded winter session". The party was opposed to the idea of diluting the percentage of reservation. But he said, his party has an open mind on sub-quotas for women from Other Backward classes and minorities with In the 33 per cent reservation for women in Lok Sabha and State Assemblies, if there was consensus among all parties.

The correspondent of the *Hindu* dt 24th December given the news, that the Government will try to work out a consensus on the Bill to give women political reservation to a lower figure, possibly 15 to 20 per cent. The more is seen as a peace offer to the Janata Dal (United) a constituent of the ruling National Democratic Alliance which is strongly opposed to giving women 33 per cent reservation in Parliament and State Assemblies even as it pacifies the BJP's own considerable number of backward caste MPs".

But how far this formula would solve the problem has to be seen.

There are already indications that this formula is likely to start a storm of protests which could jeopardise the proposed legislation itself.

Perhaps sensing the Govt's move, the Congress (I) today categorically stated that it "would not agree to a reduced quota" for women.

A day after the bill was introduced in parliament amidst confusion and by protests, the Minister for Parliamentary Affairs, Mr. Pramod Mahajan, has thrown some broad hints that on way to arrive at a consensus would be to reduce the percentage of reservation. He said the bill's aim is to provide "substantial increase" of women's representation in Parliament (Now it is eight to nine per cent only).

The Prime Minister also said that NDA Government has an "open mind" on the subject. That was taken to mean that it could accommodate the demand by some parties for a sub-quota for the BC women.

Mr. Mahajan emphasised that an important Constitution Amendment Bill such as the present one could not be passed in Parliament "even if a handful of MPs were determined to stop it". The better course of action for the Government would be to try and arrive at a consensus to ensure that the Bill was passed smoothly. A ten percent reservation would be "too low", Mr. Mahajan said at a press conference, pointing out that "since independ ence on an average every Lok Sabha had about eight to nine percent women only". Perhaps this statement implies a hint that a consensus could be achieved on 15 per cent.

But the Congress (I) made it very clear that while it is willing to discuss the question of a Sub-Quota," it is not agreeable to lowering the quota of 33 percent", as Mr. Anil Sashtri the spokesman of Congress (I) said. In fact, the party sought to take credit for the introduction of the legislation, saying that it demanded it. Mr. Sastri emphasized that the party was "committed" to giving women one-third share of the seats and that it would not agree for any reduction. However, it was made clear that Congress (I) was open to the question of "creating a Sub-Quota".

It can be recalled in this context in 1998, when H. D. Dev Gowda Govt tried to introduce the Bill some of the parties strongly opposed it. The Samajwadi Party had been brought around to accept the Bill without a quota for BCs within the larger reservation for women, if the total percentage of reserved seats was brought down to 15 per cent.

It was also a fact while the parties like SP and BJP earned a reputation for themselves for opposing the reservation bill within BJP itself, there is considerable turmoil. Now, there is added factor of some of the BJP allies opposing the Bill. Mr. Sharad Yadav, now a cabinet rank minister had opposed the Bill even when his own Party's Prime Minister, Mr. Indra Kumar Gujral tried to introduce it.

A definite pointer to the problems within the NDA was Mr. Mahajans' comment that his Government would also like to build a "consensus within our party and the NDA".

He countered the argument that the Bill had ignored the women belonging to SCs and STs, pointing out that it provided for 1/3rd of SC and ST seats to be reserved for SC and ST women. As for BCs, Mr. Mahajans argument was the entrenched caste loyalties had ensured more than 50 percent representation for BC castes without reservation and there was no reason why the same loyalties would not help the BC women to get elected.

But it appears that a section within the BJP, discussing about OBCs, quota within the women's quota. The Andhra Prabha, a well-noted Telugu daily dt 24th December 1999, reports that,the national executive of BJP, in its meeting to be held in Chennai on 27th, 28th and 29th of Dec' 99, will discuss about the point. When the women's reservation bill was introduced in the winter session of Parliament it, opposed by parties like SP, BSP, RJD and so Some senior leaders of BJP are arguing that there should be reservation for OBCs also, within the women's general quota of 33 per cent this has gone to the notice of the prime minister, the home minister, and the party's president, according to Sri Bandarv Dattatrey central minister for urban development who expressed with the journalists on Friday at Hyderabad.

In addition to him, minister in the central cabinet like Umabharathi, Kasiram Rana, Santosh Gangwar and others are also of the opinion that there should be reservation for OBCs also. They are suggesting that there should be reservation only for OBCs, he further said, and that their party never expressed the opinion that there should be reservation for minorities. To provide reservation on the basis of religion, is not their party policy and that their party' feels that there should be equal justice for all sections. Though there was sufficient majority to pass the Mahila Reservation Bill. The Prime Minister is trying to arrive at a consensus with all the parties, he explained.

6

PROPORTIONAL REPRESENTATION

Proportional representation may be the only answer to quota problem? How? Let us know in detail.

Increased participation of women in the economic activity is considered to be a favourable factor for women to enter into power positions. But this argument cannot be supported by available data. For instance, in the Asia-Pacific region there are 11 countries which have more than 70 percent of the women of the world and they are above 15 and economically active. But among these countries, only three countries have 10 percent women in their national legislatures.

It is argued that illiteracy is one of the factors responsible for this low level of women's participation in politics. It is wonder to note why developed countries which have achieved remarkable success in female literacy, could not achieve the same level of success in power sharing. 14 developed countries have less than 10 percent women in their national legislatures. Out of 46 developed countries only three countries namely, Portugal, Malta and Yugoslavia reported more than 10 per cent illiteracy.

Another point to be noted in this socio-economic argument is that the character of the political systems has a bearing on female political participation. Democratic systems tend to have more women in their legislatures. It is his dent that Democratic countries in other regions have less than 20 percent women in their legislatures. Communist regimes in Cuba, Vietnam, China and North Korea have 20-30 per cent women in their legislatures.

There is another cultural argument also. The level of female political participation is linked to the culture of the country.

Most of the Islamic countries with a lot of curbs on women in public life, have registered lowest levels of participation in national legislatures. Inter parliamentary reports that as on December 25, 1998, the Arab states have only 3.5 percent women in their national legislatures. But countries like sharing the same Islamic culture like Indonesia, Syria, Bangladesh have 9.12 percent - almost equal to the world average.

What role can the institutional factors play in determining women's representation in legislatures? An analysis of world wide data reveals, that there are different kinds of electoral laws and different voting systems.

Widely accepted single member constituency system is not found favourable to the cause of power seeking women. More women are elected in countries with the electoral system based on proportional representation this system provides for election of two candidates from a list of candidates presented by various political parties and organization from multi member constituencies.

The single member constituency system has a number of serious drawbacks. It denies representation to large sections of the electorate, discriminates against minority groups and under privileged sections. There is a fundamental flow of this system. Only those who vote for the winning candidate get representation. Everyone else, who may make up even more than 50 per cent of the electorate in a constituency get no representation.

With this background in view, if we consider latest attempt to give 33 per cent representation to women in electoral position, no doubt, it brings more women into legislatures. The number of women in Lok Sabha will increase to 182 in one stroke from the current number of 43 MPs. (8.1 per cent).

In Argentina, women were 4 percent in 1991, it rose to 16 percent 1993 and 28 per cent in 1995. In Brazil, when quotas were used in 1997 elections. number of women legislators increased by nearly 40 percent from the previous election. In Great Britain, when quotas were used in the last election to the

House of Commons, female representation doubled to 18 percent.

Having only one MP for each constituency means that each party runs only one candidate. Thus stipulating that all the candidates of all parties, are women, there is no male candidate in those constituencies.

Most of the people vote for the party and for the ideology of it and not for the individual.

7

WOMEN'S MOVEMENT—GANDHIJI'S ROLE

Any movement has as its ideal, the prosperity and well-being of the individual. Main enemies to human being, are not only famines, epidemics and population growth, ignorance, poverty, and backwardness of half of the population viz. women.

Those who can save the people from destruction are not only army men, not industrialists, not even political leaders, it is the selfless and men of integrity that can lead any nation to peace and prosperity.

Gandhiji was one such great man, who could give a clarion call to the people of India and to the whole world, especially to women. The success that Gandhiji achieved in eliminating discrimination against women is something unique and unprecedented. Indian women are really indebted to him, so, in the great movement led by Gandhiji to trans form a feudal Indian society, with tolerance and understanding, women had an equal role to play and he brought them out of clutehes of social dogmas and convictions. Even women in purdah attended his meetings and courted arrests and went to jails.

Gandhiji's successes in South Africa, are tremendous. His life itself is a great laboratory for many a principles required for moulding the inner life style of a human being.

Barbara Ward Jockson, writing about Gandhiji's human values, mentioned that "he is a symbol of humanism".

Ideas of self-respect and human dignity among women, spread because of his preachings.

In Paris, in the year 1932 and after, some time in Switzerland, Gandhiji addressed women and said "I don't think,

I have courage to address women of Europe, without causing them any anger. I request them to know about Indian women, who entered the political arena, in a big way. It is possible to know Europe about non-violence, only through their women".

Gandhiji entrusted responsibility to women of India, in all his constructive programmes on par with men. For in-stance, anti-liquor movement was a grand success because of the participation of Indian women. Khadi movement and burning of foreign clothes was taken up by women only. They came out of the four walls of their houses, went to jails, and ran the families in the absence of their husbands. During his tour over India, Gandhiji once said, "I think the responsibility of exhibiting true colour and form of nonviolence rests only with the women......... for taking up innovative decisions and to implement them, women are well suited more than men because in self-sacrifice, women excel men.

Thus, Gandhiji has tremendous confidence in the capability of women. He led them with love and affection to the forefront.

A few days, before his assassination in Birla Mandir, Gandhiji expressed that his desire was to see that a Harijan woman is elected as the 1st President of India. If such a thing happens, I will dance with joy".

Moving in his footsteps, Pandit Jawaharlal Nehru, the first Prime Minister and the architect of modern India, furthered his cause and gave women of India equal status in the Indian constitution as well as in society.

He gave women, the fundamental right to vote and participate in elections. He brought about several changes in the Hindu Law and was responsible for bringing out the Special Marriage Act, Inheritance Act. and several other Acts concerning women.

But he could not bring out the inheritance by women on property of the father, as the conservatives fought against it.

He wanted to change the very spirit of our laws but some forces worked against his progressive ideas. But because of his towering personality, he could issue "whip" for all the Congress members of Parliament to vote for all the Bills he introduced.

But now, there is no such person, who could see the Women's Reservation Bill passed in the spirit in which it was needed.

Feminist Prospecting: Some Valuable books.

"Women and the politics of class" By Johanna Brenner articulates some scholarly ideas about women's issues.

What do feminists really want? Johanna regards herself as a social activist and a feminist and is at present the head the Women's studies Dept. at Portland State University. She has some reconciling theories between precept and practice. Her book is an attempt to bring together feminist and socialistic politics to provide conservative perception of women's issues. Recounting the debates going on in USA on welfare abortion, women's and workers rights in the context of social policy on gender, family and class politics. She tries to trace the possibility of the spirit of socialism in a family and community life that is democratic and participatory. She attacks the capitalist system as regards the nuclear family for the reproduction of labour and so pinning down women into care-giving roles, which they may not freely choose.

Outside the nuclear family, the woman is often poor because of her lower wages, due to the constraints in her job search, lack of flexibility in her situation, balancing of her domestic duties and due to the fact that women work places are not unionised properly.

Her analysis connects to the issue of female poverty in India, on account of early marriage, inheritance practices and difficulty of enforcing divorce settlements.

As a sociologist, she describes the contradictions seemingly in our needs, we need security in a marriage and we want self development as individuals. We want autonomy but we cannot survive without community.

Analysing power relations based on class, gender, sexuality and caste in India, Johanna believes that they should be looked at, not separately, but at their in intersections. We have multiple identities based on gender, class, race, ethnicity nationality etc. and hence we are called upon to negotiate on these overlapping identities.

What do women want? Johanna tells that women want equity, social and legal justice. But she has ignored the role of religion.

Women of India-colonial and post-colonial periods edited by Bharati Ray. (Sage publications)

This book is a monu mental compilation, comprising 24 contributions spread over 600 pages, sweeping across two centuries. The editor described her underlying message of the volume as follows. "Gender is about power. And if it is about power, it is about politics".

The essays in this volume explore the operation of power and resistance to it. The space that was denied to women.

Breaking Barriers: stories of Twelve women by Parvati Menon is another book, that is to be read to understand, how women have got much of what they take for granted.

As the name suggests, it speaks of the lives of 12 women, who challenged social stereotypes and were crucial in laying a firm foundation for the women's movement in India.

The Gender Gap Persists Globally

The gender gap study released by the World Economic Forum in the year 2005, indicates the huge gaps between men and women in the developed economics. According to the study, no country could eliminate the gender gap, although Nordic countries with a long tradition of serval democracy and welfare system could narrow down the gap to some extent. Sweden, Norway, Iceland, Denmark, and Finland occupy the five top spots among the 58 countries covered by the study. They took up 30 organizations and 28 from the emerging market for study. United States ranked 17 trailing behind East European countries from the former socialistic bloc, like Latvia Lithuania and Estonia.

According to the study, USA fared poorly on account of maternity leave, lack of maternity benefits, and limited facilities for child care. Provided by Government. The low score in economic opportunity tallies with the image of Glass ceiling"

Nordic welfare states are scoring high in educational attainment, political empowerment, and economic opportunities. But they do not perform well in economic participation of women. The former socialist countries, in contrast, score in economic participation and education but failed in the area of health, women in the developed countries "Opt out" of work and economically developed East-European countries on an overwhelming share of the chores at home.

Thailand, which ranks 44 overall, is right at the top when it comes to economic participation of women. Among Asian countries, China ranks highest (33) followed by Japan (38), India at 53, is in virtually at the bottom of the ladder. In health and well being, India is ranked 34, in economic opportunity 35, in economic participation 54 and in educational attainment, a shocking 57. Only Pakistan, Korea, Jordan, Turkey, and Egypt fare worse overall.

The High-School drop-outs among girl children and wage inequality are the key factors in India's ranking. So, in the era of globalization the lesson for India and other poorly ranked countries, is that they should strengthen and enhance the Government support systems. As economic inequality increases within a country, so does the gap between males and females.

Gender Equality: National Advisory Council

The National Advisory Council (NAC) chaired by Sonia Gandhi, has suggested certain specific changes in the existing Laws to ensure equality to women in all matters including in heritance of agricultural land and property, in line with the commitment made in the national common minimum programme (NCMP.)

NAC has written to the Prime Minister and hoped that Government would give priority to the issue.

The council felt that access to arable land was an important instrument for the economic empowerment of rural women and their status.

In several states, rules of succession are different relating to agricultural land than personal laws. The tenurial laws of

Himachal Pradesh, Jammu and Kashmir, Punjab, Delhi, and Uttar Pradesh were cited to show that specified rules of devolution had a strong preference for males.

The council members also felt that the 9th schedule of the constitution still had laws which discriminated against women. The committee also felt that all those laws should be examined separately within a time-frame and steps should be initiated to amend them appropriately.

Since, some of these laws are to be modified by the state Governments, the centre could consider initiating an arrangement, in which, in respect of resources allocated under the existing centrally-sponsored schemes, an appropriate system could be imposed in the event of a state not fulfilling relevant criteria.

This could include amendment of laws denying equal land rights to women and actual recording of women as land-owners.

The rights of women, as co-owners of property could not be confined to land only but to other productive assets like houses and trees.

They felt that the land records could be verified to show the entry of the wife's name as owner of the property.

The state Governments could also be advised to make allotment under the programme relating to waste-lands, surplus ceiling lands, village common lands, developed house sites, assets in rehabilitation packages and ration cards in the name of the women, with priority to BPL women, who are widows, are unmarried or victims of harassment, the NAC suggested.

Under the centrally sponsored schemes like Indira Awas Yojana and the Balmiki Yojana the allotment should be compulsorily made in the name of wife, with priority to those below poverty line, the council felt.

Sonia's Appeals for Greater Focus on Women's Issues

Chairman of UPA, Sonia Gandhi stressed on the need for focussing attention on gender issues in clouding female foeticide, illiteracy and discrimination against women.

"Women may have more opportunities now. But we still have a long way to go" she said, after unfurling the national flag on the eve of the International Women's Day. Mrs. Gandhi said that the Indian constitution entitled women to equal opportunities and rights but in some parts of the land, the note of foeticide is high and the gender ratio terribly skewed. "Girls are not being sent to schools in many places and women face prejudice and discrimination at the work place" she said.

She asserted that the Government was giving top priority to the welfare of women and children.

According to M/s Gandhi, the Panchayat Raj System brought women to positions of responsibility. About 12 lakh women in Panchayats had disproved the scepticism that they would be proxies for men or mere rubber stamps.

Earlier to this meeting, Ms Gandhi unfurled a theme flag on women's empowerment designed by Farook Ambalapurathe of the United Nations population fund. The flag which depicted the colours of a rainbow under the national tricolor against a white background and it will be hoisted all over the country on International Women's Day on 8th March.

The week long celebrations of the international women's Day began on 8th March, with the inauguration of a film festival, that would show case movies based on women's issues.

8

AWAKENING OF WOMEN

The development of women, we see, around us today was not achieved in one day or by one single person. It was the effort of some luminaries who contributed their time and talent to achieve this. Their role should be recognissd and respected by all generations to come.

Dr. Annie Besant and Margaret Cousins, though foreigners, studied the problems of our Indian society and worked for the awakening of sleeping women of India. Gandhi brought out women from the four corners of the house and tried to mould them into full personalities. In fact he gave them special recognition and awakened in them thoughts of independence and individuality. Women of the country should remember his role for ever.

After achieving independence, the first Prime Minister of India and the architect of modern India, Pandit Jawaharlal tried to awaken women of India by granting 'voting right'. For this voting right, women of Britain had to struggle a lot though it was a developed country.

In 1917, Indian women met the Viceroy and demanded that "when the franchise is being drawn up, women may be recognised as people'. As a result of this representation agitation throughout India was started and several meetings were held. Use resolutions passed. As a result women were enfranchised on equal terms with men.

Later on, at several stages women began to conduct hartals and dharnas and could bring a thorough change in the minds of people. After the success of the salt satyagraha, started by Gandhi, role of women in society was recognized by society.

Several women's organisations were started and they started working for women/women's activists could achieve some tangible results.

United Nations also started efforts to awaken women of all countries and several programmes were taken up.

All nations have realised the importantance of womens development as an important factor in the development of societies. This is a good omen.

The Battle of the Vote

In 1917 a deputation of Indian Women representing the various provinces waited on the Viceroy and the secretary of state and demanded that "When the Franchise is being drawn up, women may be recognised as people".

As a result of the representation and following agitation throughout India and in England women of India were enfrachised on equal terms with men. Madras taking the lead. It is to be remembered that whatever was achieved in the field of civic and political rights during those early years was entirely due to the ceaseless and untiring efforts of Mrs. Cousins who piloted resolutions and laboured hard through public meetings, petitions, deputations, to authorities and appeals to prominent men and women of every province.

Annie Besant

Annie Besant was born in London on October 1, 1847. Her father was half-Irish and half-English His name was William Page Wood and he belonged to a family of distinction—one of his ancestors having been the Mayor of London and another a Lord Chancellor. Her mother, Emily Morris, however, was of pure Irish descent, and Annie Besant says in her own autobiography: "the Irish tongue is musical to my ear and the Irish nature dear to my heart". Her father belonged to the medical profession, and while she was still a child, he died on October 5, 1852. The Woods had only two children—Henry, a son and Annie, a daughter. The son later on became Sir Henry Wood and was well-known in London in the last years of the nineteenth and in the beginning of the twentieth centuries.

The family belonged to the well-to-do upper middle class. The death of Mr. Wood left the family in serious financial straits, and it was not easy for the mother to live on the slender income that she had and to give her children the kind of education that she wanted them to have. After a great deal of thought, she selected the Harrow and took a house where the family lived for the next twelve years.

At this time a very important event happened which was a turning-point in Annie's whole life. She met Miss Marryat, sister of the well-known writer Capt. Marryat, at the house of some friend. Miss Marryat was greatly attracted to little Annie and offered to Mrs. Wood to take over the education of her little daughter and keep Annie with her. The children living in her house were taught in the evening by Miss Marryat herself in subjects such as English, French, German, etc. For music she engaged another teacher. Annie Wood loved Miss Marryat very much and her gratitude to her was very great. She learnt to speak fluent French. Alongwith this education Miss Marryat insisted that all her young pupils should interest themselves in social service. In 1861 Miss Marryat requested Mrs. Wood for permission to take Annie abroad. They first went to Germany and afterwards spent seven months in Paris perfecting French. From Paris they came back to England and in 1863 she finished her education with Miss Marryat and went back to Harrow to her own home. She was by, this time a highly accomplished girl of sixteen.

In the year 1866 she met Rev. Frank Besant, a young graduate from Cambridge, who was serving as a Deacon in a little mission church in Clapham, a poor suburb of London. She married Frank Besant, though she had no special love for him. She married in the winter of 1867 and she herself considered that it was a fatal blunder. Two children were born to her, a boy, Digby, and a daughter, Mabel. Her married life was not happy because her husband did not understand her at all and demanded complete and unquestioned obedience which was not in her to give. They finally separated in 1873. Her mother was made bitterly unhappy by her separation from her husband. Annie had no money. However she found some work in

Folkstone as 'headcook, governess and nurse'. In 1874 she and her mother set a house together. But in the same year Mrs. Wood become very ill and died, nursed devotedly to the last by Annie Besant.

In July 1874 she happened to read a copy of the National Reformer which was the official Journal of the National Secular Society of England. The leading spirit of the Society, which called itself "atheist", was the famous Charles Bradlaugh. In August 1874 Mrs. Besant become a member of the National Secular Society. Later on she become co-editor with Bradlaugh of the National Reformer and used her great gift of eloquent expression in the cause of free thought. She became known as Bradlaugh's second-in-command.

Slowly she started to work for social reform in many directions. She was instrumental in helping to start the first trade unions in London. Her famous struggle in connection with the amelioration of the working conditions of the girls who worked in match factories is a classical instance of the early struggles of people who worked for such unpopular things as associations of workers. She joined the Fabian Society and was a close associate of such people as the Sdyney Webbs, George Bernard Shaw, George Lansbury, Ramsay MacDonald and several other prominent socialists of the time. In 1889 it was said that there was scarcely any modern reform for which she had not worked, written, spoken and suffered.

In 1866, she read two theosophical books written by Mr. A.P. Sinnet, a prominent theosophist, and in 1889 she was given Mme. H. P. Blavatsky's "The Secret Doctrine" for review. This book was to her a revelation. She joined the Theosophical Society in May 1889 and became Mme. Blavatsky's devoted pupil and helper. She became a prominent worker in the Society and after the death of Col. Olcott in 1907, she was elected President of the Society, which position she held till her death on 21 September, 1933.

She first came to India on 16 November, 1893. She landed at Tuticorin and lectured in twelve towns in South India, after which she attended the Annual Convention of the Theosophical

Society at Adyar in Madras. In 1894 she toured North India lecturing in eighteen places. Her lectures were mainly on the Hindu religion and on Indian culture. In 1895, she established her home in Benares and completed her great translation of the 'Bhagvad Gita'. In the year 1898, she established the Central Hindu College at Benares. This became one of the great educational Institutions of the time and formed the nucleus of the Banares Hindu University.

In 1907, on her election as President of the Theosophical Society, she made Adyar, Madras, her permanent home. In October 1913, she spoke at a great public meeting in Madras recommending that there should be a Standing Committee of the House of Commons for Indian affairs which would go into the question of how India might attain freedom. She founded a weekly newspaper Commonwealth in January 1914 for her political work. In June 1914 she purchased the Madras, Standard and renamed it New India, which thereafter, became her chosen organ for her tempestuous propaganda for India's freedom. She called this freedom "Home Rule" for India. She was a delegate to the Indian National Congress in 1914. Her firm belief was that India should have her freedom but should remain in the British Commonwealth. In 1915, in Bombay, at a meeting called by her, she explained her plan for the establishement of the Home Rule League. In 1916 this work intensified. People eagerly read the New India for news of the progress of the movement and read Dr. Besant's editorials in the paper. The Home Rule League was started on 1 September 1916. She failed in her first effort to persuade Bal Gangadhar Tilak to combine their two movements. In 1916, after she had addressed a meeting at Cuddalore in South India, Lord Pentland, then Governor of Madras, asked her to leave India. She refused to do so. In June 1917, with G. S. Arundale and B.P.Wadia, two of the principal workers, she was interned at Ootacamund because of the wide protest all over India and abroad, the internment order was withdrawn and in August 1917 she was made the President of the Calcutta Session of the Indian National Congress.

As a result of her campaign and in deference the strength of public opinion in India, the Montagu-Chelmsford proposals were formulated and put into force. At the Congress in December 1918, Dr. Besant admitted that the Montagu Chelmsford reforms did not fulfil her hopes. However, she suggested that they should be given chance and worked in the Provinces.

By this time Gandhiji, who had returned to India, was slowly developing his technique of non-cooperation. In 1920 Gandhiji launched his campaign of Satyagraha, and of the Congress of 1920 in Lahore. Annie Besant with five others stood against the overwhelming flood of support in favour of Gandhiji's plan. A whole lifetime of fighting by constitutional means and within the law left her with a deep distrust of massive law-breaking in whatever cause it might be.

For holding these views, her popularity swiftly waned. Her voice was a single voice against the shouting of thousands. However, her creative work for India went on. Between 1922 and 1924, in consultation with such colleagues as Sir Tej Bahadur Sapru, Sir C.P. Ramaswami Aiyar, Sir P.S. Sivaswami Aiyar, Rt.Hon. V.S. Srinivasa Sastri, Sri Purshottamdas Thakurdas, Sri Hari Singh Gour and others, she drafted the Commonwealth of India Bill which was presented in Parliament by Mr.George Lansbury in December 1955. But it did not go beyond the first reading stage.

In 1917 she established the Indian Boy Scouts' Association and this was united to the International Movement according to Sri Robert Baden-Powell's request in 1921. She was made Honorary Commissioner for India and in 1932 was awarded the Order of the Silver Wolf, the greatest honour that the Scout Movement could offer.

Her work for education went on steadily. In 1915 she established the National College at Madanpalle in South India. In 1917 she started the Society for the Promotion of National Education. In 1918 the National University was established by her at Adyar in South India. The Chancellor of the University was Rabindranath Tagore, the Vice Chancellor, Sri S. Subramnia Aiyar, and the Principal, Dr. G.S. Arundale. She also started a number of schools for boys and girls. In 192 she delivered the first three Kamala lectures at the Calcutta University.

At no time did Annie Besant advocate free love. On the other hand her views on marriage were very much vedic. In her autobiography she says:

"No countenance is given to those who fain would destroy the idea of the durable union between one man and one woman. Monogamy appears to me the result of civilisation, of personal dignity, of cultured feeling; loyalty of one man to one woman is, to me, the highest sexual deal. The more civilised the nature the more durable and exclusive does the marriage union become...Hence it arises that true marriage is exclusive and that prostitution is revolting to the noble of both sexes, since in prostitution love is shorn of its fairest attributes, and passion, which is only his wings, is made the sole representative of the divinity. The fleeting connections supposed by free love theorists are steps backward and not forward they offer no possibility of home, no education of character, no guarantee for the training of the children. The culture both of the father and the mother, of the two natures of which is the resultant, is necessary to the healthy development of the child. It cannot be deprived of either, without injury to its full and perfect growth."

In 1917 she started the Women's Indian Association to which she gave her powerful support. She was assisted in this by Dr. (Mrs.) Muthuakshmi Reddi, the first woman legislator in India and Mrs. Margaret Cousins. In 1924 the Association had by 51 branches. In 1927 the first All India Women's Conference was held in Poona and it became a permanent and powerful body.

Her health began to give way very slowly in 1930, and she passed away peacefully on September 21, 1933. She herself desired as her epitaph only the simple words "She tried to follow Truth". Her whole life was a striking vindication of this determination.

"Never *yet has a nation risen to greatness unless the men and women in it walked side by side and hand in hand, As soon may you try to make an Indian nation without the education of Indian women, as a bird might try to fly high in the air with one wing broken before it starts upon its flight. It is only where the men and women stand side by side, heart with heart and hand in hand, that any great social or political progress is possible for any people."*

—*Annie Besant*

Margaret Cousins

Born in 1878 in Ireland of Irish parents, since 1915 she made India her home and her country. Her husband, Dr. James Cousins was a poet, artist and author. Both came to India at the call of Mrs. Annie Besant, another Irish woman who had made India her home and who worked unceasingly for the advancement of India and particularly its women who led the National Movement of India.

"With my first year of landing on Indian soil, I was dedicated to the service of India, i.e., service to that half of India-its womanhood......" says Margaret Cousins and inspired the Indian women with inspiration and patriotism!!

A vibrant, lovable personality, full of zeal, vigour and enthusiasm, she infected those around her with her enthusiasm and ardour. It was she who started the Women's Indian Association in 1917 in Madras, and this was the forerunner ; of the All-India Women's Conference. She was one of its joint H.Secretaries and for years the Editor of its monthly journal-"Stri Dharma".

Mrs. Cousins was responsible in calling together the first ever deputation of Indian women from different provinces, which was led by Mrs. Annie Besant to the then Viceroy of India, Lord Chelmsford and to Mr. Edwin Montague M.P., the Secretary of State for India. The deputationists demanded that when the Franchise Bill be drawn up, women of India should be given the same rights as the men. It was the ceaseless efforts of Mrs. Cousins, writing to important men and women, calling meetings etc, which gave the lead, by granting the Franchise, as well as the right of representation to the women of Madras in 1925, followed by Bombay on 1927 and other Provinces later.

Constantly travelling, lecturing, writing to rouse the women from their age-old lethargy, she was an inspiration to many. In 1917, she organised the first All India deputation of women to the Viceroy, Lord Irwin, to ask for Votes for Women.

In 1923, she was appointed an Hon-Magistrate in Madras, the first woman to be so appointed, a position which she held with distinction for many years. But in 1932, she was imprisoned for one year, because she launched her own individual Satyagraha protesting against the inclusion of emergency ordinances under the Indian Penal Code. She helped every good cause. She was one of the founders and guiding spirit with Dr. Muthulakshmi Reddy, of the Women's Home of Service. Child Welfare work had also just been introduced in Madras, and she was also instrumental in getting the Madras Children's Act passed. The Madanapalle Theosophical College of which Dr. Cousins was the Principal. She was the guiding spirit to the students and staff and also Mummy to the women students in the hostels.

A Doctor of Music and an exceptionally good pianist and artist of no mean calibre, a writer, a lover of Indian Art and Culture, she advocated the national and artistic spirit wherever she went. Indian women owe a great debt of gratitude to this intrepid woman pioneer, a staunch believer in women's rights from her early youth who pave her all to the cause of Indian womenhood. She helped her husband in various ways when he organised the museum for the Trivandrum Palace. She was the General Secretary of the All India Women's Conference in 1926 and 1927. She was also the President of the A.I.W.C. in 1936 and at the Eleventh Session of the Conference was held at Ahmedabad in 1936 under the Presidentship of Mrs. Margaret E. Cousins. Visitors from England, Australia, USA and Holland attended the Session.

She was a model woman and a true friend of Indian Woman and All India Women's Conference.

Political [Career] For Women

Leela Damodara Menon, M.P.

If Margaret Cousins who launched the first passive campaign for women's education for their total emancipation in India were to put in her appearance now, she would be taken by surprise to see the tremendous changes that have taken place and the transformation to the All India Women's Conference itself which she had organised and of which she was the guiding spirit. The multistoreyed A.I.W.C. Complex fwill be symbolic of the progress of the Indian women. Constitution of free India has given Women equal rights and opportunities. Many Social Laws have been enacted to prevent discrimination. Serious efforts are being made to promote women's education and reduce illiteracy. Equal remuneration for equal work now law. Job opportunities for women are being expanded. Special consideration is being given to rural women. India has had a women Prime Minister, Women Ministers, High Court Judges, Engineers, Doctors, Scientists and Technicians. Many are even now at their jobs doing extremely well. All that would gladden the heart of Mrs. Cousins.

But she also will see that there are millions of Indian women who are backward socially, economically and politically, it would shock her that the early enthusiasm of women to join political activity is not so evident now. Political power is still the prerogative of the male. Even in a democracy where about 50% of the voters are females the control of the administration and political power is vested with men alone, whatever party may be in power. It is true that the Constitution guarantees equal political rights and the Indian women have deserved that right on the strength of their contribution to the freedom struggle. But to day the degree of equality and freedom really enjoyed by women is very slight and the Constitution and provisions are only on paper for most women. The few women who have reached outstanding positions as Prime Minister and Ministers, have attained their place inspite of their being women and have had to face manifold hardships.

Politics became a way of life for many women during the freedom struggle because of the inspired leadership of Mahatma

Gandhi who called upon women to join the Nonviolent Resistance Movement which suited their temperament as it involved self sacrifice. Women could reach leadership by the extent of their suffering and not by her learning on connections only. The Independence movement therefore became an area for all sections of women to get together. It was also pointed out by Gandhi who had the vision to see the truth, that politics is not merely for assumption to power, but for welfare of the people, for eradication of their poverty, illiteracy, ill health and irregularies and that was additional reasons why women also should join the stream of political life. Today that truth is being accepted by the United Nations and other World organisations.

What role can women play in politics? She can be just a voter fully conscious of her duties, privileges and power, exercising her rights. She can be part of an organisation or group which can, wherever necessary, cry for changes if all do not go well with the national programmes or she may be a full time political worker engaged in striving for the great national objectives as a citizen. This groups will form the hard core of political women workers and are unfortunately few at every level, including the highest decision making bodies. Most women do vote, but they do not do so consciously. A survey done in an urban area of 200 families in Kerala show that 95% of them who voted did not make the decision for themselves. Either the father, husband, brother or son gave them directions to vote. Sometimes, it is the neighbour's advice, but rarely because of one's individual preference. Being shut in within their homes, they do not know the candidates. The respective merits or drawbacks of the contesting parties are not usually understood by them and they vote anyhow. The active group has a very difficult time. Our tradition bound society still can't envisage women taking up full time political work and consider such women with curiosity and suspicion. Even educated women do not understand the need for interest in politics. Some years ago while organising a political conference, I happened to request an educated friend to attend the Conference. She told me she had no time for politics and asked me why I did not remain at home looking after my husband and children and leave politics to men. She said she believed in giving her full attention to home. It was quite a surprise when this same friend met me years later to take my advice in my capacity as the Secretary General of the All India Women's Conference, regarding divorce laws because she was thinking of leaving her husband as he was neglecting her. She was also unhappy with the way her children were growing up, indisciplined and indifferent to their studies. I tried to help her as best as I could. The incident showed that even if one lives inisolation from one's surroundings, happiness does not depend upon individual effort alone. I felt that if the friend had taken more interest in matters outside her house, her life could have been more real and happy and she could have been better equipped to solve her problems.

The report on the Status of Woman and recent high level discussions at Government level prove that India is being aware of the problems of women. It is true that women should have education, training, employment and encouragement to take up their full responsibilities at the national, local and community levels and also are made aware of problems that effect society not only as they hit them directly, the others as well.

Goals, strategies and time tables should be set for increasing the number of women in elective posts and public offices. Legislation alone will not guarantee eligibility to hold public officers.

Special efforts should be made to get Government to reaffirm the official policy of equality. Governmental instructions for complication of periodic reports should insisted to watch the progress of equitable representation. Research Studies should be made available as and when necessary on general information, prevalent trends as well as on competence of women for recruitment, nomination and elections to political offices. Special efforts and campaigns should be made available, as well and when necessary on general information, prevalent trends as on competence of women for recruitment, nomination and election to political offices. Special efforts and campaigns should be organised to enlighten the female electorate on political issues and the need for their active participation. Propoganda programmes as well as study should help women to get clearer picture of the existing conditions so that they can formulate plans on their own

Realisations that their active political interest can help them in their own domestic spheres in however small way, it may be, will motivate women to take interest in politics. A well organised group of women can get things done to improve their community life in no small measure. If drinking water or light or other such civic amenity is not available as required, united, they can clamour for it and no civic body can ignore such force the League of women Voters in U.S.A. which was organised to make women aware of their political and civics duties have successfully proved what a force women can be if well organised. At present they can do everything else but get a women to be the President of United States. They have already made their impact on the national life of the country. In many other countries also women are trying to organise greater awareness of political problems. Their experience would be useful guidelines for us also.

There are national Women's Organisations and Women's wings of political parties who have been trying to work on women's involvement in political life. What they have so far succeeded in doing, is to list out the disabilities and discriminations women suffer and to attempt to get Governmental and other action to remove them. The social legislation in India has first been lobbied by these organisations and today at the national level, the discussions and dialogues are already started once again.

The most important factor that will help women to establish their rightful place in political life is united action. National organisations and women leaders should offer a writed front to face issues. There must be a women's unit in every village so that the voice of the women will be heard at all levels in public life of the nation. Education and training are necessary. Not merely at the formal level, but study classes must enable women to make their own assessment and decision and such orientation at the lowest level in village. Whatever be the economic on social position, if the organisations can be alert and alive to community problems, they will automatically become politically conscious also.

There should be women represented at all elected and representative bodies. Equal rights do not provide equal opportunities. Having no representation at all inspite of having equal rights, it will be better to consider whether a certain percentage of seats can be reserved for women as minimum scale of representation. Care is to be taken that this minimum should not overlook the strength of number of women population. To equip women to successfully function as political workers, they must feel that they are involved in the action for the welfare of their children, home and nation. Concrete programmes like drawing up the Rights of the child, the Rights of the women and other social safeguards could be taken up to focus their attention. Study of wellknown experiments in other countries could be done so that similar struggle and unity will benefit our problems. There should be a great deal of systematic coordination between the Village, State and National level programmes.

Only self confidence and determination can lead women to the goals of political positions. They have to forget that they are women hemmied in, by all the hardships of tradition. With the world in front of them, with legal sanction, they have to march forward. Let the mother replace the 'abala' so tint the mother's zest for the welfare of her children will extend to the world of politics and development. That will bring new dimensions to developmental action and a greater future to the emancipated woman and the nation.

The Awakening of Women

—Mrs Annie Besent

The position of women in the ancient Aryan civilisation was a very noble one. The great majority married, becomings as Manu said, the Light of the Home; some took up the ascetic life, remained unmarried, and sought the knowledge of Brahman. The story of Rani Damayanti, to whom her husband's ministers came, when they were troubled by the Raja's Gambling, that of Gandhari, in the Council of Kings and warrior chiefs, remonstrating with her headstrong son; in later days, those of Padmini of Chittoor, of Mirabai of Marwar the sweet poetess of Tarabai, of Thoda the warrior, of Chand Bibi of Ahmednagar, Ahalya Bai of Indore the Great Ruler-all these and countless others are well-known.

Only in the last five or six generations has the Indian woman slipped away from her place at her husband's side, and left him unhelped. In his public life. Even now, they would great influence over husband and son, but lack thorough knowledge to aid, Culture has never forsaken them. But the English education of their husband and sons, with the neglect of Sanskrit and the Vernacular, and that of the wife, have shut the women out from her old sympathy with the larger life of men. While the interests of the husband have widened, those of the wife have narrowed. The materialising of the husband has tended albo, by reaction, to render the wife's religion less broad and wise, and by throwing her on the family priest for guidance in religion, instead, as of old, on her husband, has made the religion entirely one of devotion; and lacking the strong stimulus of knowledge, it more easily slides down into superstition, into dependence on forms not understood.

The wish to save their sons from the materialising results of English education awoke keen sympathy among Indian mothers with the movement to make Hinduism an integral part of education. It was, perhaps, the first movement in modern days which aroused among them in all parts of India a keen and living interest.

Then the troubles of Indians outside India roused the ever-quick sympathy of Indian women, and attack in South Africa on the sacredness of Indian marriage drew large numbers of them out of their homes, to protest against the wrong.

The Partition of Bengal was bitterly resented by Bengali Women, and was another factor in the outward turning change. When the editor of an extremist newspaper was prosecuted for sedition, convicted and sentenced, 500 Bengali women went to his mother to show their sympathy, not by condolences, but by congratulations. Such was the feeling of the well-born women of Bengal.

The Indentured Labour question, involving the dishonour of women, again, moved them deeply and, even sent a deputation to the Viceroy composed of women.

These were, perhaps, the chief outer causes; but deep in the heart of India's daughters arose the Mothers' voice, calling on them to help her to arise, and to be once more mistress in her own household. Indian women, nursed on her old literature, with its wonderful ideals of womanly perfection, could not remain indifferent to the great movement for India's liberty. And during the last few years the hidden fire long burning in their hearts, fire of love to Bharatamata, fire of resentment against the lessened influence of the religion which they passionately love, instinctive dislike of the foreigner as ruling in their land, have caused a marvellous awakening. The strength of the Home Rule movement is rendered tenfold greater by the adhesion to it of large numbers of women, who bring to its helping the uncalculating heroism, the endurance, the self-sacrifice of the feminine nature. Our League's best recruiters are among the women of India, and the women of Madras boast that they marched in procession when the men were stopped, and that their prayers in the temples set the interned captives free. Home Rule has become so intertwined with religion by the prayers offered up in the great Southern Temples—sacred places of pilgrimage—and spreading from them to village temples, and also by its being preached, up and down the country, by Sadhus and Sannyasins, that it has become in the minds of the Women and of the ever-religious masses, inextricably intertwined with religion. That is, in this country, the surest way of winning alike the women of the higher classes and the men and women villagers. And that is why I have said that the two words, "Home Rule", have become a Mantram.

"...out of the past is built the future. Look back, therefore, as far as you can, drink deep of the eternal fountains that are behind, and after that, look forward, march forward and make India brighter, greather, much higher than she ever was. Our ancestors were great. We must recall that. We must learn the elements of our being, the blood that courses in our veins; we must have faith in that blood, and what it did in the past, and out of that faith, and consciousness of greatness, we must build an India yet greater than what she has been."

-Annie Besant

INTERNATIONAL YEAR OF THE FAMILY

Proclamation of United Nations

1. The United Nations General Assembly, in its resolution 44/82 of 8 December 1989, proclaimed 1994 as the International Year of the Family. The theme of the Year is "Family : Resources and Responsibilies in a Changing World".

2. In proclaiming the Year, the Assembly decided that the major activity for its observance should be concentrated at the local, regional and national levels, assisted by the United Nations system. It designated the United Nations Commission for Social Development as the preparatory body and the Economic and Social Council as the coordinating body for the Year.

(A) The family constitutes the basic unit of society and therefore warrants special attention. Hence, the widest possible protection and assistance should be accorded to families so that they may fully assume their responsibilities within the community, pursuant to the provisions of the Universal Declaration of Human Rights, the International Covenants on Human Rights, the Declaration on Social Progress and Development, and the Convention on the Elimination of All Forms of Discrimination againt Women.

(B) Families assume diverse forms and functions from one country to another, and within each national society. These express the diversity of individual preferences and societal conditions. Consequently, the International Year of the Family encompasses and addresses the needs of all families.

(C) Activities for IYF will seek to promote the basic human rights and fundamental freedoms accorded to all individuals by the set of internationally agreed instruments formulated under the aegis of the United Nations, whatever the status of each individual within the family, and whatever the form and condition of that family.

(D) Policies will aim at fostering equality between women and men within families and to bring about a fuller sharing of domestic responsibilities and employment opportunities.

(E) Activities for IYF will be undertaken at all levels—local, national, regional and international, however, their primary focus will be at the local and national levels.

(F) Programmes should support families in carrying out their functions, rather than provide substitutes for such functions. They should promote the inherent strengths of families, including their great capacity for self-reliance, and stimulate self-sustaining activities on their behalf. They should give expression to an integrated perspective of families, their members, community and society.

(G) IYF will constitute an event within a continuing process. Measures will be needed to ensure appropriate evaluation of progress made and obstacles encountered both prior to and during IYF, in order to ensure its success and adequate follow-up.

This document is based upon : 1994 International Year of the Family, "Building the Smallest Democracy at the Heart of Society" United Nations Vienna, 1991.

Objectives

The objectives of IYF are to stimulate local, national and international actions as part of a sustained long-term effort to:

(a) increase awareness of family issues among Governments as well as in the private sector. IYF would serve to highlight the importance of families; attain a better understanding of their functions and problems; promote knowledge of the economic, social and demographic processes affecting families and their members; and focus attention upon the rights and responsibilities of all family members;

(b) encourage national institutions to formulate implement and monitor policies in respect to families;

(c) stimulate efforts to respond to problems affecting, and affected by, the situation of families;

(d) enhance the effectiveness of local, regional and national efforts to carry out specific programmes concerning families by generating new activities and strengthening existing ones;

(e) improve the collaboration among national and international non-governmental organizations in support of multi-sectoral activities;

(f) build upon the results of international activities concerning women, children, youth, the disabled as well as other major events of concern to the family or its individual members.

Relevant Policies

As most policies impact on families, "family-sensitive" approaches should be built into their development and implementation.

Economic changes

Economic changes, including cutbacks in government and social services, increase burdens on families and especially women.

Equality within Families

Unequal family relationships, exploitation and abuse result in slow personal development and initiative.

Appropriate Intervention

The extent to which society should intervene and influence family structures and patterns or the rights and behaviour of family members.

Family Image

Acknowledging that policies affecting the family should avoid promoting a single, ideal image of the family.

Changing Family Values

Families are becoming smaller, and individuals often feel less responsible for family relationships. Many families are unable or unwilling to meet the basic needs of some members. These needs must then be filled by public and private organizations and charities.

Indian Culture and Modern Women

—Dr. Lata Sinha

Recently there has been a trend in modern societies to divide human beings into two rigid sex-groups. There is a harsh competition between men and women. This trend is getting more and more stratefied. It has disforted the very premises, led to erroneous conclusions and resulted in un-happiness in the family and society.

Women should not try to copy man in each and every sphere, as it is not going to lead any solution of the present complex problems faced by the world. Also, it gives an impression that somewhere in their sub-conscious mind, they themselves regret being born as women, because of several natural functions, that go with it.

Indian culture believes that role of man and woman in life are complimentary in nature, not adversary or competitive one. There is a perfect equality between them. Men are known for their "Paurusha" or physical strength and are responsible for taking care of woman and children of the family. Women are known as "Prakriti" symbolising nature with all its qualities of creation, nurturing and sustaining the life in this cosmic world. They are the integral part of the cohesive society. In isolation, they just cannot live.

In India, right from the childhood, the girls are emotionally moulded and mentally conditioned to be wives, mothers and house-wives. Towards this, they are taught to be self-reliant in their domestic domain during normal times. During emergencies also, they rise to the occasion with courage. They are able to face the challenges of life outside the four walls of their home. They shoulder enormous physical and social responsibilities without any complaint.

Indian approach may be regarded as conservative. But it makes everybody happy and comfortable, organises the economic and social life, smoothens various relationships within the family and the society and sets healthy conditions for bringing up the coming generation. And also it gives Indian woman confidence, a confidence emerging from sense of security which many societies in other nations do not have. There is always the family to fall back upon. The emotional support of parents or the network of relatives and friends—and old ramies—is her safety net—particulary for single woman and even more so single mother—divorced or widowed.

Though the demands on Indian woman are growing day by day and so is the stress and the path to achieve liberty, happiness in life is not a smooth one for her, still she is trying her best to move onwards. Crossing courageously ail the hurdles on her way. Most of the Indian women are facing the challenges of life gracefully. They are shouldering their duties with zeal and try to give everybody in the family and society, their best effort.

The roles assigned to woman since ages by the society and nature are mainly:

— That of a home-maker;

— That of a mother;

— That of a career-woman;

— That of being a true partner to man in the moment of joy and sorrow.

And in each uf these roles, she does invaluable service directly or indirectly to the humanity, to the nation, to the society and to the members of the family.

Inspite of all this, in most parts of the world, she has been relegated to a secondary position by the nation and the society. Why?

— Is she weak—Physically she may be, but mentally not at all.

— Is she incapable—The answer is no as she has proved second to none in any field of work. She has tremendous self confidence, courage and inner strength.

— Is she incompetent—Again the answer is no. She accepts the challenges of life unhesitatingly. Also she is imbibed with patience, persuance, devotion to duty, the qualifies any task calls for its efficient performance.

The Position of Woman in India

— Indian philosophy and ancient India gave great respect to women as she has been visualised as Laxmi (protector of wealth), Saraswati (Goddess of Knowledge) and Annapurna (Goddess of prosperity, health and life).

— After Mughal invasion, she was confined within the four walls of the house due to safety reasons. This was the time when many restrictions were imposed on her and she became the victim of illiteracy, ignorance, completely male dominance and many other social evils.

— In the beginning of 20th Century, reformists worked on her liberation from social injustices and indiscrimination done against her in the society.

— Independence in 1947 brought a new hope for women in India as the right of equality, freedom and access to education and employment were given to her.

— By 80s, woman became aware of her strength and rights. She has discovered a whole new world within herself. She is ambitious but not dependent on others for its fulfillment and has become self-confident in an effort to make her own identity in the society.

— Nineties and the dawn of 21st century hopes for the better.

— Today, three types of groups for women are extent in Indian society.

— Those, who choose the life of home-makers only. Maximum number belongs to this group.

— Those, who choose the career only. The number is very small.

— Those, who opt for both the roles of a home-maker and a career woman. According to a study, the number has gone up to 42.3%.

— **The position of home-makers only is not very encouraging.**

— Housewives belong to the most neglected section of society. They still remain a vast reservoir of human resource, which remains untapped and unutilized to a great extent even today.

— Patriarchal system and male chauvinism prevalent in most of India, has imposed on woman many levels of restrictions and made her victim of unequal laws and traditions.

— Modern Indian society regards home-makers as ignorant, dull unworthy of interest and not smart enough to move in modern society.

— Home-makers usually loose their own identity in order to make everyone else comfortable.

— They always remain economically dependent on others, may be father, husband or son.

— Therefore, they become victims of many social evils.

— Due to their patience and self-sacrifice, fathers usually become careless and leave parenting to mothers alone.

— Their contribution remains invisible and under-rewarded.

— Household activities and responsibilities strenuous (24 hours job), repetitive in nature, and thankless occupation. Therefore, now-a-days instead of staying back at home, women prefer to take up a job or a career. But there are many difficulties on their way.

— In a male-dominated society, it is difficult to get a suitable job for a woman.

— She has to work doubly hard to prove her worth as her capacity to work is always doubted.

— It is very difficult to meet the responsibilities of household and workplace simultaneously.

— For rearing up the children, woman has to depend on somebody else, which is always expensive, unsatisfactory and unreliable.

— Proper growth of a child is hampered due to very busy schedule of both the parents, and lack of time to devote on child.

— Children feel neglected and do not develop the feeling of interdependence, or being wanted and loved in the family.

— It is mainly the mother, who rears, nurtures and guides the growth of the child, develops child's character and moulds him/her into a civilized young citizen. And her absense from the house usually make children insecure, resentful, having unresolved emotions.

— Quarrels between husband and wife due to the increasing burden of work within and outside often results in divorce and in each case, the position of children becomes pitiable.

— Due to craze of comforts, the values have already been shifted from "being" to "having". The values of life have given way to sheer selffishness, materialism and commercialism and irresistable desire for luxurious life-style. Seeing all this one wonders;

— Does employment not make women economically strong and free; but socially and emotionally broken;

— With divided attention, is she able to contribute her maximum in her workplace and at home; and

— Does it not take away from children the sense of security, belongingness and emotional stability.

The question arises what steps could be taken to uplift the position of women without disturbing familial peace and social harmony.

Steps to be taken to uplift the position of women in society without disturbing familial peace and social harmony may be summarised as:

(i) Sound education and proper training for creating awareness in them about their rights as well as about their duties.

(ii) Developing ability to make appropriate junctures of life on their own.

(iii) Providing enough job opportunities at appropriate time in life.

(iv) Creating congenial atmosphere at working place.

(v) Recognising house-making a fulfilling and respected occupation, which in long run provides a sound foundation for the development of nation by giving it confident, encouraged, disciplined and healthy citizens.

(vi) Her contribution for providing sound management at home, contended husbands, who could be efficient at their place of work without having any tension about the management of the house and secure, confident and responsible children should be acknowledged.

(vii) Women should be encouraged to take-up part-time jobs, so that they could do justice with household responsibilities.

(viii) Short-time refresher courses and coaching classes for them, if they want to take up job after certain time gap.

(ix) More and more home based income generating jobs for women should be created.

Gender Perspective in the Family and Violence against Women

—Mrs. Shobha Dikshit,

Justice High Court, Allahabad

I am not amongst those pessimists who live in despair and believe that nothing can be done for women as their present condition has deteriorated beyond repair. On the contrary, I believe that society is now conscious of the plight of women and much has been done for women and is being done and the result is that there is perceptible improvement in their status.

The question which comes to our mind is why the status of women has become such that the need so much attention and enactment of special laws for their betterment. Born similarly like a man from the womb of the same mother, in the same home, and environment, why a woman is treated so differently? Our Constitution gives equality to both men and women without any discrimination, why then does she not have the same status in the society? Generation after generation this has happened and, therefore, it naturally agitates our minds. This disparity should be removed and the women should have a place in the society as guaranteed by our Constitution. I am happy at the selection of this topic 'gender perspective in the family' for it is this Gender Bias, if I may call it so, which is the root cause for this discrimination and lowering the status of women in our society. It is this Gender Bias which has resulted into illiteracy, ignorance, insecurity, economic dependence and ill- treatment of women. Once the society especially the men felt that a woman is physically and economically dependent, they took advantage of this situation and tried to have complete control over her, so much so that they did not even spare her from physical harm and sometimes violence. It is manifested in different forms in a woman's life and has made her a victim of the same.

Violence against women has become the order of the day. Physical and mental assault on her inside the home and outside is a common occurance. Such violence is increasing day by day and therefore, it has become a cause of great concern and requires immediate attention and prevention. Violence against women is not necessarily physical, it can also be mental or emotional. Right from the birth, a female child is treated with disdain. Her birth itself is a trauma for the mother and subsequently for the female child. Aminocentesis tests are now pre-birth traumas and danger to her very survival and existence. The home where she takes birth treats her differently from a boy from the moment she is born. She is fed, clad and educated differently and is throught of as a burden for the family. It is this impression of being unwanted in the family that causes greatest damage to psyche which is later on reflected in her personality. A girl child, therefore, develops into a timid, insecure and dependent person. She all the times looks upon men of family for guidance and support. She is even unable to think about herself. It is this insecure and unwanted child that is given in marriage to an unknown man in an unknown family that condescends to accept on a price in the shape of dowry and other material considerations. The girl's family thus discharges its social obligation by passing on its assumed liability to another family where again the violence continues against her but in a different form. Now she is required to work for this family and perform all jobs like cooking, washing, sweeping and to bring up children. She has now new masters and quite often is subjected to violence in the shape of physical assault, not only by her husband but also by other members both male and female of this new family. Bride burning of course is the extreme form of such violence, I need not dwell on this aspect as all of you are well aware of this shameful act.

The cause of concern is as to how to control this violence, prevent it and ultimately eradicate it. Laws have no doubt been made. Even more legislation for the betterment of the lot of women is in the making and shall be made. Courts of law are there to implement the same and to punish the guilty. Changes in Criminal Procedure Code, Evidence Act and Indian Penal Code have been made. A woman is no more to prove the guilt, it is the man or other family members who have to prove their innocence in cases of offences against women. Notable sections are Sections 498-A and 304-B in I.P.C. Section 174 in Cr. P.C. and Section 113-A in the Evidence Act. I am not elaborating on these provisions of law, all of you will have an opportunity to discuss the same in some detail.

The question before us is as to why a woman needs special laws for her protection when the Indian Constitution gives her a equal status, equal to that of a man in all spheres of life. It is in this context that one has to see as of life. It is in this context that one has to see as to who is responsible for bringing our status down to this extent and what can be done by the society and particularly by the women themselves for their betterment.

Society consists of both men and women. In our country, women constitute approximately 50 percent of the total population. Is it then fair and just to shift all blame for the plight of womon and their present status on men alone? For this, I would call upon you to do some soul-searching, to look inward, to introspect and to give a conscious thought to this serious problem. You may yourself see how a woman reacts to the birth of a female child. How she herself brings up and treats her own daughter, how a sister treats another sister vis-a-vis a brother, and how a mother-in-law treats her daughter-in-law and vice versa. I ask you that when a woman is harassed, ill treated or even physically assaulted inside the home, how many women in the house have protested, intervened or for that matter retaliated and have come to the rescue of that unfortunate woman who is being attacked for no fault of hers? It is no doubt true that more often women in the house themselves have participated in violence against one of their own sisters. The need of the time, therefore, is that we must awake. Woman must and should take up their own cause and react to the situation. The laws of society which are all man made should take up their own cause and react to the situation. The laws of society which are all man made should now be changed and women should make laws for themselves. Women should start respecting women. I may tell you, legal laws can only provide support but they can never become the base of life. Women should not continue to ask for status, respect, independence from men but they should endeavour to achieve it. They should help other women and social organisations to achieve equality and thus regain their lost status. We must achieve equality in all spheres of life as no nation can develop where approximately 50 percent of its population is illiterate, dependant and incapable of participation in the nation building. We have to take a pledge that in day to day life, you shall not tolerate violence against women, be it mental, emotional and physical. You have to assume dominant role in the family, you have to assume dominant role in the family, you have to educate every daughter, as you educate your sons and make her strong, independent, self-respecting and self-thinking person.

(*Courtesy* : Roshini)

Women and Law

We have given to ourselves the Constitution in 1950 enshrining equality before law, equal protection of laws and no discrimination on ground of sex, caste and religion. The Constitution was adopted on 26th November, 1949. *More than 41 years after this, it cannot still be said safely that women in this country, who are more than half of the population have achieved equality in all fields of the—whether at home, at work or even in political life. The bold question that we have to ask ourselves today is why so ?* What has inhibited us or prevented us from achieving equality, are we not having enough legislation, or are the laws not being properly implemented, or is it the authoritarianism within the family, or the customs and traditions which have prevented us, or is it possible to point a needle to anyone particular aspects singular cause.

It is my attempt in this paper to share my thoughts with you all and identify ourselves the areas where we women need to strengthen ourselves so as to be able to be in the mainstream of social and political life and participate equally in the development of society. I can quite see many of you shrugging your shoulders with these ideas I can guarantee that women cannot compete as equals with men. Where is the necessity of repearing to ourselves that we have equality before law, we have a right of vote, we have right to work, we have right to equal wages, there is no discrimination that cannot be set aside and is liable to be quashed under the Constitution, for the Constitution provides enough safeguards for equal rights for men and women alike.

It is not strange that in a country of India's size and dimensions which also had the privilege of being led by women leaders of importance of unparalled ability and competence, prejudice still exists against women. Competent women who make the grade in India are only exceptions and they do not prove the real. The women are in supositions of authority, be it political, social of otherwise, that they cannot be ignored and possibly because they have proved themselves to be as efficient as their male counterparts. But stray examples of handful of women who might have found successful careers, cannot justify the generalisation that women enjoy a status equality with men in our country. *By and large women are not educated nor economical independent. They are not able to command status in society in their own right*. Matrimony gives them the necessary sense of security. Matrimony in fact is considered a must for woman. It is a career by itself and for the financial security that a woman gets in marriage at the high price that she has to pay for it is that she becomes totally dependent—socially, economically and even psychologically after marriage. The decision making in family life is not in the hands of women and in this process we are losing in terms of human energy, at least half of the energy.

The makers of our Constitution were aware of this inbuilt inequality in our society for women, therefore, a provision for better protection in law for women by providing Article 15(3) of the Constitution was made, but unfortunately Article 15(3) had not been made use of for the protection of woman and for providing her better laws and to help her remove the inbuilt shackles against her In the society itself. Woman is tied down to home, to family, to the children and to all that surroundings within the home.

It is a paradox that when our Constitution makers thought that women in India are not equal and they need special treatment, and the necessity of Article 15(3) was felt and was enshrined that some of us amongst ourselves feel shy of accepting this fact. *I think that time has come that we must get over this inferiority complex and get hold of the reality and find out as to what is that special legislation that should have been there.* That woman as a class has been a weaker section of society in fact admits of no dispute and further that social justice requires State intervention to enable women to grow to their full stature and potential and avail of their natural talents. Here the words of an eminent American Judge who, after trading the historical background, explained the need for special provisions being made for women. Thus, in Muller V/s Oregon (208 U.S. 412)—

"That women's physical structure and the performance of maternal functions places her at a disadvantage for subsistence is obvious. History discloses the fact that woman has always been dependent upon man. He established his control at the outset by superior physical strength and this control in various forms, with diminishing intensity, has continued to the present. Education was long denied to her, and while now the doors of the school room are opened and her opportunities for acquiring knowledge are great, yet even with that and consequent increase of capacity for business affairs, it is still true that in the struggle for subsistence, she is not an equal competitor with her brother. She will still be where some legislation to protect her seems necessary to secure a real equality or right."

Therefore, to make a woman struggle for equality a reality, compulsory reservation of minimum 30 per cent posts in all employment under the State and in private industry in favour of women, be made. The need for such provision becomes apparent when you see that even under the Minimum Wages Act, a lesser wage is fixed for women; this giving a go-bye to the principle of 'equal wages to equal work' and the reason for this discrimination being that if a higher wage is demanded, women will not get work. Even other socially beneficial legislations like Maternity Benefit Act are also deterrent for men to take women as employees. *May be to start with, the reservation may be made for twenty years. Thus, by providing ample employment to women, you would strengthen the position of women and this would also have a very salutary effect in our society when more and more women are seen at work in all fields.* I am sure that this move of making compulsory employment for women would stand the test of constitutional validity and it is possible for the State to come out with proper and befitting legislation.

With the socio-economic changes that have taken place in the country within the last few decides, the condition of women in certain areas, has further deteriorated. One had never heard of dowry deaths before, but the factum of dowry deaths has taken a very ugly shape in our society and as a matter of fact, has become a cancerous spot. *There is need to examine whether there is any relationship between women's right to property and her status in the family.*

The various personal laws in the country are uniform in recognising the obligation of a husband to maintain his dependent wife, but the right of the wife to claim to be part owner of the property accquired and enjoyed jointly by the husband and wife during marriage is not recognised. In the socio-economic situation prevailing in the country, the contribution of the female to the family's economy is not recognised. A larger number of women participate in the family's effort to earn a livelihood and are unpaid family workers. Even *when they do not work and add to the family's budget, the economic value of their effort in running the household, assuming all domestic responsibilities, certainly allows the husband all time for his vocation, but this effort is not recognised as having brought any economic gains either directly or indirectly.* Most married women do not have any independent source of income. Many women give up their employment after marriage, or do not take up employment for many years after marriage in order to be able to devote their full time to family's obligations, particularly in bringing up children. They are, therefore, economically dependent on their husband. In most of the cases, property—both movable and immovable—acquired during marriage is paid for out of the husband's earnings. If a matrimonial home is acquired, it will be registered in the husband's name. If things are bought for the household, the legal ownership will vest in the husband as in the economic terms the wife has not contributed anything. The principle of determining ownership on the basis of financial contribution is unjust and works inequitably against women. The demand for recognition of the wife's contribution in the way of work is growing in many other countries. It is, therefore, necessary that legal recognition be given to the economic value of the contribution made by the wife through house work or purposes of determining ownership of immovable property instead of continuing the archaic test of actual financial contribution. It is, therefore, recommended that on divorce or separation, the wife should be entitled to at least one-third of the assets acquired at the time of and during marriage.

Therefore, according to me we should devote ourselves to get more and more occupation for women and reduce her burden of domestic responsibility. The equality would be achieved only when woman is in fact treated equal on all fronts and the authoritarian male family members seize to guide and control her destiny.

Girl Child

[An excerpt of India Country Office paper on Girl Child, 30th Oct. 1990 by UNICEF.]

1. The Unwanted Girl

In a culture that idolizes sons and dreads the birth of a daughter, to be born female comes perilously close to being born less than human. Today the rejection of the unwanted girl can begin even before her birth : prenatal sex determination tests followed by quick abortions eliminate thousands of female foetuses before they can become daughter? Those girls who manage to survive till birth and beyond find that the dice is heavily loaded against them in a world that denies them equal access to food, health care, education, employment and simple human dignity. Unless the girl becomes a priority in health, nutrition and education policies, can there be Health for All by 2000, or universal elementary education, or social justice or equality? It is already late. But perhaps not too late. The time is long overdue for the girl child to be given her share of human dignity and opportunity.

2. Living with Neglect

From the day of her birth, a girl is viewed as a burden and a liability. So deeply entrenched is this view of the girl as a liability and the son a valuable resource, that even when girls step over the barrier of their upbringing to become wage earners who support their parents, this is seen as aberration, a grudgingly accepted reversal of the ideal that even the neediest parents find somewhat demeaning. The low status of the girlchild is linked to the low status of the woman.

The female infanticide was outlawed more than a century ago, its detention and prevention are virtually impossible despite reports from around the country which testify to its continued prevalence. Amniocentesis, originally intended as a prenatal test to detect certain congenital abnormalities, is now widely used across the conntry to determine the sex of the foetus and abort it if it happens to be female. In a study of 8000 abortions after amnio-centesis in Bombay it was reported that 7999 of the aborted foetuses were female. Maharashtra has become the first and to date the only State in the country to ban *amniocentesis* in private hospitals.

The ratio of females to males has been declining steadily since the beginning of this century. Our country has one of the lowest sex ratios in the world not because fewer females is consistently higher than for males in every age group upto the age of 35, but it is hightest during the first five years of life. The sex ratio is lowest in the northwestern States where the positions of girls and woman is possibly the lowest in the country.

Girls suffer from malnutrition more often than boys. The route cause is not the lack of food as the lack of value attached to the girl. It is generally true that boys eat better food than girls even in privileged families. When the underweight girl with an inadequately developed pelvis becomes an adolescent bride and mother, her already burdened body is laxed beyond its resources. When the young mother dies in child birth, the cycle of mutritional depletion is complete.

Studies have shown that fewer girls are 'treated for illness than boys, and when they are treated it is usually by the local "Vaid" whereas boys are more likely to be taken to the qualified doctor.

The implications of this inequality are grave, specially when viewed within the context of Health for all by 2000 A.D. For the girl child constitutional guarantee of equality will remain. Only a gesture, a symbol of social justice we aspire to but do not realise.

3. Wasting a Human Resource

For the planners of India's Independent Future, education was seen as the catalyst that would give an Indian Woman the equality, justice and dignity. More than forty years after independence, 75% of India's females are still illiterate compared to 53 percent males. In some remote areas, female literacy ranges from 10% to 15%. The reasons for this disparity in school attendance between boys and girls are:

(i) Shouldering upto 30 percent of the work of the household by girls between the age of 6 and 11 and also work in the fields and help their mother in beedi-rolling, gem polishing or any other home-based work, she may be engaged in.

(ii) Low value attached to literacy.

Today's girl and tomorrow's responsible citizen needs to be empowered with information about sanitation, child care, animal husbandary and modern agriculture. If she is not to be marginalised forever, she also needs a basic grasp of how pumpsets, tubewells and simple farm machinery are operated just as she must have an elementary acquaintance with rural markets and distribution networks, banking and loan facilities and cooperative practices. It is this knowledge gap between boys and girls based on traditional gender stereotyping, which forces females out of mainstream economic activity and forever relegates them to low-skill, low pay and low status occupations. Only formal and non-formal education gears itself to these needs can the development of the girl child as a genuine resource become a reality.

4. Invisible toilers

Studies on the rural girl-child's labour show that she works about 9 hours every day on an average of 315 days a year in the fields and the home, providing the family with free labour. This unequal domestic labour of boys and girls must earn their keep. It is not important for boys to do so since they will compensate parents by supporting them in their old age. It is this belief that impels mothers to demand a great deal of help from their daughters.

The 1981 census reports:

(i) 4 crore child workers

(ii) 1%of all boys and 4.3% of all girls under 14 are included in this figure.

What is more revealing is the change in work participation rates between 1971 and 1981. While there was a decline in the percentage of rural working boys during this decade, the percentage of working girls has been increasing during the same period particularly in the age group of 15-19 years. This trend is expected to continue through the present decade and suggests that more girls are being inducted into the labour force while more boys are being sent to school. Far from removing disparities based on gender, it is apparent that recent trends are widening the gap between male and female development opportunities. The number of invisible toilers around us is increasing.

An integrated approach to the girl child's development is essential for the creation of a new environment in which she can be valued and nurtured. It involves a process of social mobilisation that will make her everyone's concern, the media, the family and the community, as well as Government and voluntary agencies. By supplementing formal school with non-formal education, by enlarging the ambit of child development programmes, by reinforcing constitutional mandates through widespread awareness of the rights of girls are some of the ways in which we can empower the girl child to enter the mainstream of economic and social activity.

U.N. Activities—A Report by Ms. Sudha Acharya

1. 1994 would be the International Year of the Family (IYF). This programme will seek to promote effective ways to meet the needs of families and strengthen their ability to cope with the changing situations in today's world.

2. The United Nations Conference on Environment and Development (UNCED) will take place in Rio De Janeiro from June 1 to 12, 1992. It has been named "Earth Summit". The Earth Summit expected to produce an 'Earth Charter' which should govern the economic and environmental behaviour of peoples and nations and the means to carry out the agenda. The highlights of the Conference will be the observance of "World Environment Day" on June 5, 1992, the 20th anniversary of the Stockholm Conference.

3. International Policy Action Committee on Environment and Development has planned a "World Women's Congress for a Healthy Planet" with the objective of drawing attention to the fact that women—more than half the world's populatien must have an equal say when 'the fate of the Earth is being decided before, during and after the UN Earth Summit. The Congress

will take place at Miami, Florida, USA from 8—12 November, 1991 and is expected to be very well attended.

Membership of Principal United Nations Organisations in 1991

The General Assembly is composed of all 159 United Nstions Members States.

TheSecurity Council has 15 members. Five States as permanent members are: China, France Soviet Union, United Kingdom and the United States.

The Economic and Social Council has 54 members elected for three-year terms by General Assembly.

Our representatives regularly attended these sessions.

Promoting Girls and Women's Education

One way to increase female enrolement in schools is to lower the costs of education by providing culturally appropriate facilities, scholarships, and alternative schools that offer classes in the early morning or evening. Another is to train girls and women in growth sectors of the economy and to make strong recruitment and placement efforts.

Basic education is often considered a right which nations have a responsibility to guarantee to each generation. The benefits to education are now well established. The education raises the quality of life, it improves health and productivity in market and non-market work, increases individual access to paid employment and often facilitates social and political participation.

For promoting the girls and women's education following points should be adhered to—

1. Improving access to schools
2. Building culturally appropriate facilities
3. Recruiting female teachers
4. Lowering direct costs
    (a) Lowering the cost of uniforms
    (b) Providing scholarships

5. Lowering opportunity costs
    (a) Establishing day-care centres
    (b) Modifying home technologies
    (c) Adopting flexible school schedules
    (d) Building safety nets
6. Raising the benefits
    (a) Educating the community
    (b) Providing school feeding programmes
    (c) Training for non-traditional occupations
    (d) Ensuring gender-neutral instruction

Conclusion

Improving female education should be a topic of national education policy concern, one that is integrated into education development plans to ensure adequate planning, monitoring, evaluation and financial support.

Table 3. A Summary of the Effectiveness of Strategies to Improve Girl's and Women's Education Based on Country Experiences

Objective	*Effective*	*Not effective*	*Insufficient Evidence to Draw a Conclusion*
Lower the costs of education	Culturally appropriate facilities Female teachers Scholarships Alternative (morning or evening) schools	Distributing free uniforms	Programmed instruction Home production technologies Day care School feeding programs
Raise the benefits and of education	Vocational training for Growth sectors of the economy when directly linked to employment and with strong recruitment	Vocational training in non-growth sectors of the economy not directly linked to employment and no recruitment effort	Reveamping curricula books to introduce broader roles of females Information campaigns

Environment for the Girl Child

The Convention on the Rights of the Child urges that all rights to survival, protection and development should apply equally to every child regardless of sex. In this regard, the implementation of the Convention on the Rights of the Child could be facilited by the accelerated implementation of the convention on the Elimination of all forms of discrimination against women.

Ten Policy Recommendations

Sustained political will and action are required to ensure equality of status and opportunity for the girl child 1990s. Mention below are ten recommendations:—

1. Adopt political, legislative and development policies that eliminate gender disparity and discrimination in childhood. At present there is inadequate appreciation of the problems and special needs of the girl child by all involved in the development process.
2. Undertake specialized research and investigation into the status of the girl child. Create databases on her by collection data disaggre gated by gender and age and demonstrating the anthropological, religious, legislative and socio-economic evidence of her unequal status and living conditions. Disseminate widely the findings of such research for advocacy, policy formulation and programme interventions.
3. Formulate time-bound targets and concrete actions to improve the basic health, nutrition, education and social status of the girl child.
4. Establish mechanism to monitor the situation of the girl child at the community and national levels to ensure that policies and programmes for her urvival and development successfully carried out.
5. Launch effective public information and communication programmes to create an awareness of the greater vulnea) Lowering the cost of uniforms

6. Formulate pecific legal and social provisions to counteract the unacceptable negative image of the girl in traditional and non-traditional media, education, religion and culture. Set u.o adequate mechanisms to enforce such provisions.
7. Mobilize political, religious, cultural, administrative and community resource to create an ethos of care and value for the girl child. Such an ethos should promote the elimination of gender disparities and discrimation against women.
8. Encourage the participation of girls at all levels of human development activity to enhance their self-confidence, self-worth and self-reliance.
9. Advocate equal rights for girls in all national and international flora. Multilateral, bilateral and non-governmental organisations must place the girl child and women's issues higher on their development agendas.
10. Review progress in development efforts for the girl child in the 1990s on a regular basis at the national and international levels.

INTERNATIONAL YEAR OF THE FAMILY

Proclamation of United Nations

1. The United Nations General Assembly, in its resolution 44/82 of 8 December 1989, proclaimed 1994 as the International Year of the Family. The theme of the Year is "Family : Resources and Responsibilities in a Changing World".
2. In proclaiming the Year, the Assembly decided that the major activity for its observance should be concentrated at the local, regional and national levels, assisted by the United Nations system. It designated the United Nations Commission for Social Development as the preparatory body and the Economic and Social Council as the coordinating body for the Year.

(A) The family constitutes the basic unit of society and therefore warrants special attention. Hence, the widest possible protection and assistance should be, accorded to families so that they may fully assume their responsibilities within the community, pursuant to the provisions of the Universal Declaration of Human Rights, the International Covenants on Human Rights, the Declaration on Social Progress and Development, and the Convention on the Elimination of All Forms of Discrimination against Women.

(B) Families assume diverse forms and functions from one country to another, and within each national society. These express the diversity of individual preferences and societal conditions. Consequently, the International Year of the Family encompasses and addressees the needs of all families.

(C) Activities for IYF will seek to promote the basic human rights and fundamental freedoms accorded to all individuals by the set of internationally agreed instruments formulated under the aegis of the United Nations, whatever the status of each individual within the family, and whatever the form and condition of that family.

(D) Policies will aim at fostering equality between women and men within families and to bring about a fuller sharing of domestic responsibilities and employment opportunities.

(E) Activities for IYF will be undertaken at all levels— local, national, regional and international, however, their primary focus will be at the focal and national levels.

(F) Programmes should support families in carrying out their functions, rather than provide substitutes for such functions. They should promote the inherent strengths of families, including their great capacity for self-reliance, and stimulate self-sustaining activities on their behalf. They should give expression to an integrated perspective of families, their members, community and society.

(G) IYF will constitute an event within a continuing process. Measures will be needed to ensure appropriate evaluation of progress made and obstacles encountered both prior to and during IYF, in order to ensure its success and adequate follow-up.

This document is based upon: 1994 International Year of the Family, "Building the Smallest Democracy at the Heart of Society" United Nations Vienna, 1991.

Objectives

The objectives of IYF are to stimulate local, national and international actions as part of a sustained long-term effort to:

(a) increase awareness of family issues among Governments as well as in the private sector. IYF would serve to highlight the importance of families; attain a better understanding of their functions and problems; promote knowledge of the economic, social and demographic processes affecting families and their members; and focus attention upon the rights and responsibilities of all family members;

(b) encourage national institutions to formulate, implement and monitor policies in respect to families;

(c) stimulate efforts to respond to problems affecting, and affected by, the situation of families;

(d) enhance the effectiveness of local, regional and national efforts to carry out specific programmes concerning families by generating new activities and strengthening existing ones;

(e) improve the collaboration among national and international non-governmental organizations in support of multi-sectoral activities;

(f) build upon the results of international activities concerning women, children, youth, the disabled as well as other major events of concern to the family or its individual members.

Relevant Policies

As most policies impact on families, "family-sensitive" approaches should be built into their development and implementation.

Economic Changes

Economic changes, including cutbacks in government and social services, increase burdens on families and especially women.

Equality within Families

Unequal family relationships, exploitation and abuse result in slow personal development and initiative.

Appropriate Intervention

The extent to which society should intervene and influence family structures and patterns or the rights and behaviour of family members.

Family Image

Acknowledging that policies affecting the family should avoid promoting a single, ideal image of the family.

Changing Family Values

Families are becoming smaller, and individuals often feel less responsible for family relationships. Many families are unable or unwilling to meet the basic needs of some members. These needs must then be filled by public and private organizations and charities.

International Year of the Family

I want to give you some information about the International Year of the Family. The United Nation's General Assembly in its resolution 44/82 of 8th December, 1989 proclaimed 1994 as the International Year of the Family. The Theme of the year is "Family : Resources and Responsibilities in a Changing World".

In proclaiming the year, the Assembly decided that the major activities for its observance should be concentrated at the local, regional and national levels, assisted by the United Nations Commission for Social Development as the preparatory body and the Economic and Social Council as the coordinating body for the year.

Activities for International Year of the Family will be undertaken at all levels—local, national, regional and international; however, their primary focus will be at the local and national levels.

The objectives of the International Year of the Family are to stimulate local, national and international actions as part of a sustained long-term effort to:

(a) increase awareness of family issues among Governments as well as in the private sector. IYF would serve to highlight the importance of families; attain a better understanding of their functions and problems; promote knowledge of their economic, social and demographic processes affecting families and their members; and focus attention upon the rights and responsibilities of all family members;

(b) encourage national institutions to formulate, implement and monitor policies in respect to families;

(c) stimulate efforts to respond to problems affecting and affected by, the situation of families;

(d) enhance the effectiveness of local, regional and national efforts to carry out specific programmes concerning families by generating new activities and strengthening existing ones;

(e) improve the collaboration among national and international governmental organisations in support of multi-sectoral activities;

(f) build upon the results of international activities concerning women, children, youth, the aged, the disabled as well as other major events of concern to the family or its individual members.

(Courtesy: The Federal Co-ordinator International Year of the Family Deptt. of National Health and Welfare Ottawa Antario)

Extracts from United Nations Instruments

"The family is referred to as the basic unit of society; it is appreciated for the important socio-economic functions that if performs. In spite of the many changes in society that have altered its role and functions, it continues to provide the natural framework for the emotional, financial and material support essential to the growth and development of its members, particularly infants and children, and for the care of other dependants, including the elderly, disabled and infirm. The family remains a vital means of preserving and transmitting cultural values, in the broader sense, it can, and often does, educate, train, motivate and support its individul members, thereby investing in their future growth and acting as a vital resource for development."

I am passing on this information so that you can organise some activities in connection with the International Year of the Family in the next few months, don't forget to send the reports to the Headquarters.

DRAFT PLATFORM FOR ACTION ANNEX TO RESOLUTION 38/10 OF

The Commission on the Status of Women

18 March, 94

Sudha Acharya the United Nations representative of the All India Women's Conference at New York attended the thirty-eighth session of the Commission on the status of women on 18th March 94. Here are some of the salient points from them.

Draft Platform for Action

The Platform for Action aims to accelerate the removal of the remaining obstacles to women's full and equal participation in all spheres of life including economic and political decision-making, to protect women's human rights throughout the life cycle and to mainstream women in all areas of sustainable development so that men and women can work together to equality, development and peace.

Critical areas of Concern

(a) Economic burden of poverty

The heavy burdens of poverty generally falls disproportionately on women because women are less likely to have sufficient access to the economic and other resources necessary to improve their lives.

(b) Inequality in access to education, health and related services and means of maximizing the use:

Education is a key to development and it must be resposive to the practical needs of women. This includes training in science and technology and modern communication.

(c) Violence against women

It is global problem and it derives from the lower status accorded to women in the family and in society.

(d) Effects of armed or other kinds of conflicts on women

Women are often left with the responsibility of maintaining families when conflict disrupts to destroy social and economic life. Women are the victims of torture, disappearance and rape.

(e) Inequality in women's access to and participation in the definition of economic structures and policies and the productive process itself

Women lack equal access to, and control over, land, capital, technology and other means of production owing to the predominant division of labour between men and women in most societies. Consequently, women have been largely excluded from the shaping of economic structures and policies.

(f) Inequality between men and women in the sharing power and decision making at all levels

More women are serving as heads of State Governments, ministers, members of parliament, mayors and members of city councils than ever before. Yet, women still lack equal access to power structure that shape society.

(f) Insufficient mechanisms at all levels to promote the advancement of women

Effective mechanisms are needed at the international, regional, national and community levels to serve as catalysts for promoting the advancement of women in and human resources to perform this function successfully.

(h) Lack of awareness of and commitment to, internationally and nationally recognized women's human rights

The World Conference on Human Rights emphasized that women's rights were integral part of the mainstream of universal, inalienable and indivisible human rights. However, unless these standards are fully applied, interpreted and enforced in civil, penal and commercial codes and administrative rules and regulations' they will exist only in name.

(i) Insufficient use of mass media to promote women's positive contribution to society

The world is undergoing a communication revolution in which new image and ideas reach into the far corners of the world. These technologies are powerful tools that can be used either for social progress or to inforce stereotype.

FOUNDER OF AIWC—MARGARET E. COUSINS

When a girl was born in the middle of a cold night on November 7, 1878, God alone knew that she was going to spend the best years of the life serving India, making it her home, and going to be known as Margaret E. Cousins, founder of the All India Women's Conference.

Early Life

Being the first child of a large family she got a loving welcome from her parents and relations. Describing herself, she says in her autobiograph, "We two together", "Abundant energy and good health were mine—but not beauty." She had the reputation of being a wise child who could be trusted and who made original remarks. A born equalitarian, she rebelled against any differential treatment of sexes from an early age. She loved and respected her "Grannie", whose love of flowers and nature, admiration of paintings and pictures, and appreciation of the best in music and literature influenced her deeply.

Education

She got her early education in a co-educational "National School". As a child she was not a bit interested in dolls. She loved reading, especially biographies of women saints. She wanted to be a saint herself, but a "cheerful saint."

At the age of thirteen, she joined Intermediate school of the town. There she developed love of science. Here, she won a three year schalarship. Her talent for music was also noticed and she became the pianist of the school orchestra.

During the four years she spent in the boarding of a high school, she developed independence of character, the habit of moving easily with people and the judgement of the character which helped her all her life. Describing her independent disposition, she says, "My nature was free and original on its bent. I could be happy only in doing what I felt was right in principle, not because other people did it".

At the age of nineteen she joined the Royal Irish Academg of Music, Dublin. And there, she felt herself to be "the luckiest, freest and the happiest girl in Ireland". Later, to study the scientific aspect of music, she took up a course in acoustics (the science of sound). Here she came into contact with a professor who got her interested in the knowledge of psychic research.

Marriage

In Dublin, she came to know Mr. James Cousins, whom she did not like, initially. But, he was a poet and she loved poetry, so the final result was their marriage in April, 1903. The wedding took place on Holy Thursday (just before Easter). And, using her own words' she and her husband "learned how to be married, though happy."

She started her married life as a vegetarian, at the wedding breakfast, in a fashionable hotel in Dublin, and in her words she was "......happy to look animal kingdom innocently in the face... 'and just after that their full freedom began to make their lives according to their New Order of Peace on Eastern and Universal Kingships" which became a reality later.

Action

Involvement in women's suffrage movement filled her early married life. She started taking active part in campaigning for votes for women in Ireland. In the process she was sentenced to one month's imprisonment as a common criminal. She even went on a seven-day hunger strike during imprisonment. "My memories of that month sum themselves up as a species of living death..."

Another question closely connected with right to vote was, women's place in the Church. A new organization was set up in Liverpool. It was known as the Church of the New Ideal. A Church was opened in Liscard Cheshire, Town Hall on Sunday March 22, 1914, by a woman Res: Hattie Baker, who preached the sermon. But after one year a man preacher was appointed. At times, Mrs Cousins also preached there, during the period it was run by women.

Landing up in India

Now the time for her had come to start her journey to India with her husband on the ship 'City of London'. They sailed for India on October 6, 1915, and reached Madras in about a month's time on November 1. The world was already at war since 1914.

They started their life in Adyar (Madras) at the International Headquarter of Theosophical Society established by Mrs. Annie Besant. It took little time for this Irish couple to get used to the heat and sweat of Madras. While James Cousins started with the post of the literacy sub-editor of 'New India', a prestigious newspaper from south, he later became lecturer in English and Vice Principal of the college run by the Theosophical Society.

Step by Step

During this period Margaret Cousins developed contacts and made many friends on her trips to different places in south with Mrs. Besant. On the trip to Hyderabad she met Mrs. Sarojini Naidu was impressed by her brilliance and her self-confidence.

With her experience of women's voting rights movement in Ireland and England Mrs. Cousins soon got into the fray for Rights of Indian women. She became the organiser of "Votes for Women" deputation. Mrs Cousins was pleasantly surprised that getting voting rights for Indian woman was like a cakewalk compared to her earlier experience.

Another outcome of the subject of Vote was the unity of India as a nation. Now Margaret Cousins started thinking about uniting the women of India and bringing them under one umbrella. Health service of all India and Girl Guide movement were also creating all Indian unity among women. Besides this, in different states women had joined themselves for social service, education, economic and social activities.

The History begins

Margaret E. Cousins started the linking process to bring all these energies to a point of focus, by bringing together delegates from the state-level organisations. The Bombay National Council for Women, The Sewa Sadan of Poona and Bombay. The Saroj Nalini Dutt Mahila Samitis, The Bharata Stri Mahamandalam of Bengal, The Arya Samaj of Punjab and U.P., The Mahila Seva Samaj of Mysore, the many women's clubs for recreation. As a result the All India Women's Conference came into being in October 1926, and the first conference of delegates took place in Poona from 5th to 8th January 1927.

Thus started a long process of the development the struggle, the liberation and the ups and downs in the history of AIWC, which continues to the present day and is looking forward towards a bright future.

GENDER PERSPECTIVE IN THE FAMILY AND VIOLENCE AGAINST WOMEN

Mrs. Shobha Dikshit
Justice High Court, Allahabad

I am not amongst those pessimists who live in despair and believe that nothing can be done for Women as their present condition has deteriorated beyond repair. On the contrary, I believe that society is now conscious of the plight of women and much has been done for women and is being done and the result is that there is perceptible Improvement in their status.

The question which comes to our mind is why the status of women has become such that the need so much attention and enactment of special laws for their betterment. Born similarly like a man from the womb of the same mother, in the same home, and environment, why a woman is treated so differently? Our Constitution gives equality to both men and women without any discrimination, why then does she not have the same status in the society? Generation after generation this has happened and, therefore, it naturally agitates our minds. This disparity should be removed and the women should have a place in the society as guaranteed by our Constitution. I am happy at the selection of this topic 'gender perspective in the family' for it is this Gender Bias, if I may call it so, which is the root cause for this discrimination and lowering the status of women in our society. It is this Gender Bias which has resulted into illiteracy, ignorance, insecurity, economic dependence and ill treatment of women. Once the society especially the men felt that a woman is physically and economically dependent, they took advantage of this situation and tried to have complete control over her, so much so that they did not even spare her from physical harm and sometimes violence. It is manifested in different forms in a woman's life and has made her a victim of the same.

Violence against women has become the order of the day. Physical and mental assault on her inside the home and outside is a common occurance. Such violence is increasing day by day and therefore, it has become a cause of great concern and requires immediate attention and prevention. Violence against women is not necessarily physical, it can.

GENDER DISCRIMINATION: SURVIVAL OF THE GIRL CHILD

Dr. Manorama Bawa
President, AIWC

At the 51st session of UN Commission for the Status of Women from 27th February to 11th March, 2007 besides the official UN Plenary sessions, a number of workshops organized by the participating NGOs were held. The topics of the workshops centered around the theme of CSW session. This year the priority theme was "Elimination of discrimination and violence against the girl child" and also focused on issues of trafficking, violence against women, health migration etc. Besides that, the girl child - violence and abuse, adolescent girls, female foeticide and the diminishing number of the girls in the population in comparison with the ratio of boys, were issues for advocacy and lobbying activities. The important review topic was promoting gender equality as sustained change for women and girls so that gender equality becomes part of the programmes for education and social norms. The International Alliance of Women (IAW) and All India Women's Conference (AIWC) collaborated to organize a workshop on the "Missing Girls". Eventhough a few workshops were held around this topic as a part of workshops on other related topics, the workshop organized by AIWC and IAW attracted an unexpectedly large number of participants from different countries.

Dr. Bawa's presentation on the "Discrimination against the Girl Child in the South Asia Region" focused on how gender bias and deep rooted prejudice against girl children has aggravated the risk to the survival of the girl child. United Nations has very important role in propagating the principal of gender equality as envisioned in the BPFA and creating a world fit for children envisioned in the Millennium Development Goals, calling for implementation of CEDAW and the Convention on the Rights of the Child (CRC), as they have been identified as key human rights standards.

These principles of equality, justice and freedom form the foundation of the Constitution of India and prohibits discrimination on the basis of gender, race, religion, caste or place of birth. Of 12 million girls born every year in India 3 million do not live to celebrate their 6th birthday. Discrimination against the girl child takes the form of female foeticide, female infanticide, girl child neglect and excess child mortality, before and after birth. The life cycle of the girl child starts with discrimination and is reinforced throughout her life in the form of elimination before birth by abortion, low weight gender inequality, low access to education, child marriage, sexual abuse, family violence, dowry, early child bearing. Technology and preference of a male child both in rich and poor, educated and illiterate families, has led to large-scale female foeticide. The latest techniques allow sex determination within four weeks after conception and pre implantion genetic diagnosis lead to safe abortions. According to the UNFPA reports, states with high income per capita such as Punjab, Haryana, Gujarat, Maharashtra with higher education and income per capita recorded a 50-point drop in girl child sex ratio where the ratio is less than 840. Kerala is one of the few states of India where girls out number boys. In India in 2006 the ratio of girls is 917 to 1000 boys especially in the land owning families. It is becoming increasingly the practice to determine the sex of the unborn child and eliminate if the foetus is a girl. This practice involves two stages: determination of sex of foetus and induced termination of female foetus. The gap between number of women and girls who should have been a part of the population and the number of girls missing, needs to be investigated.

Preference of Male to Female Child

These trends can be attributed to India's traditional patriarchal society where attitudes towards girl child, have not kept pace with economic progress. The girl child is a part of society that idolizes sons, and where she is seen as a curse than a blessing. The son performs the last rites of the parents. The family lineage and inheritance runs through the male line. Sons are bread winners and a support for the parent in the old age whereas daughter, when she goes as a new bride to her husband's home, is given blessing to produce eight sons. A daughter's birth affects the status of the mother in the family and daughter's share in the inheritance affects her acceptance in the family.

The issues emerging because of the declining sex ratio have national implications - resulting in imbalances in the human species, unsafe abortions affecting the woman's health giving rise to maternal mortality. Policies and initiatives do not address specific concerns of updating the programmes for the girl child. Gender based data is required for accurate need based assessment in programme design for social and gender based development services require specific programmes to serve women and children. Examination of sex determination laws to identify flaws and practical mechanism for enforcement, are required.

Recent Measures Set in Motion

The Preconception and Prenatal Diagnostic Techniques, Prohibition of Sex Selection Act came into force in 2005. These measures regulate the use of prenatal diagnostic techniques such as ultrasound and prohibit sex selection before or after conception. Doctors found violating the Act, will lose their license and persons seeking help in sex selection will get stiff fines and imprisonment for 3 years. So far in one city only one medical practitioner has been prosecuted.

Action required

Strict enforcement of the Preconception and Prenatal Diagnostic Techniques Act, advocacy campaign against female foeticide and infanticide to create awareness and respect for female life, increased efforts and networking by women NGOs to create a conductive environment and services for the protection of female life, government policies and support for eradication of malnutrition among children, national charter for children ensuring literacy, nutrition and health care for every girl child and time bound programmes for women throughout their life span from childhood to adulthood and old age.

Representatives from other women's organisations from China, Africa etc. spoke. Interactive session followed the presentation of AIWC. Representative of All China Women's Federation spoke on the discrimination against the girl child and gender inequality in China. In China the ratio of girls as compared to the boys is much low. China also has the tradition and culture of idolizing a son in the family though the Chinese society is a product of a different ideology. The speaker from Ghana said that the status of girl child was discriminatory in Ghana also and female foeticide was prevalent in the society affecting the birth of girl children. The open house session with the participants was very interactive. The participants had a lot of interesting questions for the speakers and there was a lot of sharing of information making the interactive session very interesting.

The workshop ended on a very positive note with the representatives of various NGOs committing themselves to end the elimination of the female child before or after birth and building up public pressure for safety nets for the protection of the girl child.

The representative from India informed the house that the government of India has taken strict measures to save the girl child against violence by introducing measures such as conditional cash transfer by depositing a definite sum of money on the birth of a girl child with a commitment from the parents to spend the interest of the deposited sum on the care and education of the girl child. As soon as the girl child reaches the age of 18 years the money will be given to her for higher education. The Government has strengthened strict enforcing of laws for rape, sexual harassment, trafficking, domestic violence, and dowry to provide security to the girl child.

In conclusion, there is discrimination against the Girl Child in most of the developed and developing nations.

This is the reason that societies are showing their concern for the imbalances in the populations by building up public opinion for the survival of the girl child, setting convention on the right of the child, strengthening the Human Rights policies and strategies for the protection of the girl child.

SECRETARY GENERAL'S REPORT

(79th Annual Conference, 13-15 February 2007, Hyderabad)

The emphasis during last year was mainly completing and reviewing the ongoing programmes, refine them and allot new programmes in health, nutrition, education and skill-centric literacy to more branches. Efforts were made to formulate the course design comprising the programme schedule, training methods to be used and the suggested resource persons along with the budgetary guidelines. The idea was to guide the branches so that the programme is implemented properly and the objectives of the programme are not lost. Some of the highlights of the major programmes are awareness programmes on 'Anemia free society', Female foeticide, HIV/AIDS; Health Camps for detection of Cancer, T.B., Dengue, Malaria and Gynae problems; Literacy and Skill Development programmes; National Environment Awareness Programmes and Research and Documentation programme.

As a follow up of the formerly allotted Anemia free camps, review camps were held to assess the impact of these camps on people and the results were found to be very encouraging. Review camp at Madan Pur Khadar showed improvement among the anemic patients. Out of 143 cases consisting of 97 females and 37 males, 30 females and 13 males were found to be normal.

Health Camps

Health camps were conducted by Kerala Ikeya Mahila Samajam. Palakkad branch Upahar Social Service Organisation, Moradabad, Meerut, Kakinada and Jammu. In each health camp around 50-60 patients were examined for various diseases like cancer, Gynae problems, general check-up, Malaria, Dengue etc. The new Health camps for the year 2006-07 have been sanctioned to Priya Darshini Women's Association. Gyanasundram - Chennai, Perumpoor Branch-Kerala, Manipur and South East Delhi Women's Association-Delhi. North East Suburban branch, Kolkatta and Manipur.

Programmes for Adolescents on 'Life-Skill Education'

Branches at Batala, Raigang, Surat, Pune and Manipur have conducted the programme and submitted the reports according to the guidelines provided to them. The new lot for the year 2006-07 is sanctioned to the following branches- Kerala Iykya Mahila Samajam-Kerala, Gandhi Nari Kalyan Samiti-Dhampur, Amritsar branch, South West Delhi Women's Association, Delhi. The branches were given guidelines along with the detailed course content and the programme schedule and also the break up of the budget so that the programme is conducted successfully. Two branches have completed the programme and report is submitted to head office.

The feedback received suggests the usefulness of the training programme as various topics like health.

WOMEN IN CHINESE AND INDIAN TRADITIONS

Reproduced from EvesTouch, March 2007

–Jaya Kothai Pillai

I happened to read the book *Wild Swans - Three daughters of China* by Jung Chang, winner of the NCR book award,

London 1992. The book tells the story of three generations of women in a family in China, grandmother Yu Fang (1909-1969), mother, De Bong born 1931, and the author, Jung Chang, born 1952. The book describes the life of people in China before the Communist regime, what led to the Cultural Revolution, what happened during the regime of Mao, what her parents, herself, her siblings and her family went through during that regime and, finally, how she found a haven in London.

We get glimpses of the traditional beliefs and practices of China as we read the narrative. They are so similar to ours. The Chinese were deep rooted in Confucian ethics, and filial piety was one of the most honoured traditions. To quote the author, "In an ordinary Chinese household, the younger generation had to be subservient to the older, with suitable decorum to mark their relative positions. In the Manchu system, the younger generation had to pay their respects to the older every morning and evening, the men kneeling and the women curtseying. At festival times, the men had to do a full 'kowtow'."

The importance that was given to 'sons' in the Chinese tradition is so amazingly similar to Indian traditions. Talking of her great grandfather, Jung Chang says, "The only son made him of supreme importance to his family—only a son could perpetuate the family name—without him the family line would stop, which to the Chinese amounted to the greatest possible betrayal of one's ancestors." How similar to our theory of Three Debts—'Pithru runa'—according to which, only by producing a male progeny can one's debt to the ancestors be cleared and the parents be prevented from going to the hell called 'puth.'

The Chinese peasants considered it a complete waste of time for girls to go to school. "They get married and they only belong to other people. It is like pouring water on the ground." Even when girls were sent to schools, the aim of education for girls was to turn them into "gracious wives and good mothers". The single most important thing that was imparted in school to a girl was how to please one's husband... The curriculum comprised cooking, sewing, tea ceremony, flower arrangement, embroidery, drawing, appreciation of the Arts etc. The traditional saying was, "Women have long hair but short intelligence." Just compare this with Richard Bronsley's "Thought does not become a young woman" and Freud's theory, "Because of their anatomy, women are emotionally unstable, submissive, passive, masochistic and devoid of creative intellectual potential."

Another Chinese traditional belief was "a good woman was not supposed to have a point of view at all, and if she did, she certainly should not be so brazen and talk about it." It was also expected that "a virtuous woman should suppress her emotions and not desire anything beyond her duty to her husband."

In the Chinese traditional culture, "marriage was seen above all as a duty, an arrangement between two families." Failing in love was almost considered shameful, a family disgrace. "Marriage was a transaction, not a matter of feelings. There was no question of consulting one's daughter; she would be informed when the wedding was arranged."

The advice given to girls was, "If you are married to a chicken, obey the chicken; if you are married to a dog, obey the dog." Traditionally, an important way in which a woman expressed her love for her man was by agreeing with him in everything. Compare this with the rule of conduct laid down by our Dharma *shastras:*

— "Though destitute of virtue or seeking pleasure else where, or devoid of good qualities, yet a husband must be constantly worshipped as a God by a faithful wife."

— "By violating her duty towards her husband, a wife is disgraced in this world; after death, she enters the womb of a jackal and is tormented by diseases of her sins."

— "She who controls her thoughts, words and deeds, never slights her lord, resides after death with her husband in heaven and is called a virtuous wife."

Regarding the position a Chinese woman in the family, the author says, "There was strict segregation prevalent and men did not even meet their daughter's friends; a woman was not supposed to talk to a man who was not her husband."

Chinese tradition permitted little physical contact even between father and daughter. Rich men would take concubines. "Wives were not for pleasure - that was what concubines were for. For wives, to enjoy sex was considered shameful." They showered jewels and gifts on their concubines because they believed that this was the only way to a woman's heart. How similar to the practice of our kings and zamindars having a number of women in their harems.

Talking about the beliefs of agricultural communities, Jung Chang say, "Planting rice could only be done by married women with children, particularly sons. The more sons a woman had, the more she was in demand for this job. The belief was that a woman who had produced a lot of sons would produce more grains in the rice she planted — sons and seeds have the same sound 'zi' in Chinese." In Indian villages also we find the same kind of popularity of fertile women.

In Chinese tradition, the person with most power over a married woman was always her mother-in-law to whom she had to be completely obedient and who would tyrannise her. When she, in turn, became a mother-in-law, she would bully her daughter-in-law the same way. Talking of feminine identity in India, Sudhir Kakkar says, "In the social hierarchy of her new family, the Indian bride usually occupies one of the lowest rungs. Obedience and compliance with the wishes of the older women of the family, especially that of her mother-in-law, are expected as matter of course. Communication with the older men is minimal, if it exists at all."

In Chinese custom, it was considered a great humiliation for a man to move into a woman's family just as we in India consider a man living in the house of his father-in-law as demeaning.

Similar to our thinking, pale skin was the main criteria for beauty in much of the Chinese countryside The Chinese also observed the practice of considering women unclean during her menstrual period. They believed that noodles would sag if the woman touched the bowl during those three days.

As late as the 1970s "Much of Chinese society still expected its women to hold themselves in a sedate manner, lower their eyelids in response to men's stares, and restrict their smile in a faint curve of their lips which did not expose their teeth. If they contravened any of these canons of behavior, they would be called 'flirtatious'." womb, as well as the voices of others nearby. Sunshine on her tummy begins her world. She hears music and singing, and yelling and the effects of her sadness, anger, and happiness. We are all familiar with Abhimanyu's story in this context.

After his birth, 'a baby learns much about communicating by his mother's responsiveness to his cries, his method of communication. As she watches and learns his squirms, his funny faces, his whimpers - and responds to meet his needs accordingly, their level of communication goes up and their relationship blossoms.

He feels calmed when she holds him close, and he is secure when he sleeps next to her. Her gentle touch makes him relax: He loves the way she smells. As she nurses, sweet, warm milk fills his/her tummy and makes him/her feel good inside.

The loving, peaceful atmosphere a mother creates for her baby, her responsiveness to his cues, their almost constant interaction—spoken and unspoken—provide a rich learning environment for her child. Her arms, her voice, her touch, all that a mother is and does, help her child to learn about life, love, trust, communicating, and relating to others. Hers is an awesome responsibility which can give blessings which are immeasurable.

The mother is the first teacher of the child. Children, at the beginning of life, are fresh and tender as young twig, and can be trained in any fashion you desire. If you rear the child to be straight, he will be straight, in perfect symmetry. It is clear that the mother is the first teacher and that it is she who establishes the character and conduct of the child.

Research is continuing to prove that the child's pre-school years are the most important years in his intellectual development that the experience in childhood has a crucial formulative influence on the personality, later on. According to Freud, innate motives and the behavior are established in the first few years of life. Bloom in his thesis on human, intellectual development states that by the time a child is four years old, 50% of his organized thinking pattern are established. Hunt's extensive work with young children says, 'it is possible to raise the intellectual quotient of children considerably by restructuring the environment to provide more stimulation'.

An abstract of the research studies that have gone into the effects of social class background upon educational performance indicates that the poor living conditions, the economic problems, the verbally unstimulating environment and the lack of cultural and leisure facilities experienced by lower social and economic status families inevitably act as a powerful handicap to the educational progress of their children. Thus, we can see that the early years are the most important and special care therefore needs to be taken to protect the child during this period. Due to more involvement of mothers in economic activities, the early years of child tend to be neglected, whether upper class, middle or lower class families.

India has around 157.87 million children (about 15.42%) below the age of six years as per 2001 census. Only a society that cares of its children can be said to be truly developed. Importance of optimal nutrition for health and human development is well recognized. According to National Family Health Survey III, nearly half of the young children in India are under weight (47%) and one in six children are wasted (16%) The prevalence of under nutrition is among the highest levels found in any country in the world. Economic situation of the household is a strong predictor of under nutrition children.

According to National Family Health Survey III, the infant mortality rate in India is 57 per thousand, %age of children age under 3 who are stunted is 38, children who are under weight is 46. Vaccination coverage is 44 and age of children fully immunized {12-23 months} is 43.5 and % age of anemic children 6-35 months is 79.2.

The United Nations declaration on the Rights of the child (1959) maintains that "mankind owes to the child the best it can give". The U.N. convention of 1989, the most exhaustive international expression of children's rights starts with the statement, "Children, because of their vulnerability, need special care and protection". The human rights of the child includes civil, political, economic, social and cultural rights. The civil rights under the convention include the right to a name and nationality, protection from torture and maltreatment. The economic rights include the right to benefit from social security, the right to a standard of living, and right for protection from exploitation at work. The social rights include the right to highlight attainable standard of health and access to medical services, the right to special care for handicapped children, protection from abduction and social exploitation and regulation of adoption. Cultural rights include the child's right to develop fully through education.

If we want our mothers to be ideal teachers and home to be the first ideal school, we need to make the mothers aware of the various factors affecting child's development and growth. There is need to emphasise on pre-school education combined with parental and community education so that the parents may be enlightened on the needs of children and the importance of health (vaccination, immunization, safe drinking water sanitation), nutrition (proper balanced diet for healthy growth), moral education etc. ICDS is doing some work on these lines but catering only to a small section of the society. There is need, to cover larger section on these lines. Suggestions for improvement.

Here I would restrict myself to something which can be undertaken immediately with a slight increase in training facilities, within the scope of the limited funds available but with a very considerable increase in our own initiative. The following tips may prove useful for the parental/community education as an intervention programme for improving the environment for healthy growth of the child during the early childhood years.

1. Health Education should consist of information on developmental milestone, proper vaccination and immunization in time. Identification of delayed milestone and information about referral services, nutritional

deficiency diseases, worm infestation, importance of balanced diet and ideal diet for the child for his/her proper growth.

2. Information on the importance of safe water supply and simple but efficient drainage system in the area.
3. In the field of nutritional gap an attempt should be made to close the caloric gap first by provision of inexpensive calorie containing supplements. It is much easier and cheaper to close the caloric gap, which, incidentally, by conserving protein, will help to close the protein gap also.
4. Programmes for educating parents so that they understand the importance of early years and provide suitable stimulating experiences and opportunities for spontaneous play to their children within the available resources should be developed.
5. Mass media resources could be harnessed for the purpose of language development, cognitive development, socio-emotional development and development of basic skills to advance learning readiness in young children.
6. Home/family is the primary social institution for the care and protection of the child. Helping the families to ensure conditions of health, development and growth of the young children should be given priority of attention.

I would like to conclude, quoting Dorothy Law Note- "If a child lives with criticism, he learns to condemn."If a child lives with hostility, he learns to fight. "If a Child lives with ridicule, he learns to be shy. "If a child lives with tolerance, he learns to be patient. "If a child lives with encouragement, he learns confidence. "If a child lives with praise, he learns to appreciate. "If a child lives with fairness, he learns justice. "If a child lives with security, he learns to have faith. "If a child lives with approval, he learns to like himself and "If a child lives with acceptance and friendship, he learns to find love in the world".

9

INTERNATIONAL WOMEN'S DAY OF 2007—WOMEN PARLIAMENTARIANS

"Women parliamentarians had their say in both the Houses of Parliament on the occassion of International Women's Day on Thursday i.e. on 8th March's but were unable to secure a concrete assurance from the Government on the introduction of the Women's Reservation Bill.

All they got was a reiteration of the Government commitment to bring the Bill to Parliament before its term ended. In the Rajya Sabha, Prime Minister Man Mohan Singh said our Government remains Committed to, work towards broad-based consensus on the Bill". Some months back the initiative nearly succeeded but some problems arose and we could not bring it in the last session of parliament. Reports the Hindu dated 9th March' 07. Responding to the demand for a commitment on the introduction of the Bill in the Lok Sabha, Union Parliamentery Affairs Minister Priya Ranjan das Munshi said "a consensus building exercise was on since it was a constitutional Amendment requiring Two-Thirds majority for passage. "We will introduce it before our term is over".

Before this declaration by the minister, Lok Sabha speaker, Sri Somnath Chatterjee made a reference to International Women's Day before setting aside time from Question Hour to allow women members to speak about their views on the Bill.

Women members refused to speak for a minute each and nearly half of the question hour was taken up.

The speaker dripped "I made a mistake, I find".

Setting aside applications of Party Politics, women MPs pointed out that every year platitudes are offered to women's empowerment both inside and outside parliament. But the Bill remarked an elusive goal.

Women have to improve their managerial skills. Kiran Bedi, the first IPS officer of India and the Director-General, Bureau of Police Training and Development attended a grand function arranged in Ravindra Bharati on the eve of the International Women's Day by the member of the Andhra Pradesh Secretariat Women Employees Welfare Association. She gave her personal impressions. On the present Day society in the following words. "Women as a class did not yet make a difference to the role played by men. If they had, they would have ushered in a new management culture Barring a few individuals, women did not pave path to a new work culture. Many women, like men, were also asserted for corruption.

In the new age, one was not looking for more employment percentage of women but for the good governance they would bring in with a fair, positive and fearless attitude.

Addressing the women who gathered there, Ms Bedi in an innovative and motivating voice said "Ask yourself if you are the new age woman capable of taking right decisions. It is only when women working in every possible field have the right attitude, new face of management and leadership will emerge. Furthering her speech in clear terms, the magsasay Award winner, Ms. Bedi demolished the eternal dilemma of women about their primary responsibility. In her own words, she said "Give up dichotomy in thought. Woman's duty is to become her own decision maker and architect of her own destiny, by being confident, independent, contributing and self-respecting".

The situation in the present day society is leading to dichotomy of thought due to a clash in between age old traditional values and the modern values. Due to illiteracy and poverty and backwardness and also sentimental approach to life, to fit in the family system, a large chunk of women are not able to participate in what is happening around them. They are clinging simply to the old systems.

Barring a few highly educated urban women, women living in rural India are far away from the modern concepts as an individual. She is not able to take her own decisions either in career or in personal life.

Even professionals are not able to take their own decisions because of the influence of the parents or families.

In the same meeting Smt. Rachel Chatterjee IAS, CMD of Transco, advised women to be the agents of change. If women wanted a change in the perception of society at large, they have to change and shoulder responsibilities in a befitting manner.

Ideologically speaking, these words seem to be very commencing to achieve empowerment of women in the near future.

Women's organizations are holding seminars and conferences on the eve of the International Women's Day to bring about awakening among women. Even political parties are speaking on the platforms voce foriously about women's empowerment but are not able to allot even 1/3rd reservation in the assemblies and the parliament.

Lenin said "every woman working in the kitchen should become a politician" when an Indian woman comes to the stage, Indian society will automatically change. Inequality, corruption and the feeling of high and the low would disappear.

For instance, if we take into consideration Andhra Pradesh, as per the statistics of 2001, women are 49.4% in the population of 76.21 millions. In the rural areas, percentage of women among the work force is only 43.48% when men's force is 58.30 percent. In Andhra Pradesh, when child mortality among girls is 58% as per 2005 figures, it is only 15% in Kerala. We are lagging behind Tamil Nadu and Karnataka also. When death rate among women in Kerala is 5.2% it is 6.9% in Andhra Pradesh.

Education is basic for any progress. As per 2001 figures, literacy rate among women in Andhra Pradesh is 50.4%, it is 87.7 in Kerala, 64.3% in Tamil Nadu and 56.9% in Karnataka and in Orissa, it is 50.5%. As per an African Proverb, if a man is educated, it is only useful for him but when a woman is educated, it is useful for the family and the society because her influence is more on the children, who form the coming generation.

Budget allotment for women's welfare programmes is 11.7 per cent out of the entire budget expenditure. The rate of drop-outs among girls in between Ist and 10th classes is 65.20% during 2005-2006. It is 72.2 per cent among scheduled castes whereas it is 83.88% among scheduled tribes. So, it is clearly evident that every effort has to be made to spread literacy among women, especially girls. How long will it take to educate all these girls and by what means? Who is answerable ? Who is responsible ? More hollow promises or platform speeches will not do. They cannot achieve any good results.

Even if many women's days are celebrated, there is no change in the life of women. Many women are expressing that in all the fields, women are being looked down.

March 8th is fixed up as women's day by the famous German Communist Clara Jetkun and the second international meeting was celebrated in 1911 in Lokcers Hegan trying to unify women of the world. Since then, women in all countries have been celebrating it with an inspiration to solve their problems. India had been participating in the international conferences and accepting the resolutions passed. But Birth of a girl is becoming appreciated. That is why mother throwing away the girl child on the dustbins soon after birth or taking up abortion when it is declared by the PSDT that it is a girl is becoming common. Dowry deaths are also increasing even in the modern days.

Though women are shining in every field on par with men equally. They are facing many problems. Many women's organizations especially AIDWA, on the eve of the women's day conducted a conference in Sundarayya Vigrnana Kendram, Hyderabad and ventilated the grievances of women in achieving equal rights, on account of the policies of the Governments and globalization. Cases of sexual harassment at the work spot, dowry deaths, kidnaps are increasing in number. On account of the increase of prices, education and health have become very costly and many women are suffering in the absence of a proper living place. Reasons may be many for this situation. Remedies also may not be nearer.

Of course, women's status has slightly improved but much is to be achieved. If women have to get their due place, each and everyone have to be educated. Economic independence and property right is to be ensured.

Wise-men's club of Hyderabad conducted International Women's Day in YMCA, Narayanaguda and Dr. Lakshmi Bhavani project officer of UNICEF attended as chief guest on the oecasion. She addressed the women who gathered and said that women should improve their self-confidence and individuality and for achieving this goal, sound system of education is required. We are celebrating International Women's Day to bring out the thinking capacity of woman to serve the humanity. The awakening among women, brought about by such gatherings is enabling her to work on par with men in every field and this is a good indication of women coming out as good professionals.

"We are committed to women's empowerment", says the Hon. Chief Minister of Andhra Pradesh, Dr. Y. S. Raja Sekhara Reddy. Speaking on Gender Budgeting, in the AP Legislative Forum, he expressed the view that if a country or state wants to prosper, women's progress is essential. Only when women develop economically, the country would also develop. Women are coming forward from the last ten years because of the self-help groups formed in the rural areas and they are achieving results. There are 6.2 lakhs of self-help groups and 82 lakhs of women are taking benefit out of the loaning system. As much as 3,500 rupees were provided as loans to these women during 2006-2007 from different Banks and now during the present year Banks are coming forward to increase this loan amount to 5,000 crores.

Even the team of the World Bank is taking interest in standing studying this system and in the programmes being implemented for the development of women. Speaking on the accession, M/s Maxinyason, coordinator of women of United Nations, told that Governments have to take up programmes for the sake of women in the fields of education, health, and livelihood, so as to improve their conditions. When Governments take interest in taking up total literacy among women, women's development is possible,

Gender Equality Still a Distant Dream

A recent survey by the world economic forum finds that full economic and political empowerment of women remains a dream even in the western world.

Images of high-profile women running multi-million dollar business empires or taking over male traditional male bastions are misleading in measuring the status of women in view of the depressing stories of their plight and oppression.

In some areas, indeed, women in the third world countries like India are said to be better off than women in the more advanced countries.

The report says that "no country has yet managed to eliminate the gender gap "but the Nordic countries like Norway, Sweden, Iceland and Denmark and Finland have "succeeded best" in narrowing the gap. They are seen to provide a "workable model" for the rest of the world to follow other "female-friendly" countries like Britain, Germany, New Zealand, Australia and serval East European countries where women still benefit from the support system built during the communist era.

Poor Record of USA

America with its restricting maternity rights regime and poor child welfare system does not figure even in the top 10, women-friendly countries. Even Britain,which makes it to the top 10, fares badly in a range of areas, lagging behind even India in terms of economic opportunity. The most glaring gender inequality in Britain relates to wages, where women still earn less than men for the same work and this situation remains in spite of the Equal Pay Act passed 30 years ago. This fact is confirmed by official figures which show that the average income of women in Britain is almost half that of men.

What is the rank of India as per the Survey? Despite scoring high in economic opportunity, India is at the bottom of the heap by most criteria—above only Pakistan, Korea, Jordan, Turkey and Egypt. India is at the 53rd position, most embarrassingly behind economically less developed countries like Bangladesh and a good member of Latin American and African nations, which have done better in narrowing gender gap.

Cherie Blair, wife of the British prime minister, has expressed concern over the inequalities faced by women and called for positive discrimination. She unequivocally supported quota for women in parliamentary elections as a means of "political empowerment".

Saadia Zahidi, a co-author of WEF survey says, that there is a link between how a country treated its women and that countries ability to compete globally. The report underlines the "clear economic incentive" behind empowering women. "Countries that do not fully take advantage of one half of the talent in their population are misallocating their human resources and undermining their competitive potential".

The survey is based on hard data from leading international organizations. The countries have been ranked on the basis of five main criteria by UNIFEM - economic participation' economic opportunity Political empowerment, educational attainment and health and well-being.

This is the first time that WEF had attempted such a survey and commentators said that it reflected a recognition by the international business community that women's status was an area of critical importance for development.

Give Women Their Due—Says the Prime Minister

Prime Minister' Dr. Man Mohan Singh reiterated on the International Women's Day, that his Government is Committed to evolving a consensus on the contentions of the Women's Reservation Bill. Political parties also have given their verbal support to the Bill.

But the goal of reserving one-third of the seats in the Parliament and in the State Assemblies seems to be elusive though the support of the left parties was consistent.

Women's Reservation Bill was first introduced in Parliament in the year 1996. But on account of several objections from the political parties, it was not possible to get the Bill passed.

Of course Women's Reservation Bill was a priority item in the Common Minimum programme of the United Progressive Alliance. But several road blocks and several arguments are blocking the passage of the Bill. Some demands are put forward for sub-quotas for women from the scheduled castes, scheduled tribes and other backward classes within the 33.3 per cent quota. this springs, it appears from an argument that the quotas would be dominated by the elite of the upper strata women. The provision for rotation is also rejected by the same who are afraid of their power of position in their constituencies. There is another objection such as increase in the number of wives and daughters of politicians capturing the political scene. These arguments deep-rooted and are preventing women taking their legitimate place in political arena.

In a progressive democracy like India, only 8.3 per cent of the members of Parliament are women, according to the data published by the inter-parliamentary union in February 2007. India is behind countries like Pakistan and China in this regard.

In a patriarchal tradition a bound society if more women can be elected to positions of power, it would solve many of the problems like oppression, violence, discrimination confronting women. Equality of opportunities to work together to make just representation to women in Parliament and State Assemblies a reality for the betterment of society. Immediate passage of this very important legislation should be ensured by one and all concerned.

Women Members Call for Quota Bill

The Rajya Sabha was adjourned twice as the members simultaneously insisted on raising various issues. The House also saw most women members demanding early introduction of the Women's Reservation Bill.

The first one to demand Rashid Alvi (Congress) who claimed that he had been promised that he would bé allowed to speak. The Dy. Chairperson, K. Rahman Khan, said that there was no zero hour on Friday and assured him that his demand would be considered on Monday.

Mr. Khan had to adjourn the house for 15 minutes when Mr. Alvi insisted on his demand.

Sushma Swaraj (BJP) called for a statement on the Women's Bill. Najma Hepatullah (BJP) wanted to know from government whether the bill would be introduced in this session of parliament or not. Brinda Karat (CPI-M) also supported Ms. Hepatullah. Other members including Maya Singh (BJP), Alka Balaram and Prema Kariappa (both Congress) also called for a statement from the government. Jaya Bachan (Samajwadi party) refrained from demanding the tabling of the Bill.

Ramdeo Bhandari (Rashtriya Janata Dal) said his party supported reservation bill for women but there should be sub-quota for socially disadvantaged groups.

Minister of State for Parliamentary Affairs Mr. Suresh Pachauri said the Government and its allies were in favour of early tabling of the bill and the legislation was passing through a "process". *Hindu* dated 17th December '05, states that the fate of the Women's Reservation Bill was uncertain became obvious on Friday (17.12.05) when Brinda Karat (CPI-M) raised the issue in the Rajya Sabha during the post-lunch session.

Pointing to the presence of Prime Minister, Man Mohan Singh, Ms. Karat said the session was coming to a close in a week and the Government should give some "Signal" as to when it intended to table the Bill.

Sushma Swaraj said at least a draft Bill be introduced in parliament. "A Draft Bill should be introduced after clearance from the Union Cabinet".

Janta Dal (United) leader Sharad Yadav objected to the raising of the demand "all of a Sudden". He said the Bill could not be introduced without consultations with the political parties.

Unfortunately, there was no response or any kind of reaction from the Treasury Benches.

Left Parties—Not in Favour of Increasing Seats

The Left parties have demanded that the Government should come forward to present the Bill in its present form and put it to vote instead of seeking consensus "We are confident that the Bill will come up in the next session of Parliament. The Left parties are not in favour of increasing the number of seats" a senior Left Party leader said after a 3-hour UPA-Left coordination meeting that discussed a range of issues based on the exhanstive note submitted by the Left Parties.

Left parties said the, objection to the Government approach on the issue of women's reservation centred around Union Home Minister Sivraj Patil's suggestion to increase the number of state to arrive at a consensns. This led to a brief verbal sparring. Sonia Gandhi, President of the Congress party, said, That despite her own efforts consensus on the issue was elusive and sought a way forward.

Non-Passage of Women's Reservation Bill Criticized

Speakers at a national consultation on "Gender and Governance" expressed varied opinions on the status of women in governance, though all agreed that there were gaps between policies and implementation. Referring to non-passage of Women's Reservation Bill as "defeat of democracy" in independent India, which gave a right to vote, while their counterparts in other parts struggled hard to achieve it.

Organized by the World Bank and the United Nations Development Programme, the consultation focussed on promoting gender equality and strengthening decentralizations. Describing reluctance in passing the Women's Reservation Bill, and provision of reservation of Women in Parliament and the Assemblies, as "institutionalization of discrimination", the former member of Parliament, Smt Jayanti Natarajan said women were asking for reservation on the basis of equal status enjoyed by them under the Indian constitution.

"There was no talk of dual membership or increasing the number of seats when Dalits were given reservation. Importantly, the experience of women in Panchayats has been excellent, though with some aberration", she said, adding that it proved women were good administrators and should not be discriminated against on the basis of sex.

The greatest achievements of women in the post-independence era have been reservation in the local Self-Governments and the success of the Self-help groups.

George Mathew director of Indian Social Institute felt that only political empowerment could bring about a societal action and reservation of women was the one way of achieving this.

"We keep women as cultural emblems. They are required in the field of art and culture but unwanted in political, social and economic structures" he said.

Striking a different note, the noted sociologist, Sarojni Ganju Thakur, admitted that while there were gaps between policies and implementation women had been empowered by the power of right to voting. The number of women in civil services is also a positive indicator when compared with the ICS, where there were no women. According to her, The key challenges were to bridge the gap between planning and its implementation and better monitoring.

Women on the March—For a Better Share

Member of various organisations staged a protest demonstration in New Delhi, demanding the Women's Reservation Bill be brought in the current session of Parliament in 2006 on August 3rd. Along with some members of Parliament, including CPI (M) leader, Brinda Karat. They met Home Minister, Sivaraj Patil and urged him to take the initiative. In the Lok Sabha, the speaker adjourned the House abruptly during zero hour following on uproar over are the issue.

Introduce Women's Bill without Delay -Yechury

Hindu, dated 20th November '05 reports that the CPI(M) Politbureau member and MP, Sitaram Yechury has demanded that the Central Government introduce the Women's Reservation Bill in the Parliament in the coming session of Parliament instead of delaying its enactment in the name of obtaining consensus on it.

Participating in a workshop organised by the party on the issue, he said that, though all the major political parties were supporting the Bill it was not introduced so far, on the ground of evolving a consensus, which was difficult to reach." Let the Government bring the bill first and let those opposing it, vote against it" he said.

A few political parties were opposed to the introduction of reservation to women and the alternatives, that were suggested by the same sections of society, were aimed at blocking its enactment. Alternatives such as increasing the number of seats in the Parliament and incorporating the caste quota with women reservation would only delay its enactment.

"The previous NDA Government which convened a joint session of the Parliament, to pass POTA, after failing to arrive at a consensus on it. Let the UPA Government explore any such options to ensure the passage of the bill" he said.

"The CPI (M) had no illusions that the quota bill would stop atrocities against women in various forms. It was only a beginning towards emancipation of women from their struggle and give them their equal right.

The CPI(M) floor leader in the Rajya Sabha, Nilotpala Basu, criticized some of the North Indian political parties that were trying to resist the introduction of the bill, as it would trigger a set of changes in society enabling women to play their role. though there was no principled disagreement in the Lok Sabha and State Assemblies on the Bill, it was unfortunate that such a social legislation met with such a fate.

Since the issue was a political one, the CPI(M) had decided to mobilise public support, and mount pressure on the Government for its enactment." It is not confined to women's organizations. All the progressive thinking sections of society must come forward to mount pressure on the Government" he said.

Excepting some statements here and there nothing moved forward and no decision to introduce the bill was taken to introduce the bill in Parliament.

Days rolled on. The year 2007 came. Taking part in the valedictory programme of the 3 day 8th convention of All-India coordination committee of working women at Sarada Nagar in the Steel Township of Visakhapatnam, Brinda Karat, a politbureau member, of CPI(M) said that her party was confident of tabling the Women's Reservation Bill in the winter session of Parliament, speaking to press reporters, she condemned the decision of UPA to achieve consensus on the bill, before tabling it in the House.

She said "Let the Government first table the bill in Parliament and then try to achieve consensus rather than just showing sympathy. If the largest party of the ruling coalition is firm, women's reservation bill becomes a reality."

"Our party is firm on this bill. We have already spoken to other parties of the coalition" she said.

Alleging that the National Democratic Alliance had utterly failed as an opposition. Ms. Karat said the Left parties mainly taken by the UPA, both in and outside Parliament. She urged all the State Governments to launch special campaigns to create awareness among the general public about the newly enacted Domestic Violence Act also.

Brinda Karat sought special economic package for Muslims.

In the year 2005 itself, Brinda Karat and her party colleagues Subhashini Ali led a march to Parliament seeking passage of the women's bill. Reminding Dr. Man Mohan Singh of his assurance given in the National Common Minimum Programme that their Government would pass the bill. Their memorandum said that it was disappointing that the bill had not been listed for discussion.

"While we do appreciate the difficulties that a coalition Government may face in passage of a legislation that is not totally acceptable to all its partners.This cannot be a justification for the non-implementation of solemn assurance", the memorandum said.

AIDWA president Subhashini Ali told the prime minister that thousands of their members from all over the country had assembled to press for the passage of the Bill.

"We appeal to you to make a clean break with this attitude which smacks of not only gender insensitivity but insensitivity to the process of making democracy more inclusive and vibrant. We would request you to place the Bill for a thorough discussion in Parliament and to ensure that a vote is taken on it. If this is done with sincerity, the enactment of the bill will become a reality "the memorandum said,

Commitment Stands: Says Das Munshi

A demand for tabling the long-pending women's Reservation Bill was made in both the Houses of Parliament *Hindu* dt 3rd August '06 reports. While members sought its passage in this session, the Government reiterated its support for the measure, which seeks to provide 33 per cent reservation for women in Parliament and State Assemblies.

In the Rajya Sabha JD(U) President, Sharad Yadav and Samaj Wadi Party leader Amar Singh stood up in protest when Dy. Chairman K. Rahman Khan observed that the entire House was in agreement on the issue.

Raising the subject during zero hour, CPI(M) leader Brinda Karat demanded that the bill be debated in this session itself "Let there be amendments but at least, let it be tabled and debated".

The Bill was not a question of men versus women, she said. It was a question of democratic system.

"This Lok Sabha has only 8% women members several members associated themselves with her but as soon as Mr. Khan said, the entire House was in agreement. Mr. Yadav said "This is wrong".

BJP Dy. leader Sushma Swaraj said the bill was introduced during the Dev Gowda regime and it came up for discussion twice during the NDA rule but did not see the light of the day during UPA regime.

In the Lok Sabha, CPI leader, Gurudas Dasgupta raising the matter during zero hour, said the Government should not make the bill a matter of political controversy. He drew the attention of the House to thousands of women staging a dharna at Jantar Mantar, demanding early passage of the bill. Intervening Parliamentary Affairs Minister, Priyaranjan Das Munshi, assured the members that there was no going back" by the Government on its commitment to the Bill. However as it was a Constitution Amendment Bill, the support of all sections was required. Home Minister, Sivaraj Patil was engaged in talks with various parties. But before the matter was further discussed speaker Somnath Chatterjee adjourned the House for lunch.

Later, a delegation led by Ms. Karat met Sivaraj Patil, who assured the team that the Congress. supported the Bill and was working hard for its passage without a hitch. Ms. Karat said she had sought time from the prime minister and would take up the issue with him also.

CPI's plea to Man Mohan: The CPI urged the prime minister Man Mohan Singh to bring forward the women's bill. According to Mr. Das Gupta, the prime minister informed them that discussions were on to arrive at a consensus on the Women's Bill. There was a possibility of the quota being lowered.

Reorganisation of Constituencies First—Women's Bill Next

Vaartha a prominent Daily in Andhra Pradesh dt. 13.10.06, states that all the parties arrived at a consensus that passage of the Women's Bill should not be linked up with the issue of reorganisation of the constituencies of parliament and state assemblies.

In an all meeting held at New Delhi, all parties come to a conclusion that in addition to accepting the Women's Reservation Bill if the Parliament decides to increase the number of seats, taking up reorganisation may be necessary and for that sake, it is not now necessary to take up this issue as a precautionary measure.

So, as per the delimitation Act of 2002 Constituencies of parliament and assemblies of the states may be continued upto 2009 general elections. In this meeting which was presided over by Sri Pranab Mukherjee union minister for defence, almost all parties except Trinamul Congress came to an agreement. After the meeting, Pranab declared that reorganization process would be taken up as per the delimitation Act. Pranab gave an assurance to all the parties that before considering the objections by North Eastern States, urban-rural constituencies and the difference of their numbers, rotation of SC reservation constituencies, opinions of all parties would be received.

Till the year 2026 the year number of the present assembly and parliament constituencies would not be changed and the present set-up would not be continued until then and population figures of 1971 would be taken into consideration. If reorganisation is done depending on the new population figures, states like Tamilnadu and Andhra Pradesh, where population growth is less, would be put to loss and so as this problem is applied to all over India, since 50 per cent of the reorganisation is completed, recoganisation process, has to be completed, said Yerram Naidu, leader of Telugu Desam party in the Parliament.

If population is taken as the basis in both urban and rural areas, the number of rural constituencies would be decreased and so 10% of the population relaxation in the rural constituences, should be there some parties felt as per Sri Ascar Fernandez, Chairman of Elections Wing of AICC.

Reorganisation has not reached even to drafting of notification level in Andhra Pradesh, the issue of rural-urban constituences can be taken up but this should not delay the delimitation process, said Yerram Naidu, declaring his party's attitude.

On account of the proposal to increase parliament and assembly constituencies, reorganisation process should not be delayed or stopped and this was declared to be the opinion of all parties, as per the version of secretary of delimitation cell of the Congress party and MP Raya Sabha Sri JD Sedam. Hence it is better to think of Women's Reservation Bill after completion of the delimitation process.

MP, TRS, Sri Vinod Kumar demanded increase of the number of Parliament and Assembly constituencies. Delimitation process had been completed in 12 states and seats of SCs and STs are to be increased by six more. So if matters are delayed still further, they will be put to loss, said Suravaram Sudhakar Reddy, MP (Lok Sabha) of CPI.

BJP made it clear. that if delimitation process which is already started is delayed' and if women's bill is linked with this process by 2009 elections, delimitation should be completed at any cost.

Left parties requested for introducing the bill in its original form in the winter session of Parliament. But Sitaram Yechuri and others have not touched upon the point whether there should be OBC quota or not among the 33% quota already proposed.

Speaking on behalf of DMK, T.P.R. Balu said that reducing the difference in urban-rural constituencies is policy of their party.

Narayanan, speaking on behalf of AIDMK, said that their Jaya Lalitha is a staunch supporter of Mahila Reservation Bill.

Social Justice Required for Women

The All-India Democratic Women's Association urged the United Progressive Alliance (UPA) to ensure an agreement on the Women's Reservation Bill with its partners in order to let it be passed with the support of the Left parties.

In a press-meet during the Executive Committee meeting Subhashini Ali president, Brinda Karat MP and Sudha Sundara Raman, its secretary, said that it noted with satisfaction Prime Minister Man Mohan Singh's assurance on introduction of the bill in the winter session. They utilized the 'BJP' for its duplicity on the issue and said that AIDWA, along with other women's organisations would request the Government to display the "political will" to counter any possible disruption of the bill.

Brinda Karat said that in this country, the Governments have no proper attitude towards social justice and progress. Progress does not mean sensex points or progress of some corporate companies. When we look at the details of the 11th Five Year Plan, it is evident that our Governments have not changed their age old concepts of allotments. People, especially women who are targets of social oppression should be received of special attention. Whether special allotments are made or not is to be observed. But no such things are there in the plan.

Subhashini Ali said there are several people who are obstructing the passage of the Women's Reservation Bill. But one point is clear only with the help of men who are more in number in Parliament the bill can be passed. If you talk about reservation on the basis of caste in the bill, there are more men belonging to OBC cadre in the Parliament. If you talk of reservations, in their place, more women would come.

Charter of Demands by Women's Bodies

As early as 1995, a charter of demands was prepared by women's organisations and Mr. Madhav Rao Seindia, the then

Human Resource Development Minister said that a National policy on women would be finalized after consultation with women's organisations.

The women's organisations objected to the hurried manner in which the document was being finalized on the eve of elections.

AIDWA, along with centre for Women's Development Studies (CWDS)' Joint Women's Programme (JWP). National Federation of Indian Women (NFIW) and YWCA of India, have prepared a joint response to the draft policy document and drew a charter of minimum demands for all the political parties.

Ms Vina Majumdar of CWDS said "over the years there have been innumerable reports, laws and policies in ending discrimination against women and involving them in national development proprammes. But they have not been implemented.

According to them, issues such misuse of religion for political purposes, criminalision of politics, crucial manner of guaranteeing economic independence of women including rights on land have not been included in the policy.

They have also objected to the creation of new mechanisms like a national committee on women and the appointment of a National Commissioner for women's rights which will only serve to erode the statutory power of National Commission for Women.

10

REVOLUTION OF THE OTHER HALF-IN ASIA

Japanese women are becoming more aware of their rights and roles in the society. There is a revolution taking place in Japan and it is not by men, who brought about the economic miracle but by women who form the "other half"- the quiet invisible half.

A few years ago, corporate board rooms discussing carnival issues, were found to be empty of any women. But now, They are opening up slowly to women. "Now I hire business women not "Ochakuni" (tea powers) says an executive at Matsushita Trading Company. More women are joining the ranks of men. It is the acceptance of men, which has surprisingly set the revolution rolling.

Though the hidden energies of women have surfaced in the past two decades, the present women in Japan are very vocal about their grievances. Whether against the rape incident of a school girl or sexual harassment in offices, known as "SEKUHARA" in Japanese language. The anti -US bases rally in Okinawa turned into a major issue because it was led mainly by women's organizations all over Japan.

The turning point in Japan came in 1986, when Equal Employment Opportunities (EEO) Act, set the goal for working women. The law encourages equal hiring, training and promotion practices.

Before that only 33 percent of large companies would accept applications from female graduates as it was deemed highly risky for a firm to hire a woman for a "manly job." Male employers resisted any such move as a slap on their abilities. Now the situation has changed drastically and many companies are taking recourse to the EEO law, to silence their male employers. Now more than 80 per cent of the companies are welcoming Women to Join their manegirial eadre. As a result, many women are leaving their old-fashioned clerical jobs and joining managerial cadre even such assignments involving even construction work.

The increasing number of women in the job market has a demographic angle too. By 2025, Japan will become world's most aged society, with nearly 20 percent of the population come to 65 yrs. This ironically is going to be good for Japanese women. Major planing companies are planing to absorb women in their work force. About 15 electronic giants like Hitachi, NEC and Mitsubishi are offering one year Maternity leave to women.

Many women go to great lengths to balance between home and office. With the average life expectancy of a Japanese woman reaching 82 years, the potential to enter job market has become more.

The old imagination that the Japanese women wrapped in silk Kimonos, walked three steps behind their husbands the devoted, demure and self-sacrificing, is now getting rapidly reverted to the pre-confusion society when the empresses ruled the country with an iron-hand.

Quality of life now is their top priority. A recent survey shows that the priority of graduate girls is getting a full-time job till mid-thirties.

Vietnam's Gender Equality

"In many areas, Vietnam leads the Asia Pacific region on gender equality indicators. On an average, Vietnam performs well in delivering education and health services to girls and boys, women and men" a UNICEF official was quoted in a press release.

School enrolment rates in Vietneum show little difference between girls and boys. UNICEF representative in the country Jasper Morch said, adding that the gap between male and female literacy rates has been decreasing over time.

He said Vietnam also had one of the highest economic participation rates in the world. 85 per cent of men and 83 per cent of women aged 15-60 are engaged in economic activities, as per the data released by the World Bank in 2003.

Vietnamese women are very often required to put their families first and expected to defer to male authority. As a result of it, women may not be aware of or do not exercise the rights accorded to them by law and policy said the press release.

Due to gender inequalities, in access to productive resources women also have much less capacity to compete.

Iran-Women are fighting a Heavily Patriarchal System

This ancient land is known for its poetry' its arts, its monuments and its culture. Today's Iran is a mix of mix fascinating modern and traditional values.

For women in Iran, life is not all that easy. Of course, They have access to education and jobs. But there are limits imposed. Women are lawyers, journalists in business, in academic, and also as film makers.

But they are exceptions and do not have to confront the problems that the majority of women face by virtue of unequal laws: That places them in secondary status.

In August 2006, Iranian women began a campaign to collect one million signatures to demand the end of discriminatory laws in Iran. For this they were arrested and five of them are still in prison.

Shadi Sidr ran the Raahi legal centre, where legal help was offered to women, while Mahboobah ran an NGO training center. The courage of these women to speak out against a system, which will not permit their questioning, is to be saluted. Noble Peace Laureate, a great compaigner for human rights - Shirin Ebadi writes in her book "Iran Awakening" as follows. Iranian revolution has produced its own opposition, not least an educated, conscious women, who are agitating for their rights. They must be given the chance to fight their own fights to transform their own country uninterrupted".

It is a different image of Iran! What a change!!

Saudi Women Throw Their Hats in the Ring

Saudi women candidates in the elections to the board of the

Jeddah Chamber of Commerce and Industry, hope they are blazing a trail for women in the conservative kingdom.

"The more fact that a decision was taken to allow women to contest the elections is a success for ladies. Even If one women is elected, we would view this as a major achievement. Hanan-al-Madani, a candidate told the press.

Allowing women to stand in the Jedda chamber polls for the 1st time "will also show the world that Saudi decision makers trust women and want them to progress." Contrary to what westerners think said of fat Kabbani, another candidate. 16 women are in the run for 12 elected board seats. They are among 72 candidates in the run.

Half of 40,000 members of the chamber are eligible to cast votes including around 14,00 of 3000 women members, who in the past elections were entitled only to vote. Both M/s. Kabhani and M/s Madani are running as part of a 87- strong all-women grouping__the equivalent of an electoral list—appropriately called "Al-Awael" meaning in Arabic language "The first".

M/s Madani said" who were barred from landmark municipal elections earlier this year and are subjected to a host of restrictions in oil-rich Saudi Arabia, should similarly grab other opportunities to stand for office of women arise.

Pakistan - Woman Power on Display

Nirupama Subrahmanian, a reporter of the *Hindu* dated 29th March 2007 says that student of a prominent seminary, in the heart of Islamabad were locked up in a tense stand off with the Government Yesterday after taking three women and two policemen hostage. This is the second confront- action between the students of the women's Jamia Hafsa Madrasa with the Government this year.

In January, the women took over a poblic library for children next door and refused to vacate unless in Government rebuilt that it had demolished and introduced Islamic Law. The mosdues critics continues even after the Governments surrender with Religious Affairs Minister, Ejaz-ul-Haq laying the first bricks of the reconstruction work.

President Parvaz Musharaf's non-Islamist opponents contrasted his assertions of "establishing the government's writ" in all party of Pakistan, with the government's apparent inability to enforce the law in the capital.

The latest challenges to the government's writ came, after Hafiza students, assisted by men from the neighbourhood Lal Masjid captured three women allegedly and imprisoned them at the seminary. Women in Black burquas kept a look out from the seminary's roof while masked men and boys patrolled the road. The administrator, Mr. Ghazi said that the girls at the seminary had made it their mission to "cleanse" society of its "ills" and they had made a beginning with the neighbourhood. A large number of residents present at the press conference gave "heartfelt thanks" to the students.

Musharraf's Claim Disputed

The women who spearheaded the cause of the disappeared in Pakistan contested president Pervez Musharraf's claim that the Government was not linked to the disappearances. General Musharaf said in Rawalpindi in a meeting that most of the missing persons had been lured away to join "Jihadi" groups and that it was "sheer propaganda".

Human rights organizations have alleged that the disappeared were picketed up illegally by the Government on supicion of having links with Al-Queda and some were even "sold" to the United States in return for bounty money from the CIA.

Amma Masood, whose husband Masood has been missing since 2005, Gen. Musharaf's claim was "absurd", and that nobody "believes his version".

The human rights commission of Pakistan also contests the presidents' claim.

11

AMARTYA SEN, THE NOBEL LAUREATE SPEAKS ON GENDER ISSUES

Amartya Sen provides certain insights into what led him to examine gender issues intellectually.

He says "My early encounters, when I was a student, with the role of tilted attitudes and positional observations and slanted habits of thought, did prove, in retrospect highly educational for me. I do see for my self, in part, as a feminist economist, in addition to having other descriptions to which I respond".

Bina Agarwal, Jane Humphries and Ingrid Robeyns questioned him.

"What factors first led you to examine gender concerns intellectually? For instance, you have said often that your experience during the Great Bengal Famine shaped your interest in and work on famine. Have any such social or personal experiences shaped your work on gender".

His reply was in a way thought provoking "My interest in inequality, which goes back to my school days, was initially quite fixed on class divisions. My involvement with gender concentration on class, in standard politics (including standard student politics) and when in early 1950s, I was studying presidency college in Calcutta, it was taken for granted that class divisions were in comparably more important than other social divisions Indeed, when later on, in the late 1960s, I started working on gender inequality. Many of my class friends still saw this as quite an unsound broadening of interest involving a dilution of ones focus on class....... This was, of course, evidence of inequality between men and women as well. But its severe and brutal manifestations (on which I worked later from the late 1960s to 1990s, were hidden from immediate observation. In comparison with the firm aspirations of the boys in my class, the girls, even very talented ones, seemed far less ambitious, with much less expectation. This had the apparent outward appearance of a difference in their respective preferences.

"Who are you to tell people what they should do with their lives"? My troubling thoughts about the widely held implicit belief that men's preferences were more focussed and their interests and their interests, as a result demanded more attention than women typically seemed to be superficially by women made themselves.

I was really struck by the fact that the female students, seemed convinced as the boys, that there was no real issue of gender inequality. These discussions, confusing and frustrating as they were at that time, later helped me to understand, in retrospect, how gender inequality survives and flourishes, working in a valuational mist that engulfs all and which works by making allies out of the victims.

To another question, he says

"Many argue that although you have written extensively on gender inequality, you do not directly address the question of power within gender relations. Do you agree? Amartya Sen proceeded to reply "I do not think I can agree with that. I cannot even understand how it could be possible to discuss gender inequality extensively without going into the question of power within gender relations, since power is so central. In fact, the importance of power is part and parcel of my understanding, both directly or indirectly of gender inequality.

Women and men have both congruent and conflicting interests affecting family living. Decision making in the family tends to take the form of the pursuit of cooperation. Each of the parties has much to lose if cooperation were to break down and yet there are various alternative cooperative solutions.

There are thus far-reaching casual impacts of the presence and use of powers of different kinds, from physical powers to institutionally mediated powers, such as the social powers arising from traditional roles inside and outside the household.

Perhaps the point is not about whether the concept of power is being used, but about the frequency with which, the word 'power' occurs in my writing as opposed to the ones, I tend more often to use, such as' empowerment' or 'capability', or 'freedom' or 'agency' of 'threat' of 'vulnerability'.

The essays in a volume entitled "Women of India" colonial and post-colonial period Edited by Bharati Ray and published by Sage Publications, New Delhi, explore the operation of power and the resistance to it. The space that was denied to the disadvantaged gender-women and the space they created for themselves and the history of the mutual roles of women and men in colonial and post-colonial periods in India. This gives a historical understanding of the gendered politics, policies and programmes, and legislations.

An essay by Flavia Agres on 'Personal Laws' and the one by Patricia Uberoi on 'Family' underscore the point.

Ubero's point raises some important points and questions. The manner in which marriage practices between the north and the south were legally debated and ultimately resolved without addressing the gender question.

12

VAJPAYEE TO MEET OPPOSITON LEADER ON WOMEN'S BILL

Hindu dt 22' December 1999 reports as follows:

The opponents of the Women's Reservation Bill today forced the Government to think again before rushing through in the current session of Parliament. As the Lok Sabha witnessed noisy scenes for the second consecutive day also, the prime minister Mr. Vajpayee agreed to have a discussion with the opposition leaders to break the deadlock.

He already met them several times, but with no success. The opposition parties made it very clear that they would not even allow the bill to be introduced until it was modified to provide Sub-quota for OBCs and Muslims within 33 percent across the broad reservation planned for women in Lok Sabha and State Assemblies.

Announcing the prime minister's move the Parliamentary Affairs Minister Mr. Pramod Mahajan, told the Lok Sabha, that though the Government was committed to reservation for women in legislatures, it Favoured maximum possible consensus. Consensus, however did not mean unanimity.

Mr. Mahajan's statement followed a determined attempt by the Samaj Wadi party and the Rashtriya Janata Dal to disrupt the business. They insisted on an assurance from the Government it would not introduce the Bill unless there was a consensus. Proceedings were reduced to a farce as the members of SP and RJD parties "occupied" the "well", raised slogans against the bill and its supporters. They shouted down anyone who did not support them.

SP leader, Mr. Mulayam Singh Yadav, refused to restrain his members despite repeated and strong warnings from the Dy.

Speaker Mr. P.M. Sayeed. He threatened to "name" the SP/RJD members if they did not behave properly but they continued to raise slogans and disrupt the house. Mr. Yadav watched with amusement and told Mr. Sayeed that he could expel them if he liked.

Trouble began soon after the house met in the morning. Though the Bill was not listed on the day's agenda, the SP/RJD member were suddenly on their feet demanding that it should be put off, soon, they were in the "well" which they occupied toll the lunch time. slogans, calling the Govt "anti-Dalit" and "anti-minorities", drowned ministers' replies during question hour and "zero hour" submissions by members.

There were heated exchanges as the Cong (I) and the Treasury benches protested the SP/RJD behaviour. Amid noisy interruptions, the Cong (I)'s deputy leader Mr. Madhav Rao Scindia opposed putting off the bill under pressure.

Some Attempts for Women's Empowerment (2005)

Somnath Chatterjee Lok Sabha Speaker, is hopeful of the controversial women's reservation bill, which seeks to reserve one-third of the seats in state legislatures and in Parliament for women being passed during his tenure. Releasing a commemorative stamp and first day cover at the inauguration of an international congress on women in New Delhi, he said "This is my expectation". Expressing confidence that pressure from women's groups and other citizens would prove successful in empowering women in the political sphere in the near future.

Earlier, inaugurating the 4-day congress, Mr. Chatterjee said he was proud of the fact that the constitution provided reservation for one-third of the seats in local Government bodies for women, both in the rural and urban areas. This was a uniqe achievement. The Government was committed to empowering women socially, educationally, economically, and politically specially designed policies and programmes were in place to realise this objective. In several states, substantial progress has been made and as a result there was progress in reducing female infant mortality, maternal mortality and improving female literacy, and retention of girls in schools.

Speaking on the condition of women in other countries he said, they were always disadvantaged including in the developed countries, one way or the other. In developed countries, the problem was with the so called "glass ceiling" at work places that discriminated against them moving to top decision making positions. In less developed countries, the problem was with the societal preference for male children which translated into institutionalised in equities faced by women in all fields.

The eighth meeting of the United Progressive Alliance and the Left parties took up the issue concerning women.

The Left parties sought to know the status of the Women's reservation Bill and the more on central legislation. On the women's bill, CPI national secretary, D. Raja urged the Government to consult its allies so that some headway could be made. UPA chairperson, Sonia Gandhi is understood to have noted that opposition from some parties was known. RJD, SP opposed the bill but Revolutionary Socialist Party MP Abani Roy said the UPA would have to convince its allies on the bill.

The ruling alliance was divided with the Trinamul Congress, favouring the introduction of the Bill and the Janata Dal (U) opposing it. The JD(U) Deputy leader, Mr. D.P. Yadav had an angry argument, with the chair insisting on that he should be allowed to speak. "I am the Dy. leader of JD (U). You can't refuse me time" he shouted, shaking with rage.

Later speaking on the bill, he said, it violated the constitution which guaranteed equal rights to all citizens. Nobody was against reservation for women, but there should be separate reservation for OBCs and Muslims - a point also emphasised by the Muslim League's Mr. G. M. Banatwala and other critics of the bill.

Continuing his theory of a *"BJP– Congress (I) Conspiracy"*, Mr. Mulayam Singh Yadav said, the Government had agreed to the Congress (I)'s support to push through certain controversial bill in the Rajya Sabha, where the BJP–led alliance does not have a majority.

When the house resumed after the lunch recess, noisy seenes continued until Mr. Mahajan's announcement that the "Prime Minister would meet the opposition leaders tomorrow".

Mulayam sees a conspiracy: the Samaj Wadi Party president, Mr. Mulaym Singh Yadav, even before the parliament session, that his party resolve was not to allow parliament to pass the women's reservation Bill in the present form.

He told presspersons at Lucknow, that the Government should try to find a solution to the vexed issue through talks with different parties. If the BJP led Government tried to use brutal force to adopt the bill, his party would do everything to the warst it, he said. Alleging that the Bill aimed at curtailing the democratic aspirations of the weaker seetions Mr. Yadav said the provisions would be used to deprive the backward sections of their due share of seats in the Lok Sabha and State Assemblies. Also, the system of rotation would discourage members from nursing their constituencies.

It was wrong to think, Mr. Yadav said, that women were a homogeneous class. There were two per women, who were "Devis" and the rest 98 percent are 'Dasis'. The benefit of reservation would be cornered by these two percent women belonging to the elite class, while exploited ones would gain nothing" he said.

It looked like a conspiracy hatched by forces opposed to the interests of scheduled castes, Scheduled tribes, Backward class and minorities. The same forces had launched agitations against the implementation of Mandal Commission report. While the BJP's position over the issue was well–known, the role of the Congress (I) was in explicable" he said.

As the situation obtained today, there was not a single member of the minorities in the Lok Sabha from a number of states. This was why he had demanded caste–wise reservation of seats in the women's quota. Also, the percentage of seats should be reduced to 10 percent.

Another solution could be to introduce legal provisions to force political parties to allot 33 per cent share to women, while giving the ticket.

Position in 2007

Women's Organisations Press for Passing of Women's Bill:

Nine women's organisations demanded that government should introduce the women's reservation Bill without further delay.

In a statement, the women's organisations said they felt "deeply betrayed by the utter failure" of the UPA Government to even list the Bill for introduction in the current session" leave alone ensuring its discussion and passage."

Referring to numerous public statements made by the Prime Minister Sri Man Mohan Singh, and UPA chairperson Sonia Gandhi in this regard, the women's organisations pointed out.

"While many other contentions legislations have been passed in the last three and half years of the UPA in power, the consensus excuse has been used time and again to delay this bill."

India lagged behind many neighbouring countries vis-a-vis the representation of women in legislatures. Pakistan had 22 per cent reservation in Parliament and Nepal had planned to give 33 per cent in the coming elections.

This statement was issued by among others the All India Democratic Women's Association, National Federation of Indian Women, All India Women's Conference, Centre for Women's Development studies, Guild of service, it women's programme and Young Women's Christian Association.

Discrimination of Women Continues

A recent study commissioned by the United Nations says that the rights of women to equality and non-discrimination are enshrined in a number of international instruments including the universal declaration of human rights, the UN charter, and in the convention on the Elimination of All Forms of Discrimination against women.

States have the obligation to enact and implement effective measures to promote and protect the rights.

BJP backs EC Proposal on Quota for Women

Bharatya Janata Party indicated that it was ready to back the proposal of the Election Commission that 33 per cent reservation for women in allotment of seats by all the political parties should be supported by all concerned. At a press conference, senior BJP leader Smt. Sushma Swaraj said that as there was no consensus on the issue of reservation for women for the past 11 years the Commission's proposal would find higher acceptability not only with NDA but also with those forming part of UPA.

"The proposal will resolve all the problems, including the fear of rotation and losing seats. It will not require a constitutional amendment as originally proposed and passage of legislation through simple majority would make the whole thing work" she said.

Asked if this indicated a shift in the BJP's stand, from what was endorsed by the former prime minister, Atal Bihari Vajpayee, Mrs. Swaraj said this was the best possible option in the current scenario that comprises lack of consensus, conflict on the kind of reservation and what categories should be concluded.

The BJP had held talks with its allies and they were agreeable to the new proposal. Mrs. Swaraj said her party felt that legislation should be introduced during the Budget session and the bill passed. This would facilitate women to get reservation in allotment of party ticket for the 2009 Lok Sabha election.

13

WOMEN'S BILL : SOMNATH'S DREAM, 2008

Sri Somnath Chatterjee, Lok Sabha Speaker said on March 9th, 2008, that "Every session, I hear that the bill will be moved and it is my dream that during my tenure it is passed by parliament, releasing a book marking the International Women's Day.

He, being a staunch supporter of the bill, he said he was convinced that it would be the "Single most powerful catalyst" in ensuring equity and justice for women. Advocating enhanced gender participation in democratic institutions at the state and National level he said" women were grossly under represented and he found it embarassing to even quote the decimal figure of 8 per cent in Parliament.

Mr. Chatterjee said further the picture was not very different in states as in some of them such as Mizoram, Manipur and Nagaland, where women outnumbered male voters, there were no women legislators. In Kerala there were only seven out of 140 legislators though the state had highest literacy rate.

"It is a matter of great sorrow as well as concern that democratic institutions have not measured up to the expectation of women. The Government of the day should not be spared in parliament or the assemblies. If it is found wanting in dealing with activities which result in denial of rights to women" he suggested.

Acknowledging publicly that the reputation of democratic institution has hit "an all time low," Mr. Chatterjee said devaluations of conventional parliamentary norms' disruptions, disorder and disrespect for the chair, have led to widespread cynicism. There should be zero tolerance for discrimination, abuse and violence against women with democratic institutions taking a lead in this fight.

All Party Meet on 20th March to Arrive at a Consensus

A delegation of women, which included members of parliament, called on the prime minister, on the occassion of the International Women's Day and he assured them that the long pending Women's Reservation Bill would be tabled in Parliament. He also told the delegation that an all party meeting would be convened to arrive at a consensus and also "hinted" a "breakthrough" in negotiations with the other political parties on the issue". Dr. Singh said that he was confident that the Bill would be passed, though he regretted that it had taken so long" Akhila Siva Das of CFAR told the *Hindu*.

The delegation presented a charter to Dr. Singh demanding that the political class go beyond rhetoric and give 33 per cent representation to women in legislatures, and provide gender sensitive governance.

A similar charter was presented to Vice-President Hamid Ansari who exhorted the women to make the spirit of International Women's Day an every day phenomenon.

Presenting the charter, Congress Member of Parliament Krishna Tirath said 33 per cent representation in Parliament and Assemblies was a pre-requisite for the empowerment of all sections of women.

Congress Women MPs Plea to Man Mohan

Almost on the eve of the Budget session of the Parliament, a delegation of Congress Women MPs met Prime Minister Man Mohan Singh to demand the tabling of the Women's Reservation Bill in the current session. itself (2008).

In a memorandum, the MPs said, that during the first phase of the Budget session, the Prime Minister had given assurance that the Govt would evolve a consensus among all United Progressive Alliance partners on the Bill, which calls for reservation of 33 per cent seats for women in Parliament and Assemblies.

"Today the Mahila Congress and various NGOs, working on women's issues, looking up to you and your Government, with great expectations to get this important Bill tabled in this session, so that, by ensuring their participation in national politics and in decision making in the process of their political empowerment". The memorandum submitted to Mr. Singh said.

The delegation led by senior Congress leader, Smt Mohsina Kidwai, noted that while the Congress-led UPA has committed to get the long pending Bill passed, due to non-cooperation of some of the alliance partners, the Government could not present the proposed legislation in Parliament.

Don't Dodge Women's Bill any Further

Women's activists staged dharna outside Parliament that the Women's Reservation Bill be introduced in the ongoing session itself (2008).

They were supported by P. Seetha Devi, and C. S. Sujatha, MPs from the Communist Party of India (Marxist).

Leading the protest, the former MP, Subhashini Ali said it was a paradox that the Government was still keen on going ahead with the introduction of the Women's Bill, in spite of the fact that many national parties are favouring it.

The women's groups said nothing less than its swift passage would satisfy all those who were supporters of not only gender justice but also democratic processes.

"We urge the United Progressive Allowance Government not to adopt any further delaying tactics".

According to Annie Raja of the National Federation of Indian Women, though women had been fighting for this just demand for more than 12 years successive Govts have failed to pass the bill. The UPA's Common Minimum Programme curtains this promise, but no sincere effort had been made to fulfil it.

Whenever the issue came up, the Government tried to delay the bill taking cover under consensus. The delay in bringing the bill for a debate, showed lack of political will and commitment on the part of the UPA Govt. Ms. Raja said.

The activists, who staged the protest belonged to All India Democratic Women's Association, the National Federation of

Indian Women, the Joint Women's Programme, the Muslim Women's Forum, the Center for Women's Development Studies, the Young Women's Christian Association, and the Guild of Service.

Seetharam Yechury appealed to all parties to allow the Govt introduce the Bill in its original form in Rajya Sabha. He said a debate could be held on the floor of the house. "We have been saying for the past 10 years that the Bill should be introduced in its original form. Whatever issues, other parties have with it (the bill) should be discussed as part of the debate in Parliament" I am appealing to all political parties not to prevent introduction of the Bill in the name of their objections and modifications, which can be debated on the floor of the house" he said. Mr. Yechury told a press conference that RJD and SP were apposed to the Bill, as they had certain concerns with it. However, these could be discussed through amendments also.

Contrary to the claims made by BJP that all the National Democratic Alliance parties had agreed to the new formula of providing for 33 per cent reservation for women in the allotment of party ticket for assembly and Parliamentary Polls, the Janata Dal (U) announced that it did not approve the formula of reservation and stick to its stand.

JD(U) President Sri Sharad Yadav, said that the party was for reservation within reservation for Dalit women.

"Our Party's stand is totally different. We want quota within the quota for Dalit women and it should be proportionate to their population" Mr. Yadav said, when asked about the BJP's stand the Government should go ahead with the formula of the Election Commission to provide for 33 per cent reservation for women in the allotment of party tickets. Mr. Yadav's comments came out a day ahead of the proposed rally by the BJP Mahila Morcha in support of the demand for quota for women.

Mr. Yadav categorically said that unless this was done, his party would not support the Bill in the Parliament. Mr. Yadav also said that the JD(U) Parliament Party will meet to discuss the issues to be raised in the budget session (22.2.08).

Anticipating such a situation perhaps, Congress members formed a cordon around Mr. Bharadwaj when Mr. Azmi continued his attempts, Minister for Women's Development and Child Welfare, Mrs. Renuka Chowdhury and Panabaka Lakshmi, Union Health Minister physically held him back, when Prime Minister, Man Mohan Singh and other senior leaders were watching.

Congress spokesperson Jayanti Natarajan, put herself in the way of Mr. Azmi and Minister of State, Vilas Muttemwar also obstructed him.

Mr. Bharadwaj tabled the bill by voice vote. P.J. Kurien, who was in the chair declared the bill as introduced and immediately adjourned the house for lunch.

Several SP members raised slogans opposing the bill, while their colleague tore a copy of the supplementary list of business and threw it into the well of the house.

In a rare show of solidarity, several women MPs placed themselves next to members belonging to RJD, JD (U) and those who were opposed to the bill.

JD(U) sticks to its stand on quota within quota for Dalit women.

Women's Bill Tabled in Rajya Sabha on 6/05/08

An emergency meeting was held in the residence of the Prime Minister to discuss about the Women's Reservation Bill and the Union Cabinet approved for introduction in the Rajya Sabha.

The bill was originally drafted and introduced in Parliament in September 1996 when HD Deva Gowda was Prime Minister in United Front Govt.

Law Ministry has prepared two drafts, the first envisaging reservation of 33.3 per cent seats for women within the existing strength of Parliament and Assemblies and the second calling for increasing their strength by 33.3 per cent.

Under the second option the strength of the 545-member Lok Sabha increases to 900 in number. An alternative was also suggested by the Election Commission making it mandatory for parties for reserving seats for women in each state.

This involves an amendment to the Representation of peoples Act, 1951 and the parties could lose recognisation if they failed to preserve reservation and sharing of seats, which were not acceptable to women's groups.

The Bill introduced in 1996, was sent to a Joint Parliamentary Committee headed by Geeta Mukherjee, a Left MP. But it lapsed when the United Front Government fell. When it was again Introduced in the year 1999, by the then Law Minister, Sri Ram Jeth Malani, during the NDA regime, the Bill was snatched from his hands and torn up with the Samaj Wadi Party, the Rashtriya Janata Dal, the Lok Jana Sakti party and the Janata Dal (United), opposing the proposed legislation and insisting on reservation within reservation from the minorities and backward classes.

Amidst High Drama, Women's Bill Introduced

The UPA Government introduced the much delayed constitution (108th Amendment) Bill, 2008, in the Rajya Sabha amidst unruly scenes and protests by Samaj Wadi Party (SP) and Janata Dal (United) members.

As soon as the Law Minister, H. R. Bhardwaj rose to introduce the bill, Abu Azim, Azmi, an SP member, who was protesting with his party colleagues in the well of the house, moved toward the minister and made an attempt to Snatch the bill from his hands-perhaps a possible repeat of 1998 incident in which the bill was torn up in the Lok Sabha, after its introduction.

Chequered Journey

The *Hindu* dt 8th May 2008 writes an editorial on the chequered Journey of Women's Reservation Bill as follows:

"Mainstream political parties have reacted with a sense of triumph to the introduction in the Rajya Sabha of the Constitution (108th Amendment Bill) providing for one-third reservation of seats for women in Parliament and the State Assemblies. The elation must be understood in the context of the Bill's failed journey though three successive Lok Sabha. Bills tabled in the Upper House enjoy a longevity in available to those introduced in the Lower House. Yet the chequered history of the women's Quota Bill is a warning against any undue optimism regarding its early passage. That a progressive measure on women has had to wait for a decade for being brought again before Parliament, and that too in near battle field conditions. Is indeed a sad commentary on 21st century India. Proponents of the bill, including the ruling coalition, section of the Bharatiya Janta Party, and the Left had to employ guerilla like tactics to prevent the papers from being torn up-as happened in 1998 in the Lok Sabha. In a heartening sign of general solidarity, women MPs cut across party lines to ensure the physical safety of the bill papers. Unfortunately, this bonding also served as a reminder of the surmountable difficulties awaiting the future course of the legislation from its 1996 Avatar, as the 81st amendment Bill, it has got only as far as the first stage of the legislative process. Just how tortuous the next steps can be is underscored by the fact that it would be examined by what is currently an All-male standing Committee on Law and Justice".

This is a sad story of the whole process.

Of course, the names of Brinda Karat and are added later on, which give some relief!

"Hindu" further adds" the opponents of the women's reservation bill argue that in the absence of a Sub-Quota, for the other backward classes (OBCs) and minorities, it will benefit only the affluent upper caste women. The reasoning is spewons for election to parliament and the various Assemblies, have brought in an increasing political representation, for the backward classes in recent years. What better proof of the power and muscle of OBC lobby in parliament than the fact that the bill has been successfully, blocked all these years. It is inconceivable that in practice party leaders can afford to ignore the demographies of the constituencies: when allotting tickets from the women's quota. That the Bill's opponents appear willing to accept it, in its present form provided its passage is accompanied by a proportionate increase in the number of Lok Sabha and assembly seats, shows up their stand to be duplicitous. The suggested alternative that political parties be mandated to nominate women candidates to at least one-third of the seats contested is equally flawed. For, where is the guarantee that women will not be relegated to unwinnable seats? None of the usual obstacles to the women's bill seems to have been cleared as yet."

Women's Quota Bill : Plea for Consensus

The All-India Democratic Women's Association has urged the United Progressive Alliance (UPA) to ensure an agreement on the Women's Reservation Bill with its partners in order to get it passed with the Left parties' support.

Briefing reporters on AIDWA's two-day central executive committee meeting, which commenced on Friday, Subhashini Ali, president and Sudha Sundararaman, general secretary, said it noted with satisfaction Prime Minister Manmohan Singh's assurance on introduction of the Bill in the winter session. They criticised the BJP for 'duplicity' on the issue and said that AIDWA, along with other women's organisations, would petition the Government to display the 'political' will to counter any possible disruption of the Bill.

14

CONSENSUS ALONE CAN SEE WOMEN'S BILL THROUGH PARLIAMENT

Hindu dt 18 June 2008 reports that the Communist Party of India has urged the parliamentary standing committee on Women's Reservation Bill to come up with a report based on a "Broad consensus"

"Only such a consensus report can steer the matter through parliament" a party delegation led by general secretary AB Bardhan said in its presentation to the committee in Delhi".

While reiterating the CPI's support for one-third reservation for women without a Sub-Quota in the state Assemblies and the Lok Sabha, the delegation pointed out that there was no change in the stated positions of political parties on the Bill. Efforts at arriving at concensus outside parliament had proved elusive through the years. For, it was an open field where every party and individual could air/his/ her views for "political effect" or other suggestions without any obligation to reach a conclusion".

However, the CPI was optimistic, the discussions on the standing committee, being structured time-bound, and with basis, could move towards a "broad consensus".

Its leaders asserted that there was no need for a Sub-Quota within the quota. "When we talk of women, it means women from all sections of society and that it includes women from OBCs and minorities. Reservation of seats for the scheduled castes and the scheduled tribes are mandatory under the Constitution. This applies to seats reserved for women as well" questions on the quantum of seats, sub-quotas and the Principle of rotation should be addressed on the basic premise that significant steps must be taken for gender equality and for progressively empowering women who constituted one half of the society. "At the same time when we talk of women, it means, and should mean, women from all sections of society", the CPI memorandum said.

Within the larger women's Quota, a view opposed by others on the ground that there is no over all OBC quota in legislative bodies, unlike a quota for the scheduled castes and the scheduled tribes.

Pointing out that the Bill mentioned quotas for 15 years, the NFIW demanded a provision for "review" after that period. It said it had no objection to women's reserved seats being rotated. For all elected representatives were chosen for five years during which they represent their constituencies.

Letters Sent to Parties

Mr. Nachiappan told the *Hindu* that he had sent letters to all recognised parties at the national and state levels, asking them to send their submissions in writing by June 10. Their representatives would depose on 17 or 18.

The Communist Party of India (Marxist) would send its representatives on June 17. Earlier on June 10, it would make a written submission.

Hindu dt 4th June 2008 report that the CPI has objection to quota within quota for OBCs. Neena Vyas writes that process of organizations deposing before the standing committee attached to the Ministry of Law and Justice, which is looking at the Women's Reservation Bill, has begun and political parties are scheduled to make their representations on June 17 and 18.

Four representative of the National Federation of Indian Women (NFIW), a frontal organisation of the Communist Party of India, met the committee chaired by Congress MP Sudarsana Nachiappan and said they did not want dilution of 33 per cent reservation in the Lok Sabha and the State Assemblies. The reservation, the NFIW said could go upto 50 per cent but it should not be less them 30 per cent.

The NFIW wanted representation to women from all categories and walks of life and said it would have no objection to creation of a quota for women belonging to the other backward classes within the over all reservation for women.

Contentious Issue

This is a contentions point, which the Rashtriya Janata Dal, The Samaj Wadi Party and the Janata Dal (United) have raised repeatedly. In fact, the utmost opposition to the Bill came from parties which are demanding an OBC quota.

Speaker Optimistic about Women's Bill

Lok Sabha Speaker Somnath Chatterjee has expressed the hope, that the Women's Reservation Bill will get parliaments nod during his tenure as chairman of the Lower House.

Delivering the EMS memorial lecture at the inauguration of the year-Long EMS centenary celebrations, planned by the Institute of Parliamentary Affairs, at Thiruvananthapuram on Friday, on 13th June 2008, Mr. Chatterjee said, the revived interest in the Bill (to provide 33 per cent reservation for women in the Lok Sabha and State Legislatures) was a good development.

"I feel women's participation and empowerment at all levels of society is undoubtedly the key to propelling democracy forward - a large section of our population is looking forward to it with great interest" he said.

Women's Quota Impresses Syrian First Lady

If these is one thing that Syrian First Lady Asma-al-Assad takes back with her from India, it is the Indian experience with Women's Reservation in Panchayats and local Self-Governments.

"I will take the quota system in Panchayats back home with me to encourage local level participation of women in politics and governance", she said in an informal interaction with journalists at the Indian women's press conference in Delhi.

Though Ms. Assad is impressed with the Indian system of quota for women at the grass roots level, she has reservations about extending it to national politics.

Admitting that it is an issue of debate in her country-which has the highest percentage of women in parliament at 13 per cent -the 33 year old first lady fears that quota, at the national level for women would make the women's movement complacent and result in the loss of passion and drive to fight for women's empowerment.

"Syria is a pioneer in women's empowerment in the Arab world, but it is no longer an exception. We got franchise along with men in Syria. Our president is a woman and we have women in the Army, in Business........ The bottom line in women are everywhere. The challenge we face is that there are few. Women involved at the local level in politics and Governance".

Asked about the recent percentage of women's who wear the hijab" she said "I can say what is important is not how women dress, but how we use our mind. Hijab and physical appearance is not our pre-occupation. What is important is that women who wear the hijab are active in public life. For our women, it is a matter of choice."

Women Bodies Draw up Charter of Demands

Times of India dt 21.12.95 reports that Sri Madhava Rao Scindia, human resource development minister classified that the National policy on women would be finalised only after wide consultations but several women's organisations rejected the draft policy saying "It is not a policy at all but a mere document of good intentions reflecting the Government's electoral considerations".

While not questioning the Government's right to come out with a national policy, on women, women's organisations objected to the hurried manner in which the document was being finalised on election eve without proper consultations.

The AIDWA along with the center for Women's Development Studies (CWDS), Joint Women's Programme (JWP), National Federation of Indian Women (NFIW) and the JWCA of India, have prepared a joint response to the draft policy document and drown up a charter of minimum demands for all the political parties.

Addressing a joint press conference, in Delhi on 21.12.95 the women's bodies said, they will approach all the political parties and "urge them to state clearly their position regarding the minimum demands repeatedly raised by the women's movement and commit themselves to their basic demands".

Coincidentally Mr. Scindia, who was addressing the Parliamentary Consultative Committee meeting of his ministry, said the draft policy on women had already been discussed at several regional-level meetings and will be finalized only after wide consultations. A revised preliminary draft, incorporating some of these suggestions, was also circulated at a meeting convened on that day.

However, the women's organizations were unaware of the revised draft. They admitted that the Government had held a series of meetings with various women's bodies, but said these "Consultations were a farce for the Government had merely appropriated the language of the women's movement but had rejected its concerns".

Ms. Vimala Farooqui of the NFIW said the policy makers made no mention about funds and resources adding that unless budgetary allocations are made for the women's programmes, the policies will always remain unimplemented. Ms. Vina Majumdar of CWDS, said that over the years, there have been innumerable reports, laws and polices on ending discrimination against women and involving them in National Development Programmes but they have not been implemented.

It appears that political will on the part of Government is lacking to implement any new policies concerning women.

When we recall the incident of passing of voting right to adult women in Parliament, soon after Pundit Nehru became the Prime Minister, there were reports that he issued a "whip" to all the Congress members to vote for the bill. His towering personality could win the situation in an amicable manner. Out of his strength of conviction in his progressive ideas, his could take instant decisions, though some conservative people were objecting to the passage of such bills.

I am very sorry to say that there is no such leader who could take some firm decisions. Dodging and dodging of passage of the bill on some pretext or other is a very unpleasant trend and lack off proper leadership is the only reason for the delay.

33 per cent Quota for Women in Cong. (I) Posts

Neena Vyas writes in *Hindu* dat 19.12.98 that Cong (I) became the first political party to change its constitution to give one-third posts to women at all levels of the party structure from the working committee down to the block level, signalling its in tent to bring about a major change to empower women politically.

Besides, the party reserved 20 per cent of all posts for dalits, Scheduled Tribes, Backward Castes and minorities, with the provision that the party president could enhance this representation whenever necessary.

The radical move at the one day. All India Cong (I) committees session in Delhi was expected to be a trend-setter, a step which other major political parfies might have to follow. It also meets the general criticism that though the Congress and the BJP and the Left have declared their support for the proposed legislation to give 33 per cent reservation for women in the Lok Sabha and the Assemblies.

Some of the major changes included, the Pradesh Cong (I) Committees and the Working Committee from two to three years. This also meant that party election could take place every 3 years.

The strength of the CWC (I), the PCC (I)s and some other bodies was also increased. The CWC (I) which comprised the party President, and the leader of the Parliamentary Party, 10 elected members and nine nominated members, would now have the party president, leader of the Parliamentary party, 12 elected members and 11 nominated members. The strength of the Parliamentary Board was increased from 7 to 11. It is expected that Mrs. Sonia Gandhi would fill up the extra seats with women and member's from the weaker sections. The increase in the number of berths in various Committees creates the space for Sonia Gandhi to promote some new faces before the next round of elections.

She was also authorized by the AICC (I) to reconstitute committees at various levels and this included the Working Committee. This touched off Speculation that the CWS (I) itself might be revamped but reports suggested that was unlikely to disturb the sitting members.

The resolution seeking the amendments, described as "historic" and "fulfilling the dream of Rajiv Gandhi" to empower women and the weaker sections of society was moved by Mr. K. Karunakaran and put to vote after the debate by Mr. Pranab Mukherjee.

It was at the Party's Pachmarhi conclave that Mrs. Sonia Gandhi had promised to revitalize it and today she expressed satisfaction at the changes made in the party constitution. It was a new milestone but the task ahead was to train women for their new responsibilities in the party structure, she said in her concluding remarks at the session.

CPI (M)'s Stand/Introduce Women's Bill Without Delay

CPI (M) polit bureau member and MP Sitaram Yechury has demanded that the Central Government introduce the Women's Reservation Bill in the Parliament in the coming session instead of delaying its enactment in the name of obtaining a consensus on it.

Participating in a workshop organized by the party on the issue, he said that though all the political parties were supporting the bill, it was not introduced so far on the ground of evolving a consensus, which was difficult to reach. "Let the Government bring the bill first and let those opposing it vote against it," he said.

A few political parties were opposed to the introduction of reservation to women and the alternatives suggested from certain sections of society were aimed at blocking the enactment. Alternatives such as increasing the number of seats in the parliament and incorporating the caste quota with the women reservation would only delay its enactment.

"The previous NDA Government, which convened a Joint Session of the Parliament to pass POTA after failing to arrive at consensus on it. Let the UPA Government explore any such options to ensure the passage of the Bill" he said.

The CPI (M) had no illusions that the quota Bill wont stop atrocities against women in various forms. It was only a beginning towards emancipation of women from their struggle and give them their equal right.

CPI (M) floor leader in the Rajya Sabha Nilotpal Basu, criticized some of the north Indian Political parties that were trying to resist the introduction of the Bill, as it would trigger a set of changes in society enabling women to play their role. Though there was no principled disagreement in the Lok Sabha and State Assemblies on the Bill. It was unfortunate that such a social legislation met with such a fate.

Since the issue was a political one, the CPI (M) had decided to mobilise public support and mount pressure on the Government for its enactment.

"It is not confined to women's organizations, all the progressive thinking sections of society must come forward to mount pressure on the Government" he said.

Table Women's Bill Left (2006)

Hindu dated 5th October 2006 reports from Delhi that the Left parties insisted on the UPA Govt to bring forward the Bill providing one-third reservation for women in Parliament and state legislatures in the next session of Parliament.

The Left parties demanded that the Govt introduce the Bill in its present form and put it to vote instead of seeking a consensus that has remained elusive.

"We are confident that the Bill will come up in the next session of Parliament. The left Parties are not in favour of increasing the member of seats" a senior Left Party leader said after a 3-hour UPA-Left coordination's meet that discussed a range of issues.

Left sources said the objection to the Government's approach on the women's reservation issue central around Union Home Minister Shiv Raj Patil's suggestion to increase the number of seats to arrive at a consensus. This led to a verbal sparring.

Congress President Sonia Gandhi said despite her own efforts, consensus on the issue was elusive and sought a way forward. Besides Mrs. Sonia Gandhi, UPA was represented by Prime Minister, Man Mohan Singh. Defence Minister Pranab

Mukherjee, MR. Patil, Finance Minister P. Chadambaram, Minister of State in PMO Pridhviraj Chavan and Ahmad Patel.

The Left leaders present at the meeting were Communist Party of India (Marxist) general Secretary Prakash Karat, Polit Bureau member Sitaram Yechuri, CPI general secy A.B. Bardhan, its national secy D. Raja and Revolutionary Socialist Party secy, Abani Roy.

Non-Passage of Women's Reservation Bill Criticized

Speakers at a National Consultation on "Gender and Governance," expressed varied opinions on the status of women in governance, though all agreed that there were gaps between the policies and implementation, which needed to be plugged.

Organized by the World Bank and the United Nations Development Programme, the consultation focussed of promoting gender equality and strengthening of decentralization process.

Describing the reluctance in passing the women's Reservation Bill providing for Reservation of one-third seats in parliament and State Assemblies, as "institutionalization of discrimination" the former member of parliament Jayanti Natarajan, said women were asking for reservation on the basis of equal status enjoyed by them under the constitution.

"There was no talk of dual membership or increasing the number of seats when dalits were given reservation. Importantly the experience of women in Panchayats has been excellent though with some aberration," she said adding that it proved women were good administrators and should not be discriminated against on the basis of sex.

The greatest achievement for women in the post-independence era have reservation in the local self-governments and the success of the Self-help groups that have a saving of up to 12,000 to 13,000 crores in the banks.

George Mathew, Director of the Indian Social Institute felt that only political empowerment could bring about a societal action and reservation of women was one way of achieving this.

"We keep women as cultural emblems. they are required in the field of art and culture but unwanted in political, sociál and economic structures" he said.

Striking a different note Sociologist Sarojini Ganjn Thakur, admitted while there were gaps between policies and implementation, women had been empowered by the sheer power of right to voting.

The number of women in services, especially civil, is also a positive indicator when compared with the ICs, where there were no women, she pointed out.

According to her, the key challenges were, to bridge the gap between playing and implementation and better monitoring.

Hindu dt 9/12/06 reports that Rajya Sabha was adjourned twice on Friday as members simultaneously insisted on raising various issues. The house also saw most women members demanding early introduction of Women's Reservation Bill.

Members were on their feet as soon as question hour ended. The first to demand the chairs attention was Rashid Alvi (Congress) who claimed that he had been promised that he would be allowed to speak Dy. Chairman Rehman Khan, however, said there was no zero hour on Friday and assured him that his demand would be considered on Monday.

Mr. Khan adjourned the house for 15 minutes as Mr. Alvi insisted on his demand.

When the House reassembled, he again wanted to speak, triggering a demand from BJP and Trinamul congress members they may be heard on an important issue in West Bengal. This drew protests from the Communist Party of India (Marxist) Mr. Khan then announced a longer adjournment till after lunch.

Earlier, Sushma Swaraj (BJP) called for a statement on the Women's Bill. Najma Hepatulla (BJP) wanted to know from the Government, whether it would be introduced in this Session. Brinda Karat (CPI-M) who was not in this House came back to support Ms. Hepatulla soon other women member's including Maya Singh (BJP) Alka Balam and Prema Cariappa (both Congress) also called for a statement from the Government, while, Jaya Bachchan (Samaj Wadi Party) refrained from demanding the tabling of the Bill.

Ram Deo Bhandari (Rashtriya Janta Dal) said his party supported reservation for women but there should be sub-quotas for socially disabled groups.

Minister of State for Parliamentary Affairs Suresh Pachauri said the Government and its allies were in favours of early tabling of the Bill and the legislation was passing through a process".

Commitment Stands: Says Das Munshi

A demand for tabling the long-pending Women's Reservation Bill was made in both houses of Parliament on Wednesday, reports the *Hindu* dt 3/8/06.

While members sought its passage in the present session, the Government reiterated its support for the measure, which seeks to provide 33 per cent reservation for women in Parliament and State Assemblies.

In the Rajya Sabha, JD (U) President Sharad Yadav and Samaj Wadi Party leader Amar Singh, stood up in protest when Dy. Chairman K. Rahman Khan observed that the entire House was in agreement on the issue.

Raising the subject during Zero Hour, CPI (M) leader Brinda Karat demanded that the Bill be debated in this session itself "Let there be amendments but at least let it be tabled and debated."

The Bill was not a question of men versus women she said. It was a question of democratic system. "This Lok Sabha has only 8 per cent women members" several members associated themselves with her but as soon as Mr. Khan said, the entire House was in agreement, Mr. Yadav said "This is wrong"

Yet to See Light of Day

BJP Dy. Leader Sushma Swaraj said the Bill was introduced during Deva Gowda regime and it came up for discussion during the NDA rule but did not see the light of the day during the UPA regime.

In the Lok Sabha CPI, leader Gurudas Das Gupta, raising the matter during zero hour, said the Government should not make the bill, a matter of political controversy. He drew the attention of the House to thousands of women staging a dharna at Jantar Mantar demanding early passage of the Bill, intervening, Parliamentary Affairs Minister, Priya Ranjan Das Munshi assured the members that there was no "going back" by the Govt, on its commitment to the bill However as it was a constitution Amendment Bill, The support of all sections was required. Home Minister, Shiv Raj Patil was engaged in talks with various parties. But before the matter could be further discussed, speaker Somnath Chatterjee adjourned the house for lunch. Later, a delegation led by Ms. Karat met Mr. Patil, who assured the team that the Congress supported the bill and was working hard for its passage without a hitch. Ms. Karat said, she had sought time from the Prime Minster and would take up the issue with him also.

CPI's Plea to Man Mohan

The CPI has urged Prime Minister, Man Mohan Singh to bring forward the women's bill and also expedite the Unorganized Workers Bill.

According to Mr. Das Gupta the Prime Minister informed them that discussions were on to arrive at a consensus on the Women's Bill. There was a possibility of the quota being lowered. The Unorganized Workers Bill was being Processed.

Position in 2005

"Women's Bill in Next session" says Man Mohan. All India Democratic Women's Association (AIDWA) led a delegation to Man Mohan and he assured them that the Reservation Bill will be tabled in the next session of Parliament as negotiations were going on with other political parties to arrive at a consensus on the issue.

According to Sudha Sundararaman, general secy. of AIDWA, Man Mohanji told the delegation that he supported the bill and felt that it should be passed at the earliest but some political parties had reservation over it.

The 10-member delegation called on the Prime Minister after women from across the country participated in a mock women's parliament. The session reflected attitudes of various political parties towards the Bill. At the end of which, the Bill was passed.

Reminding Dr. Singh of the solemn assurance given in the National Common Minimum Programme, that the Govt would pass the Bill, the memorandum said, that it was disappointing that the Bill had not been listed for discussion in the current session.

"While we do appreciate the difficulties that a coalition Govt. may face in passing legislation that is not totally acceptable to all the partners, this cannot be a justification for the non-implementation of solemn assurances" the memorandum said.

AIDWA President Subhashini Ali told the Prime Minister that thousands of their members from all over the country had assembled to press for passage of the Bill.

They represented millions of women whose patience was now being exhausted by the refusal of successive Govts to initiate even a serious discussion on the Bill, let alone ensure its passage.

"We appeal to you to make a clean break with this attitude which smacks of not only gender in sensitivity to insensitivity to the process of making democracy more inclusive and vibrant. We would request you to place the Bill for a thorough discussion in parliament and to ensure that a note is taken on it.If this is done with sincerity, the enactment of the Bill will become a reality" the memorandum said.

15

WOMEN'S RESERVATION BILL ON THE ANVIL FOR 12 YEARS

The women's reservation bill providing 33 per cent reservation for women in Parliament and state assemblies has been gathering dust for 12 years with no government willing to give it the push that will make it an Act.

Here are some facts about the bill which has been introduced and reintroduced time and again but never passed.

- In 1996 the Deve Gowda government introduced the women's reservation bill on September 4,1996 as the 81st Constitution Amendment Bill.
- The bill was referred to a Joint Parliamentary Committee chaired by Communist Party of India (CPI) MP Geeta Mukherjee.
- The Joint Parliamentary Committee presented its report to the Lok Sabha on December 9, 1996.
- The bill was reintroduced on June 26, 1998, by the National Democratic Alliance (NDA) government in the 12th Lok Sabha as the 84th Constitution Amendment Bill.
- It was once again introduced by the NDA government in the 13th Lok Sabha on November 22,1999.
- The NDA government brought the bill to the Lok Sabha twice in 2002 and 2003 but never could get it passed even though the Congress and the Left, constituting a majority, had assured NDA of their support.
- The United Progressive Alliance (UPA) government elected in May 2004 announced its intention to pass the

bill as part of its commitment in the Common Minimum Programme (CMP).

- With a couple of days to go before the Budget session ended, the UPA government tabled the Bill in Rajya Sabha on 06.05.08.
- The Bill has again been referred to a Parliamentary Committee which has been asked to submit its report within three months.

Dare we hope that the bill will be passed before the term of this parliament expires in less than a year? Or will it be allowed a quiet exit as on earlier occasions?

Women's Reservation Bill Reports in the Media (May-June, 2008)

8 May, 2008

The Hindu

Don't dodge Women's Bill any further

Women's activists on Monday staged an impromptu dharna outside Parliament demanding that the Women's Reservation Bill be introdued in the ongoing session itself...Welcoming the announcement by Prime Minister Manmohan Singh on introduction of the Bill this session, the womens groups said nothing less than its swift passage would satisfy all those who were supporters of not only gender justice but also inclusive democratic processes.

Women's Bill to be tabled today in Rajya Sabha

The Union Cabinet on Monday approved for introduction in the Rajya Sabha the contentious Women's Reservation Bill. The nod came at an emergency meeting convened by the Prime Minister at his residence late in the evening and the Bill will be tabled on Tuesday. The Law Ministry has prepared two drafts, the first envisaging reservation of 33.3 per cent seats for women within the existing strength of Parliament and Assemblies and the second calling for increasing their strength by 33.3 per cent.....An alternative was also suggested by the Election Commission making it mandatory for parties to reserve seats for women in each State......The other options suggested were rotation and sharing of seats which were, however, not acceptable to women's groups.

7 May, 2008

The Times of India

High Drama as Govt. Outsmarts Opponents to Table Women's Bill

The planning would have done a military strategist proud. The defence was deployed with skill and guile. The back-up was forceful and arrived in time. And even though the 'enemy' managed to land a few punches, the skirmish was brief and ended with the contentious women's reservation bill being introduced in Rajya Sabha on Tuesday......It was evident that even 12 years after it was first introduced, the bill's opponents remain just as implacable.

BJP Slams 'Haste' in Tabling the Bill

.....Though the fate of the bill remains uncertain, the Constitution (108th Amendment) Bill, 2008 will go to the standing committee attached to the law ministry. The haste with which the bill was tabled—it was listed at supplementary business at the last minute and was obviously not circulated after being cleared by a late night meeting of the Cabinet on Monday—drew sharp criticism from BJP......JD (U) and Samajwadi Party members were again on their feet claiming that the government had 'bulldozed' the introduction of the bill by ignoring rules of the House.

Editorial

Half the sky—Women's Reservation Bill is a Good Starting Point

It's a woman's world in the Spanish cabinet. For the first time in the country's history, there are more women ministers than men and what's more, they don't hold just token portfolios...... Even as we cheer this development, the unfortunate opposition to the Women's Reservation Bill plays out here at home...... It drives home the fact that some of the men in the House cannot bear the thought of creating place for women and will do anything to keep them out....... It is heartening that the UPA has mustered the courage to reintroduce the Bill. It will no doubt take a long and winding road to fruition. But it is a good and necessary step in the right direction. Meanwhile political parties would do well to field more women candidates voluntarily.

The Hindu

Vayalar Ravi Confident of Getting bill Passed during UPA Tenure

Parliamentary Affairs Minister Vayalar Ravi on Tuesday expressed confidence that the Bill would be passed during the tenure of the United Progressive Alliance government on the basis of consensus......He hoped the bill would be back from the standing committee before the start of the monsoon session in July.

No Woman on Standing Committee

The Standing Committee on Law and Justice of the Rajya Sabha to which the Women's Reservation Bill has been referred does not have a single woman member.

8 May, 2008

The Hindu

Bill will only Favour Top Crust of Society

Lok Janshakti Party (LJP) president Ram Vilas Paswan said his party was in full support of the Bill. He, however, suggested an increase in the number of seats in the Lok Sabha by one-third to accommodate more women and fixing a quota for SC's, OBC's and minorities......"Not only has the population of the country increased almost three times since Independence, the number of voters has also increased tremendously. Increasing the number of Lok Sabha seats would be a good option to accommodate more women MPs," he said.

Editorial

Chequered Journey

Mainstream political parties have reacted with a sense of triumph to the introduction in Rajya Sabha of the Constitution (108th Amendment) Bill........ The elation must be understood in the context of the bill's failed journey through three successive Lok Sabhas. Bills tabled in the upper house enjoy longevity unavailable to those introduced in the lower house. Yet the chequered history of the women's quota bill is a warning against any undue optimism regarding its early passage. That a progressive measure on women's empowerment has had to wait for a decade for being brought again before Parliament and that too in near battlefield conditions, is indeed a sad commentary on 21st century India..... That the bill's opponents appear willing to accept it in its current form, provided its passage is accompanied by a proportionate increase in the number of Lok Sabha and Assembly seats shows up their stand to be duplicitous. The suggested alternative - that political parties be mandated to nominate women candidates to at least one-third of the seats contested - is equally flawed. For, where is the guarantee that women will not be relegated to unwinnable seats? None of the usual obstacles to the women's bill seems to have been cleared as yet.

Hindustan Times

Women and India's Political Vocabulary

The Indian political terrain has never been woman friendly and the opposition to a bill to reserve 33 per cent seats for women in Parliament and state legislatures is just another example of a long standing battle.......Despite the low number of women — 22 Lok Sabha members in 1952 and 50 in 2008 — India has produced several remarkable women leaders who commanded such power than their male competitors stooped low to conquer but still failed.

Editorial

It doesn't fit the Bill

More than anything else, the annual noise made about the Women's Reservation Bill is a tiring affair. Everyone makes the right noises knowing well that it is a token gesture that allows them to be politically correct without having to do the hard work of pushing for real gender equality........India's unempowered women need all the help and opportunities they can get. According to the 2000 estimates, the female literacy rate is as low as 39.42 per cent compared to 63.86 per cent for men........The maternal mortality rate is 4.6 per cent per 1000 live births and a scary 60 per cent of pregnant women in the country suffer from anemic conditions...... These are the real issues that need to be tackled head-on with war-like purpose....... Marking out specific 'women's constituencies' as a way forward to encourage gender equality looks lopsided. It would make better sense even if each political party were to set aside a certain proportion of deserving women from its fold, empowering them with representational power — rather than having a woman candidate contest against another woman candidate simply to project a skewed version of gender equality. There are real obstacles — and real solutions — facing India's women. This government's approach is like trying to fix the roof when the foundation is tottering.

The Indian Express

PM says Allies Agreed to Women's Bill, RJD differs

The Prime Minister, speaking to the media said, "If there was no consensus, we would not have been able to bring the Bill to the House....We have taken the first step but there are concerns about backward communities which need to be discussed."...... Earlier in the day RJD MP Devendra Prasad Yadav had said, "The Cabinet decision was not unanimous. Our leader Lalu Prasad Yadav had forcefully raised our party's reservations on the Bill in its current form in the Cabinet meeting."

The Asian Age

Lalu's Party gives UPA big jolt over Women's Bill

Rashtriya Janata Dal has 'warned' the Congress led UPA government of 'withdrawing support' if its demand for a 'quota within quota' in the Women's Reservation Bill is not met........ "If the government does not agree to our amendments, we will use our strength in voting against the bill in Parliament along with parties like the Samajwadi Party and the Janata Dal (United)," Devendra Prasad Yadav told this newspaper........ The RJD had given its consent for the tabling of the bill in the Rajya Sabha on Tuesday on the condition that it not be passed in the House.

9 May, 2008

The Indian Express

Sena Now Questions Women's Bill, Prefers EC Formula

While JD(U) president Sharad Yadav registered his Opposition to the Women's Reservation Bill in the Rajya Sabha on May 6, another NDA partner. Shiv Sena, has now vowed to oppose the Bill in its present form. "We do not support 33 per cent reservation of constituencies for women in legislatures," Sena spokesperson and Rajya Sabha member Sanjay Raut told *The Indian Express* on Thursday. "On the other hand we find the Election Commission formula - making it mandatory for parties to allot a certain percentage of tickets to women - far more pragmatic."......... In an editorial in the party mouthpiece *Samna,* the Sena is even more critical of the Bill. Terming the 'hurriedly introduced' legislation a 'political hypocrisy', the editorial says it may be passed by Parliament due to majority support, but reservation would not benefit women. The move, according to the daily, is intended to reap political benefits and not to ensure the welfare of women.

10 May, 2008

Hindustan Times

Third front trips on women's quota

The UNPA-Left relationship seems to have hit an air pocket over the SP's opposition to the women's reservation bill and its belligerent charge that the Congress brought forth the legislation under pressure from the Brinda Karat - Sushma Swaraj combine....... "We cannot compromise our stand for the sake of upholding the third alternative idea," senior SP leader Janeshwar Mishra said........ Stating that the third alternative was based on the principle of 'issue-based politics', he said the women's quota bill was an issue on which the Congress, BJP and the Left were on one side and the SP and certain other parties on the other.......... Former Defence Minister George Fernandes has also criticized the 'disgraceful behaviour' of 'socialist colleagues' while calling upon all members to allow the bill to be passed.

11 May, 2008

The Indian Express

Why India must make haste to welcome Stree Shakti

(Sudheendra Kulkarni)

At a time when politics has become increasingly divisive, with few bridges of dialogue and cooperation to link rival political parties, it was heartening to see women MPs joining hands in front of Parliament building on the day that the UPA government introduced the much awaited bill on women's reservation in the Rajya Sabha last week........ Some political parties opposed to it resorted to a show of muscle power inside the House, but to no avail....The Bill has finally crossed a major hurdle. Its final enactment may still be a long way off, but India has taken a big step forward on the path of women's political empowerment...... In recent decades, India has witnessed a silent social revolution after the introduction of 33 per cent reservation for women in panchayats and municipal bodies. Thus, out of nearly 30 lakh elected representatives in these bodies, one third are women, which fact gives India the proud distinction of having the largest number of women in democratic institutions anywhere in the world...... The actual representation of women in panchyati raj institutions has risen to 42 per cent. In other words, women are being elected in large numbers even from general seats. If you add to this figure the tens of lakhs of women who are either members or in leadership positions in Self Help Groups or cooperative bodies in rural and urban areas, you get an inspiring picture of the march of women's empowerment in India. Reservation for women in Parliament and state legislatures is a logical extension of this process......... However, on a cautionary note, it must be stated that increase in quantitative representation does not necessarily result in qualitative empowerment. Most political parties, including those supporting the bill, have still not adopted a new mindset of encouraging women to take up crucial assignments. .... The need for training, capacity building and leadership development among women activists is also an area that has received scant attention. It seems that our political establishment is still not ready to reform itself to both accept and promote women's empowerment. Nevertheless, the process itself is now unstoppable. The beneficial aspects of more and more women playing an active role in the social, economic and political life of the nation are so numerous, and their combined transformational effect so revolutionary, that India must make haste to welcome Stree Shakti — Women's Power. Perhaps the most compelling reason for doing so was articulated by Mahatma Gandhi who said, "If by power is meant moral power, then woman is immeasurably man's superior... if nonviolence is the law of our being, the future is with women."

15 May, 2008

The Indian Express

RJD Filed its most Vocal Anti-women's Bill MP in Panel

Rashtriya Janata Dal (RJD) leader and Railways Minister Lalu Prasad Yadav has nominated his most articulate anti-quota MP, Devendra Prasad Yadav (Jhanjharpur), to the parliamentary standing committee set to examine the Women's Reservation Bill........ The move indicates that Lalu has been forced to join hands with anti-quota hardliners from Samajwadi Party and Janata Dal(U) on the committee after having yielded to the Congress pressure to let Law Minister Hans Raj Bhardwaj introduce the Bill in the Rajya Sabha on May 6. Lalu's detractors from the JD (U) have been forecasting a split in the RJD in case he backs the Bill providing for a reservation of 33 per cent seats for women in state legislatures and the Parliament......... That the fear of a split within the RJD ranks is real is clear from the fact that a day after the Bill was introduced, Lalu had fielded Yadav to attack it. Speaking to the media, the RJD deputy leader described the introduction of the Bill amidst disorder as "a murder of the democratic values". .....Charging the Government with the addition of "a shameful chapter to the book of Parliament", he said, "If they had the courage, they should have introduced it in the Lok Sabha."

The Asian Age

Women's Bill Faces a Bumpy Road Ahead

(Dr. Nitish Sengupta)

.....The two anti-feminist Yadavs, Sharad Yadav and Mulayam Singh Yadav, have now been joined by a third: Lalu

Prasad Yadav, leader of the Rashtriya Janata Dal and a prominent member of the UPA. He was one of the initial supporters of the bill but then did a volte face. It is difficult to understand or appreciate the reasons for the dogged opposition to women's reservation from the Yadav troika. They say that women's reservation will ensure that upper class women will hog most of the seats reserved for women. But why this apprehension? Why are they not sure of their ability to persuade dalit women to vote for candidates from among themselves in preference to upper caste women candidates? Why are they so sanguine that under the women's reservation dispensation the 'short haired English speaking women' (an expression used by one of the anti-reservation stalwarts in the early days of the controversy) will necessarily get elected and will thereby upset the quota reservation for the dalits? Instead of retreating to such an inferiority complex, they should rather engage themselves in a massive awareness drive among the women of the backward classes so that they can produce sufficient numbers of appropriate candidates from among themselves. Or could it be that the anti-bill leaders are essentially casteist and are cold towards radical changes such as this, which might upset their rural caste base? Questioning the pro-Muslim women stand of the Yadav troika, Sayeeda Hamid, a member of the Planning Commission has asked, "To how many Muslim women have they so far given tickets?" Instead of opposing the proposal for 33 per cent reservation for women, they should start selecting 33 per cent of their candidates from among women........ The logic behind this proposed legislation is clear. Although India went far ahead of even some of the Western countries in appointing or electing women to top positions, and today we have a woman President, women chief ministers and Union ministers, and women secretaries to the government, there is still a vast charm between them and millions of housewives confined to the kitchen. The latter must be politically armed and brought into the forefront of the country in order to make visible and fast progress, both politically and economically. Women's reservation is a necessary step in that direction.

(Dr. Nitish Sengupta, an academic and an author, is a former Member of Parliament and a former Secretary to the Government of India)

16 May, 2008

The Statesman

Women's Bill Panel Gets Female Representation

Correcting an anomalous situation, the Rajya Sabha Chairman today nominated two women members to the parliamentary standing committee on the women's Reservation Bill. He nominated Ms Najma Heptullah of the BJP snd Ms Prabha Thakur of Congress to the Parliamentary Standing Committee.

19 May, 2008

The Times of India

House Panel Report on Women's Bill in August

The UPA government's CMP which promises to 'fully empower women' is deftly worded on the women's reservation bill. The UPA government will take the lead to introduce legislation for one-third reservation for women in the Vidhan Sabhas and in the Lok Sabha", it says. That commitment has already been met, although enactment of the bill may not follow........... "Introduction" and "enactment" are distinct legislative processes and, as the history of women's bill itself shows, not necessarily interlinked. Compare this promise with what the CMP offers just next. "Legislation on domestic violence and against gender discrimination will be enacted", it says. This has been done months ago........ The government reserved the "introduction" of the bill to almost the fag end of the current Lok Sabha session, which can at best have three more sittings before elections are called....... If the bill's enactment, as the PM has promised, is on the UPA government's radar, time doesn't seem to be on his side........ That however is not the only problem.......The RJD's quota-within-quota demand for OBCs and minorities in the bill, for instance, violates the Constitution, which does not reserve electorates on the basis of caste and religion, except for the special case of SCs and STs........ The women's bill, for now, has been referred to the Parliamentary Committee on personnel, law and justice, which is to give its report within three months, that is, by August, 2008.

The Statesman

Reservation for Women a Bad Idea

(excerpts from a debate on the issue)

The concept of reservation, whether based on caste or gender, is retrogressive. It means bringing in less competent people through the back door, shutting out opportunities for the more competent........... Let political parties draft in more women members in their parties at the grassroot level, educate them in the management of state affairs and put up more women candidates in elections for people to judge their suitability as members. *(P K Bhattacharjee)* ..... It should be remembered that the legislative proposal calls for an amendment to the Constitution, requiring endorsement by two-thirds of Parliament. It would be highly optimistic to expect that the standing committee to which the Bill has been referred will clear the proposal in time for it to be processed in the monsoon session. It would also be optimistic to expect political consensus on the Bill, which has been elusive for so many years. *(Arun Kumar Bhaduri)* The Congress-led UPA government must take a tough stand and push through the long pending Women's Reservation Bill......Certain regional parties have now backtracked and are trying to scuttle it in its present form ....These leaders are nothing but hypocrites - they talk about the uplift of women on the one hand and block the Bill on the other, instead of introducing amendments during the discussions on the Bill in Parliament........ It is a pity that no sincere effort has been made by ruling parties during the past decade to forge a consensus for the smooth passage of the bill........The tabling of the bill just before the Karnataka elections will benefit the Congress........ There is a further question: why don't the parties that want the bill to be passed voluntarily field more women candidates? *(Asabari Sen)*

22 May, 2008

Hindustan Times

Women's bill sparks interest in House panel

Until the women's quota bill came to it, no one bothered

about the 31-member standing committee of personnel, public grievances, law and justice (SCPPGL & J) headed by E M Sudarsana Natchiappan........ Suddenly the panel has acquired tremendous political significance and its recommendations on the question of earmarking one-third seats for women in the Lok Sabha and state assemblies are likely to alter the complexion of Indian politics. It is no surprise then that the parties that failed to nominate their full quota to the panel are hurriedly trying to fill it up before the May 27 meeting........The stage is being set in the SCPPGL & J for a battle royale, with the pro- and anti-bill forces trying to bring their most vociferous and determined voices on board. A staunch opponent of the existing bill, RJD's Lalu Prasad Yadav replaced Sadhu Yadav with the very vocal Devendra Prasad Yadav to press for a sub-quota for OBCs and minorities. An equally vociferous proponent of the bill, CPM's Brinda Karat has walked into the panel.....The BJP and Congress have fielded Najma Heptulla and Prabha Thakur respectively....... The bottomline: Parties have started flexing their partisan muscles on the Bill. This is a marked departure from rising above petty party interests away from the media glare to evolve a consensus. Whether a consensus emerges in this case is another question.

The Times of India

Lurching Towards Equality

(Ratna Kapur)

......Note how our neighbour, Nepal, has achieved a startling 33.2 per cent representation of women in the recent constituent assembly elections, despite a decade of conflict and political instability. This victory places Nepal at number 15 in the world in terms of representation of women in parliament. Pakistan ranks 43 and Afghanistan is at 26. War-torn Iraq ranks 32 while Rwanda tops the list at number 1. However, India is 105 out of 135 countries......... The Bill tabled in the Rajya Sabha does nevertheless represent a sign that India's democracy is lurching in the right direction as far as gender equality is concerned........Fortunately, both the legislature and courts are moving away from a model of gender equality based on protection and shifting towards one that recognizes and provides remedies for discrimination produced through historical disadvantage.......

(Writer is Director, Centre for Feminist Legal Research)

28 May, 2008

The Hindu

Three Month's Time-frame Suggested for Finalizing Report on Women's Bill

A time-frame of about three months has been suggested for finalizing the report of the standing committee considering the Women's Reservation Bill at its first meeting here (New Delhi) on Tuesday........ One of the suggestions that came up at the meeting was that the committee should study women's reservation as obtaining at the panchayat level, a point to which one member reportedly remarked that no study has been made of how male members had been functioning in panchayats....... The question of rotation of seats also came up. One member wanted to know how the seats reserved for women in the Lok Sabha and State assemblies would be rotated and which authority would identify the new seats that would be reserved for women........ While some members felt that the bill should not be rushed through, others (mainly the three women members) pointed out that the Bill has been pending for over a decade. It was not at all a question of rushing through with the legislation, but a question of not delaying it further.

Hindustan Times

Stormy First Meeting on Women's Bill

There were heated exchanges as the parliamentary committee had the first of its stormy meetings on Tuesday amidst strong indications that its opponents were out to scuttle the existing draft legislation unless there is a sub-quota for OBCs, dalits and minorities....... "Since it is a constitutional amendment bill, we want the broadest possible consultations on it. And if necessary, we will seek an extension in term after three months", said a member.......... Devendra Prasad Yadav highlighted the contradiction in the women's bill and the provision of quota in jobs and education for OBCs. He made two basic points: one, if there are quotas for OBCs in jobs and education (as manifest in the reservation of seats for OBCs in central institutes of higher learning) there should be reservations for them and dalits and minorities too in the women's bill; two, if the creamy layer has been skimmed from the quota-in-education bill, how can it be allowed to dominate the women's bill.

1 June, 2008

The Statesman

More Women Power in Panel on Quota Bill

Four more women members today joined the parliamentary committee on the women's reservation bill taking its female strength to seven in the 31-member panel. All four are from the Lok Sabha. They are Tejaswini Sreeramesh Gowda and Krishna Tirath (both Congress), Kiran Maheswari (BJP) and P. Sathee Devi (CPI-M)........ The Bill which seeks to provide 33 per cent reservation for women in Lok Sabha and state legislative assemblies does not cover, as of now, either the Rajya Sabha or the state legislative councils......

4 June, 2008

The Asian Age

Women Bill meet raises questions

The second meeting of the committee saw close questioning of those championing the cause of quota for women. CPI national executive member Annie Raja and three other women members deposed before the committee...... The questions included whether it was proper to give such reservation to women without determining the class to which they belong because reservation was so far being given to classes which have been discriminated against and not to any gender as such......

9 June, 2008

The Hindu

Difficult to evolve consensus on Women's Bill : Somnath

Lok Sabha Speaker Somnath Chatterjee said on Sunday that it was difficult to evolve consensus among political parties on the Women's Reservation Bill........He supported the Bill saying women were not asking for any charity and political parties must shed their confrontationist approach on this important issue.........“Even after six decades of freedom, women's representation in our higher representative bodies is woefully inadequate. Any plan for the development of the country cannot be a success if we do not make women equal partners in the task of nation building,” he said.

10 June, 2008

The Hindu

Congress keen on early passage of Women's Reservation Bill

........“We hope to achieve an all-party consensus on this Bill to ensure its passage, “Congress president Sonia Gandhi said in the latest issue of the party's in-house journal......... “By encouraging women to come forward to take their legitimate place in the governance of the country, the Congress has shown its commitment to gender equality,” Mrs Gandhi said in the party magazine.

11 June, 2008

Hindustan Times

Women's quota debate rages

.......When Panchayati Raj Secretary Shalini Singh appeared before the parliamentary committee which is looking into the bill, she faced a spate of queries on implementation of quotas in panchayats and zila panchayats and the empowerment of women. Among the questions posed to her was why the sustainability of elected representatives in the lower rungs of democracy showed a decline. According to the data presented to the panel, of the 84. per cent first time women pradhans, only 12 per cent got re-elected the second time and a bare 3.4 per cent the third time. “Why this sudden fall?” was among the first queries to which the secretary will have to send a written response.....

14 June, 2008

The Hindu

Speaker optimistic about Women's Bill

Lok Sabha Speaker Somnath Chatterjee has expressed the hope that the Women's Reservation Bill will get Parliament nod during his tenure as Chairman of the lower house........... "I feel women's participation and empowerment at all levels of society is undoubtedly the key to propelling democracy forward. A large section of our population is looking forward to it with great interest," he said......... He said that India had become a strong nation in all respects and was now being acknowledged as a significant player in the global economy..........

(Compiled by Usha Nair)

(Courtesy Roshni—AIWC)

Constitution of India
Part III (Article 12-35)
Guarantees these Fundamental Rights

Right to Equality

- before laws and equal protection of laws
- irrespective of religion, vace, caste, sex or place of birth
- of opportunity in public employment
- By a bolition of untouchability and entitles.

Right to Freedom :

- of expression, assembly, association, movement, residence or profession
- of certain protections in respect of conviction for offences
- of protection of life and personal liberty
- of free a compulsory education for children between the age of 6-14 yrs.
- of protection against arrest and detention in certain cases.

Right against exploitation :

- for prohibition of traffic in human beings and forced labour
- for prohibition of employment of children in hazardous jobs

- right to freedom of religion
- freedom of conscience for profession, practice and propagation of religion.
- freedom to manage religious affairs.
- freedom as to payment of taxes for promotion of any particular religion.
- freedom as it attèndance at religious instruction or religious worship in educational instictions cultural and in educational rights.
- for protection of interests of minorities to conserve their language, script and culture.
- for minorities to establish and administer educational instituion of their choice.

Right to constitutional remedies :

- By issnance of directions or orders or write by the Supreme Court and High Courts for enforcement of these Fundamental Rights.

The Constitution of India

Preamble

We, the people of India, having solemnly resolved to constitute India into a Sovereign Socialist Secular Democratic Republic and to secure to all its citizens :

Justice, social, economic and political history : of thought, expression, belief, faith and worship.

Equality of status and of oppotunity and to promote among them all.

Fraternity assuring the of the individual and the unity and integrity of the Nation.

In one Constituent Assembly, this twenty sixth day of November 1949, do he by adopt, enact and give to overselves this constitution.

16

SUPPLEMENT

Table 1. Total Expenditure of Central and State Government on Education 1951-52 to 1996-97

State	Expenditure on education by Education Department		Expenditure on Education by all departments			
	In Rs. million	*As per cent of budget*	*In Rs. Million*	*As per cent of Budget*	*As per cent GDP*	*In constant 1980-1 prices*
1951-2	645	7.92	645	7.92	0.65	3053
1961-2	2603	11.7	2,603	11.7	1.52	10,716
1971-2	9948	9.38	10,110	9.53	2.19	22,556
1981-2	37,901	9.09	42,990	10.31	2.69	38,991
1986-7	84,503	10.5	94,790	11.78	3.24	59,942
1987-8	104,302	11.27	117,980	12.75	3.54	68,772
1991-2	187,576	11.01	214,340	12.58	3.48	83,837
1992-3	209,510	11.01	250,300	13.15	3.55	90,265
1993-4	234,131	10.71	282,800	12.94	3.49	93,125
1994-5	272,301	10.82	326,060	12.95	3.42	115,495
1995-6 (RE)	324,587	11.07	390,180	13.3	3.55	125,953
1996-7 (BE)	365,293	11.23	434,120	13.5	3.40	131,142

Notes: RE = Revenue estimates; BE = Budget estimates
Source: University News, 36938, 21 September, 1988.

Table 2. Public Expenditure on Education Publication Expenditure on

Country	*Education (as % of GNP)* 1995	*Education (as% of total) government expenditure* 1993-5	*Primary & Secondary education (as% of all levels)* 1990-5
Bangladesh	2.3	8.7	88
China	2.3	12.2	67

Country	Education (as % of GNP) 1995	Education (as% of total) government expenditure 1993-5	Primary & Secondary education (as% of all levels) 1990-5
Egypt	5.6	13.8	64
India	3.5	12.1	65
Iran	4	17.8	63
Kenya	7.4	16.1	82
Korea	3.7	17.4	79
Malaysia	5.3	15.5	76
Sri Lanka	3.1	8.1	73
Thailand	4.2	20.1	73

Note: The figures for China may not be comparable due to differences in the system of accounting.

Source : UNDP Human Development Report 1998.

"By honoring a woman, we honor a whole nation!" Ten Laureates Receive 1995 Prize for Women's Creativity in Rural Life

Two Chinese rural women, Jai Junquia and Lai Xiao, are among the ten women and women's groups who were selected to receive the 1995 *"Prize for women's creativity in rural life"*, awarded annually on *8 September* (International Literacy Day) by the Geneva based Women's World Summit Foundation. Objective : To honor the creativity and courage of rural women and women's groups in the Third World, and make known their innovative projects enhancing the quality of life for their families and contributing to sustainable development.

The list of ten women (below) who receive the 1995 *"Prize for women's creativity in rural life"* with a cash award of $ 500 each, includes women from Asia, Africa and Latin America.

Prize winners are

China: *Jia Junqiao* (Longju) teaches new skills to villagers and has built a village school; *Lia Xiao,* a Mongal herdswoman (Adunchulu Sumu), pioneered a scientific strategy for breeding and raising sheep.

India: *Samuben Ujabhai Thakore and Ranabai Jemalji Rauma* (Northern Gujarat) *share one Prize.* Together they lead a union of 14,000 women, negotiate with the government and bring employment programmes to these women; and *Madhuben Bhailal Solanki,* who formed a savings group in her village Vakharia.

Egypt: *Gawaher Saad El Sherbini Fadl* leads groups for land reclamation cooperatives.

Sudan: *Huda Abdel-Elhameid* expanded her fishing activities to making and selling fishing nets and fishing lines, and became an expert in salted fish.

Ghana: *Joan Abgo* co-ordinates networking and reaches out to rural women in farming and trading.

Mali: *Samake Nakani and Sangare Aminata share one Prize.* Both lead groups committed to fighting poverty, misery and ignorance.

Togo: *Co-Ordinating Bureau for Women's Groups* (Ms Segou Tida) trains women in poverty stricken areas to gain knowledge on how to earn and manage money, and provide health care, food, housing and clothing.

Bolivia: *Domitila Barrios,* and internationally known grass roots leader, famous for leading strikes against the Banzer dictatorship, continues to fight for justice among some of the most oppressed people of the world.

Creative and Courageous Women -Heroins of the world - We Salute and Honor You!

For further information, please contact:

Foundation Sommet mondial des femmes Women's World Summit Foundation Cumbre Mundial de las Mujeres BO Box 2001, 1211 Geneva 1, Suisse Tel. : 022 738 66 19 Fax : 022 738 98 47

Literacy ... One woman at a time

In Konkaran, a remote village in Mali near the edge of the Sahara Desert, life has stood still for centuries. The only thing that moved was the water in the Niger River, which lately has been carrying diseases, parasites and the risk of river blindness.

Some 30 percent of the children in Konkaran may die before the age of five, often due to water born diseases. Clean, safe water can save many lives. Several UN agencies have launched a literacy programme as part of a campaign about safe-drinking water.

Like most other Konkoran women, Fanta raised animals to feed her family and provide income. She was one of the first to join the literacy programme. In addition to basic skills, like reading and arithmetic. Fanta learned about oral rehydration, or "life water", as it is called here. She now treats children with diarrhoea, and has also learned better methods for raising goats and healthier ways to prepare milk. Village women who cannot read often come to her to write letters for them or to seek advice on practical matters. Literacy has given Fanta's life a whole new meaning and a new level of status in her village.

A world away in Bangkok, Thailand, lives Youphadee, her family is among the 400 who live in the sprawling Rajataphan slum, where she makes her living by selling food in the street. After Youphadee joined a literacy programme sponsored by the Government and UNESCO, she learned basic accounting to help run her business.

Together with other women, Youphadee has also formed a credit union, which provides much-needed loans for family emergencies and investment in business. *"Educate girls because they have a more difficult life', she says, "If I had to choose between sending a boy or a girl to school, I would send the girl."*

Long Ago there lived such a woman

By Ziya Us Salam

A veteran Congress leader, Jyotirmoyee Ganguli, was an intrepid agitator who lost her life demanding release of INA prisoners in 1954.

Revolutions in human history are like processions on the street. They come and go. Only a few of them are potent enough to change the course of time. Most others just peter out after sundry protests, leaving in their trail tales of anguish and anger, depression and disgruntlement. And individuals who are doomed to be associated with the vain attempts are consigned to mothballs without so much as a second thought by posterity.

One such failed attempt at revolution in Indian history came about in 1945 when a procession of students in Calcutta demanding the release on INA prisoners was fired upon by the police, leaving scores of agitators injured and only a few less dead. The heroine of this vain struggle to demand justice from the imperialists was Jyotirmoyee Ganguli, a resident of Calcutta.

Daughter of Dwarkanath Ganguli, Jyotirmoyee was born in January 1889, a few months after India's first Prime Minister, Jawaharlal Nehru, opened his eyes in this world for the first time. From the early years of her life, she was keenly interested in social and political activities and never missed an opportunity to participate in a public agitation or to take up cudgels on behalf of her compatriots.

Though she joined the Government service at an early age, her heart was always with nationalists fighting to break free from the shackles of serfdom. Predictably enough, she did not think twice before jumping into the freedom movement when the Father of the Nation called all Indians to join the movement against the British. The result was the Civil Disobedience Movement of 1930 and the attendant Salt Satyagraha and the Dandi March.

Incidentally, all Indians united across the class and gender barriers during the Civil Disobedience Movement. Women, in particular, were very enthusiastic about participating in the national cause. They took part in processions, braved lathi charge, risked long jail sentences, yet never flinched from their onerous task.

About 3,000 women were imprisoned. They wore khadi on Mahatma Gandhi's call, propagated swadeshi and resigned from Government service in large numbers. Jyotirmoyee was one such woman doing her bit for sorority at the altar of the nation.

The Civil Disobedience Movement, however, was just the baptism by fire for Jyotirmoyee, a woman who was a fierce nationalist and did not shy away from taking to the streets to get her grievances redressed. Soon enough, she was involved in a number of protests against the cruelties inflicted by the British. The most famous and dramatic instance of her hostility with the foreign masters was provided by the raw courage she displayed in protesting against the imprisonment of INA heroes in 1945.

The Indian National Army started by Netaji Subhash Chandra Bose and Mohan Singh sought to drive out the British with the use of force and intended to capture Delhi after entering the country from the eastern border, via Nagaland and Manipur. Its main heroes, who were also shining examples of India's plurality were Gurbaksh Singh Dhillon, Shahnawaz Khan and P. K. Sehgal.

The INA prisoners were regarded as national heroes and helped in uniting the country across communal lines. Even as the British came down heavily on the soldiers of the army, Indians vent their anger in no uncertain way. Streams of people came out in the open and public demonstrations greeted the British officials in every city. Intelligence Bureau admitted "There has seldom been a matter which has attracted so much Indian public interest... this particular brand of sympathy cuts across communal barriers."

The popular explosion of public anger across the country was reminiscent of the famous student days agitation in Paris during the French Revolution. In Calcutta, Jyotirmoyee Ganguli led a procession of students on November 21, 1945. The processionists, organized by Forward Bloc, sat down on the Dharmatala Street for the whole night after being prevented from entering Dalhousie Square. Communist Student Federation cadres and Islamic College students carrying green flags of the Muslim League joined them. Spontaneously, the students tied together the Congress, League and red flags as a symbol of anti-imperialist unity.

Jyotirmoyee Ganguli, who was by then a veteran Congress leader, demanded release of soldiers of INA held in prison by the British authorities on behalf of the agitationists. The British did not take kindly to the attempt at providing a broad base to the freedom movement by involving students, labourers and peasants in the agitation. Deciding to nip the potential rebellion in the bud, they came down heavily on the fulminations of the students.

Military trucks were despatched to drive away the passionate patriots. In the hullabaloo which ensued, two students, symbolically one Hindu and one Muslim, lost their lives in the police firing. Rameswar Banerjee was among them.

Trouble spread across the city. Sikh taxi drivers joined hands with Ganguli. Cars were burnt, trains were blocked and barricades came up at every nook and corner. Police inquiry noted : "The crowds when fired on largely stood their ground."

Jyotirmoyee Ganguli was left fuming. Not ready to succumb to pressure tactics, she decided to carry the body of one of the students killed the previous day in the next day's procession.

Even as Jyotirmoyee marched at the head of the funeral procession, the British were determined not to allow the nationalists to make an issue out of it. Military trucks were called in again. In one such encounter, Jyotirmoyee Ganguli was knocked down and before compatriots realized the gravity of the situation, she was mercilessly killed by the British, leaving them to mourn not two but deaths of three patriots who sacrificed their lives for the nation.

However, there is another shade of opinion on the subject. Some people believe that a day after sitting on the dharna, Jyotirmoyee was killed in a car accident and not by design by the British.

Jyotirmoyee Ganguli's sacrifice though initially in vain, bore fruit in the long run. Her sacrifice and that of her comrades inspired famous novelist Manik Bandhyopadhyay to write a novel *Chinha*. And, needless to reiterate, it imbued the INA heroes with a halo of immortality and facilitated the task of India's Independence a couple of years later.

Indian Women as Portrayed by Cornelia Sorabji in 1905

By P.J.O. Taylor

Cornelia Sorabji was a remarkable woman: a lawyer, social reformer and a shrewd observer. And she could write.

I've recently come across her "pen portrait" of the *Hindu woman of 1905,* and am wondering just how true it is of affairs today. Knowing how conservative Indian society is, I would guess things have not changed much?

Here is one description of the Indian Wife of 1905, just three generations ago: "Was there ever the world over a like conception of the married state? Chief priestess of her husband, whom to serve is her religion and her delight; one with him in the economy of the household certainly, but moving in a plane far below him for all other purposes—religious, mental, social; gentle and adoring, but incapable of participation in the larger interests of his life, incapable of participation even in his games." If to that you add a wife's two major duties i.e., to please her husband's mother, whose chief handmaiden she is in things domestic, and, secondly, the duty of giving him a son (who in turn will exercise his sway over her), it will be seen that the wife's theoretical position does not differ extravagantly from that of house-slave." Have things altered?

Incidentally, modern research has established beyond all questions of doubt that the baby foetus is sexed by the father, not the mother: just think of all those women in history who have been blamed, cursed, killed even, for bringing forth only daughters, when all the time it was the man's doing! But the Hindu wife of 1905 put everything she could into the business of producing a man child: the Gods were worshipped and prayed to, the oracles were consulted and the omens scrutinized, astrology enlisted, and charms stealthily worked to achieve the end so earnestly desired.

The Inside

"And if the Gods proved gracious, proud indeed was the Hindu lady, she was at once a creature of good omen, a being to be welcomed at feasts, to be invoked by the childless. No longer is she a failure; even widowhood would leave her with the chastened halo of that son who is worthy to offer sacrifices."

"So the little Hindu wife would, if perfection were achievable, be gentle, submissive, a perfect mistress of her house, moving softly about the women's domain — i.e., the inside, not the outside of the home. Domestic duties dominated the day, with perhaps the chance of a little exchange of gossip. The evening meal brings her again into prominence: she would wait upon her husband while he ate; silent in his presence with downcast eyes, for to look him in the face would be bold indeed. Perhaps he talked to her of village or family interests or even business affairs, but she would not have thought it strange if he had not. It was his decision."

Now do all you ladies out there recognize yourselves, or are you sitting there seething wim pent-up fury at my presumption? We have spoken of wives. What of widows in 1905? The high caste widow of those days no longer fed the flames of the funeral pyre bound to the body of her husband.. Instead she lived the life of a willing drudge in the house of her mother-in-law.

The Widow

"It was perhaps true to say of all orthodox Hindu widows that they suffered their lot with the fierce enjoyment of something approaching martyrdom, and with a kind of fanaticism of selflessness. But nothing could minimize the evils of that lot, for a widow was a thing of ill omen, to be cursed even by those who loved her. For some sin committed in a previous birth, the Gods had deprived her of a husband:" is that the theory? To the alien from the West it seems irrational, but then the whole idea of marriage in India revolves upon the conception of Life, and that too is barely understood by the firenghi.

Cornelia Sorabji firmly dismissed all ideas that, there might be determined animosity in the cursing of a widow. The person doing the cursing was as much an instrument of fate as the person cursed.

"Perhaps a woman's place in the national life could best be filled by the realization of herself: she should grow to her full stature, taking as tier due her share of God's light and air and of the gifts of the Earth Mother:" gentle womanly graces are not incompatible with independence. Listen to Cornelia Sorabji's (prophetic?) words written in 1905: "What a redemption of that curse of the widowed, what a revenge on Time, if the idow herself should take the foremost place in this regeneration of Indian womanhood."

Reservation of Women?

Gita Aravamudan

Protective legislation has always been a bone of contention even among women. Does such legislation rectify the gender injustice perpetrated over generations? Or does it put women into a neat box away from the social mainstream? Do women because of their special physical and social frailties require protective legislation? Or will such legislation actually hinder their progress? An American writer arguing against protective legislation for women, said long ago that they were not "semi-invalids stricken with the incurable disease of womanhood."

High profile sexual harassment cases also generate the same complex debate. Will there be a trickle down effect which will give courage to the more timid and lowly survivors of male attack? Or will it, as some (especially male) commentators fear trigger a spate of male victimisation in the form of molestation charges?

In the past couple of weeks Indian women have suddenly woken up to affirmative action being taken up on their behalf both by the judiciary and the legislature. On the one hand there is the high-profile Bajaj—Gill case which is supposed to send tremors down the collective spine of would-be molesters and on the other, there is the proposed legislation to introduce reservation for women in Parliament.

Both these bits of action have generated heated debate among women themselves. A feminist commentator pointed out that protective legislation implied that women belong to a special class of incompetents requiring such special care as minors and defectives needed and not covered by other provisions in the constitution. This ironically is emphasised by our politicians who always club together scheduled castes, scheduled tribes, women and other "socially handicapped persons."

As early as 1936, an editorial in an American newspaper commented that "the sign of the crutch is an old brand and always signifies a man's woman and not a woman's woman". Sixty years later, we still refer to the weaker sex whose vulnerability makes them victims of social oppression. In the eyes of die-hard feminists, protection which is a manifestation of patriarchy is counterproductive.

With our long history of protective legislation for the socially oppressed, we are actually in a better position to judge the worth of such gestures. The Mandal Commission highlighted what everyone has known for a long time ... the discrimination which exists even amongst the officially categorised victims of a discriminatory social system.

Without tackling basic issues like education for women or providing them with uniform and equal legal rights, such gestures become meaningless. Experience has shown that empowerment cannot exist when the women are vulnerable to manipulation. Even during the last elections held with so much fanfare about curbs and restrictions, among the women who were elected to Parliament, at least two were illiterate, one was a high-profile ex-dacoit and another woman very reluctantly stood "on behalf" of her estranged husband who was facing court cases. If a percentage of seats are reserved "for women, not only will they face a lot of resentment, there is a very strong chance that the women who "win" these seats will belong to the "creamy layer" of politically influential families.

Even if this bit of legislation does not get passed, at least it will highlight the issue of the need to empower women. If it does, ultimately it might turn out to be beneficial. Women's empowerment comes in strange forms. In certain social classes, they might initially get educated so that they can function as better mothers (teach the children homework) or they might be given music lessons so that they can sing for their husbands. Over a couple of generations this can lead to a total transformation of these women's daughters.

Our activist judiciary which seems to revel in high profile cases finally ended the eight year Bajaj—Gill drama with an operatic finale. The critics feel that the judiciary has over-reacted and that the case itself has farcical overtones because of the number of low profile rapists, molesters and bottom pinchers who remain at large.

If Gill were not a national hero and Bajaj was just a lowly government servant, perhaps the judiciary would not even have looked at what would be considered a high-society caper. True, but, does that trivialise the case? Should Roopan Bajaj feel apologetic about her status, her perseverance and her family suport?

Even as the news of these two events was being hotly discussed, hidden away in the corners were the mundane every day news items about teenage maid servants being attacked and tortured by their employers, of women being burnt to death by their in-laws and of girls being raped by 'friends' and relatives. Almost making us believe that all these gestures have no significance in our day to day life.

But, perhaps we should learn to take a more far-sighted view. Just as Anita Hill in the U.S. helped to focus attention on the issue of sexual harassment in the work place, so too, Roopan Bajaj, can become a rallying point for women seeking justice. Symbols ... and victorious symbols at that ... can help illustrate issues. The trivialisation of women in every walk of life ... at home, in the work place, in the popular media, on the streets ... is an intrinsic issue which normally received scant attention. Roopan Bajaj might come to symbolise a fight against that.

So, perhaps all this affirmative action is not in vain. If nothing else it has helped to trigger debate on subjects which were once considered inconsequential.

The Status of the Girl Child in India : A Journey of Discrimination Through Ages

— Dr. Gouri Srivastava

"Full many a gem of purest ray screen,
The dark unfathom cave of the ocean bear,
Full many a flower is born to blush unseen;
And waste its sweetness in the desert air.

**Thomas Gray*

The status of girl child in India is socially determined and is dependent at a particular point of time. Also there is a great deal of variation in different regions and amongst the patriarchal and matriarchal communities in particular. In this paper an attempt has been made to examine the status of girl child in the patriarchal communities of India.

It has generally been observed that amongst these communities the eldest male and subsequently other male members of the family enjoy a better social status as compared to the women. The lineage is traced through a male and in all rituals it is the male who dominate. This is sharply evident socially and even ritually. This subordination is not only internalised but legitimized by the socialization pattern existing in these families that are responsible for its transmission from one generation to another.

It is significant to note that in such families the entire life cycle of the girl child i.e., from womb to tomb is marked by discrimination, neglect and even physical elimination. This is initially practiced within the four walls of the family (natal home) and is further transmitted to her in-laws family. Infact, it continues throughout the various stages of her mortal existence i.e., childhood, marriage, widowhood and so on. Her entire contribution to the family is marginalized and even made invisible. It is ironical to note that the proverb

"The hand that rocks the cradle rules the world" does not hold true in this kind of a patriarchal set-up. This is evident from the attitude the girl child is subjected to since her very mortal existence or even before being born a female.

Elimination before being born

In recent times sex-detection tests or the amniocentesis has led to the abortion of female foetus. In other words not allowing the female child to be born. Infact, killing the foetus in the womb is a barbaric act of modern civilization. In a study conducted in Bombay regarding abortions it was found that out of 8000 abortions 7999 aborted was of female foetus. This phenomena is gradually spreading in most parts of the country and we find that one of the explanations for the decline of sex ratio of females in India lies in these kind of tests. Table I gives an in-depth account of this phenomena.

Table 1

1901	—	972
1911	—	964
1921	—	955
1931	—	950
1941	—	945
1951	—	946
1961	—	941
1971	—	930
1981	—	934
1991	—	927

Source: Census of India, 1991.

According to some scholars these modern tests mentioned above have fitted well in the Indian ethos because it has received legitimacy from our culture and tradition which gives strong preference to sons and at the same time propagates elimination of the girl child.

Infancy

Few who have the fortune of being born perhaps accidently or by chance are brought into the world full of discrimination and neglect. This begins from her very birth. When the dai (mid-wives) in the village or nurse in the hospital announces the birth of a baby — boy joyous songs are sung, sweets are distributed. This is the only occasion when the mother feels very proud of her existence because her status within the patriarchal family is elevated and she is ensured the continuity of the lineage in the family. However, the opposite happens in the case of the girl child. The main issues that keep worrying the parents since her physical existence are — "How will they find a suitable match for their daughters?", how will they arrange for the dowry to be given in the marriage? In most of the northern states e.g., U.P., Bihar, Rajasthan and even Southern states like Tamil Nadu, A.P. dowry has become a great source of problem for the middle and lower middle classes. How do parents solve this problem? They either resort to borrowing money from local moneylenders at high rates of interest and thereby become bonded throughout their lives or resort to female infanticide. It is ironical to note that infanticide which was outlawed in India as early as 1870 continues to exist till this day. Female girl child are barbarically killed by adopting various means like suffocating them to death, using pesticides, insecticides, acids and so on. Sometimes mother's roll over the child till it is dead. In Musilampatti village in Madurai district of Tamil Nadu newly born baby girls are done away with by giving them poisonous juice of erukam plant.

Those who escape from this cruel clutches of destiny are reared up in an atmosphere totally hostile to them. The girl child is very often burdened with household chores, care of siblings, helping parents in occupation. The times taken in all these activities are responsible for her discontinuation of education. It is ironical to note that despite contributing significantly to the family her efforts are marginalized and made invisible. Her crucial work in the family goes unrecognized and in return she is denied the basic right of protection and care.

It is important to note that the girl child accepts her fate without questioning it. Infact, the socialization process is such that it makes them and her lot accept discrimination and neglect by parents as something natural or designed by God himself.

Childhood and Marriage

This span of childhood is of a very short and minimal duration. Infact there is hardly any childhood for the girl child. Child marriage leads to the third stage in the life of the girl child. The age of marriage varies from region to region in India. In Madhya Pradesh girls are married as soon as they become big enough to fit in a "Thali". Despite the enactment of "The Child Marriage Restraint Act of 1978" which raises the age of marriage of girls from 15 to 18 years, pre-puberty marriages are largely prevalent even to this day. In the latest Report of the International Planned Parenthood Federation — there is a mention that 18% girls in Asia are married by the age of 15 and in India 75% are married before age of 18.

In Rajasthan the popular custom of Akha Teej gives sanction to child marriage. The impact of pre-puberty marriages have a very harmful impact on the physique of the girl child. She becomes mother without realizing the significance of this stage of existence. It often leads to complications in child birth and in extreme cases is responsible for the occurance of maternal and child mortality.

Mentally also, the child bride is not placed in a happy disposition. She occupies the humblest place in her husbands family or her in-laws and is not allowed to talk to any male member in the family accept her husband. The joys of youth are not known to her. She is suddenly introduced to a ceremony the gravity of which is not understood by her. To her marriage means a joyous occasion where sweetmeat and gorgeous dresses have to be worn. Her actions are not only critically looked at but sometime mother-in-law resort to constant rebuking her daughter-in-law. There is a tendency to find fault with whatever she does. It is ironical to note that double standards are adopted as far as mother-in-laws' attitude towards daughters and daughters-in-law is concerned. For her daughter-in-law the attitude expected from her is that of obedience, submissiveness, and acceptance of her fate, once again without questioning it. As mentioned earlier it is only the birth of a son that really bring a change in her status.

Widowhood

The last and the final stage is that of widowhood. Married at an early age the child bride has a perpetual widowhood before her. In the 19th and 20th Centuries in Bengal and Bombay Presidencies widowhood was considered to be curse. Widows were considered as bad omen and were shunned by all members of the families on all auspicious occasions. They were accepted to lead a very austere life. Even now we find widowhood is considered as a bad omen in patriarchal families and the widowhood girl child continue to face hardships.

Thus, the entire life cycle of the girl child is marked by discrimination, neglect and elimination at each stages of her existence in patriarchal communities of India.

In recent times there has been a growing awareness amongst policy makers, administrators, planners and social activists that the goals for education for all and health for all by 2000 A.D. cannot be achieved if this segment of humanity is neglected. Therefore, the need of the hour is to ensure the survival, protection and care of the girl child so that the above goals are achieved. It has been increasingly realized that this journey of discrimination and neglect can end if the girl child becomes empowered with a positive self esteem and become aware of her rights and acquire the confidence to question the well laid customs and traditions that have assigned her a subordinate status. Further as the saying goes that the answer to every problem lies in the problem itself — therefore women also need to change their attitude in different roles they perform e.g., as mother-in-laws. Also, a multiprolonged strategy is needed to tackle this discrimination e.g., at the level of family, community and school. Media both print and audiovisual can do a lot in this direction to promote gender sensitive and gender aware programmes. We have voluntary organisations, educational institutions and government already working in this direction. However, what is required is community awareness, their participation and sensitivity to the problem which will gradually bring an end to this journey of discrimination. Further attitudinal changes in family and community towards the girl child is essential so that they are no longer seen as burden and liabilities but an asset.

Swatantra Bharat Panorama

Monument of our Freedom

For the last few months we have been celebrating the Golden Jubilee of our Freedom. From all over the world we are receiving Greetings and Joyous Congratulations. It is great. We are a fortunate generation who saw the dawn of freedom and the Golden Jubilee of the same.

The Freedom of this country is the fruit of aspirations of millions of people living in this ancient land, the sub- continent of the east. Is it not necessary for us to have a permanent monument to remind our future generations of our achievement and inspire them with patriotism? Ten years ago we planned such a monument — a Panorama. You have no doubt seen them in other countries - Moscow, Paris, Berlin, Brussels and New York (Washington). They all commemorate their national achievement and successes. We are no less proud of our achievement.

This monument—a panorama showing our struggle for freedom, our freedom leaders, our hour of success, the Union Jack flag coming down and our flag hoisted on the Red Fort—the brightest ruby of our country. The Vandemataram, satyagraha, nonco-operation movements, Montagu reforms, Home Rule, Bipin Chandra Pal, Tilak, Annie Basant, Simon Commission, Kohat Rebellion, Mopla agitation, Quit India, Women's movement are the rainbow colours of our freedom struggle. Time and Tide waits for no man. These memories will be soon forgotten by our future generations who have not witnessed them. So we keep them sealed in a National panorama.

We have a beautiful ready made building, land and site and money for the same, near the beautiful Kolleru lank (Island) in West Godavari District. It can be made into a beautiful tourist area. We require a pad for aeroplanes and helicopters to descend. The tourism department can develop it into such a nice tourist centre that in two decades it can finance itself and thereafter earn a handsome income to our country.

We require technicians and the will to do it. Men may come and men may go, but the country will go on and on for ever. It is high time we begin the construction now in this year of Freedom's Golden Jubilee. Long live our Freedom and our country.

Dr. (Mrs.) K. Lakshmi Raghuramaiah

According to the Rig Veda: The three basic characteristic of a nation are Mother Tongue (language), culture and Motherland and the culture includes the mode of conduct and social customs of the people as adopted according to religious traditions, historical background and the environmental circumstances.

"The Motherland is everything for me - father and son. This is why the devotee prays. Let my Motherland bestow upon me glory, honour, truthfulness, consciousness, prosperity and all around mental, physical and moral development." Atharva Veda

"Thus, unanimity, equality and unity are the foundation stones of nationalism.

"Atharva Veda.

Golden Jubilee of our Freedom 15.08.1997

—Tenali

Fifty years ago our fetters of slavery were broken. We won freedom after a great struggle and it is precious to us.

So we are celebrating it like a festival and remembering it as an anniversary. India was freed from slavery of 300 years. Both are sources of joy.

How did we become slaves for three centuries? Let us look back and see. Perhaps our disunity was the main reason. Although we are well known for our unity in diversity we fell into evil hands because of our disunity, infighting and jealousies; why are we again in such misery and distress? Disunity again is over us like dark cloud threatening our peace and freedom. What should we do about it.

Let us retrospect a little. What did Gandhiji say when the British announced that they will give freedom to India. - Gandhiji said - that the British offer is like a post-dated cheque from a near bankrupt bank. There was no alternative to the British but give us freedom. If they had not given us freedom, they would have lost not only India but Asia and all the countries in their empire. It was no kindness nor generosity on their part but it was a must – a necessity.

So also no single individual was responsible in India to obtain freedom. It was neither Gandhi nor Nehru. How are leaders born? Time and tide makes them. The political and social circumstances in a country produce leaders - Political, Social and Religious. After the end of 19th Century and beginning of 20th Century our people got fed up with their fate, the conditions in the country and the rulers. Princely states were fighting with each other. Invaders entered our country from Kyber Pass and sea around us.

There were Muslims, French, British and Portuguese, each were trying to loot India. So at this terrible stage Tilak, Bipin Chandra Pal, Lajpat Rai, Chittaranjan Das advocated SWARAJ. Gangadhar Tilak said freedom is our birth right. Chittaranjan Das first spoke of Swaraj-self reliance-Independence.

In 1930 Gandhiji chose 73 devoted workers and led the Dandi March. He walked with them from Sabarmathi, his ashram to Dandi-Surat 241 Miles. A large number of women, some whole villages followed him very enthusiastically. He made salt at Surat, 5 grams of salt was purchased by an Ahmedabad businessman for Rs. 525/-.

Jesus Christ, Mohammed, Krishna, Socrates, Plato, Aristotle were born prophets to lead the people of the world. While our leaders were working hard for Swarajya, sacrifing their lives. Nelson Mandela in Africa was fighting for the Freedom of South Africa. Gandhiji a full fledged barrister, who supported Mandela, came from Africa to fight for the Freedom of his own country-India-Swaraj. Jawaharlal Nehru, Sarojini Naidu, Subhash Chandra Bose, Sardar Patel took up the challenges of the older generation and continued the fight. Since Independence Movement began in our country nearly ten generations have worked so far — I have been fortunate to see and live with six generations – two above and three below.

How and why we obtained freedom is history. So far we have not yet written that history properly - many authors have tried to complete the same but have not yet succeeded. Even I tried - to build a panorama - Swatantra Bharat so that the world can remember our momentous fight for eternity. I have not succeeded in building that monument but I am still trying to do it. I will do it until the end of my life.

We won freedom at great cost and sacrifice, partitions of our country - Pakistan, Bangladesh, Sri Lanka, Burma. We were friends earlier and lived like one family. Now we are near enemies building up animosity and pretend to begin peace talks. For thousands of years we lived in peace -Muslims, Christians and Hindus. Even in villages the different castes lived amicabilly. But the British trick of divide and rule has ruined us. When Gandhiji was arrested after Surat, Sarojini Naidu took over. Thus, the national movement gave birth to women's movement. When they left India, India was cut into bits. But after freedom we could have forgotten and forgiven but our good politicians did not give the priority that they should have given as our neighbours were difficult people.

I am not a politician. I have to go on confessing it as some how people have got an idea that I am a politician just because I happen to be a Ex-politician's wife. I am a follower of Annie Besant. Infact the freedom struggle gave birth to women's movement and we all got involved in freedom fight. Actually I have no label or stamp of any political or religious party on me. I believe in all religions and I hate politicians, If I was born in any other religion also I would have felt the same. All religions take you to the same goal through different rastas - Hinduism is all embracing and all pervading.

Annie Besant's Home Rule gave a thrust to Independence movement; so many leaders that I have earlier mentioned, the women movement members and the general public—thousands and millions of them worked for freedom. It was not just leaders who worked for our country's freedom. The common man and women swept the movement like sea waves. They were no white caps nor any caps. They did not shout or preach or destroy anything. They worked and worked in different ways. It was a people's victory. We obtained swarajya by the united effort of all our people.

Even in those days all leaders did not agree. They did not see eye to eye. For example, Rabindranath Tagore, Arabinda Ghosh, Rajagopalachari, Mohamed Ali brothers and even Motilal Nehru did not approve of Gandhiji's Satyagraha. The Simon Commission the Kohat rebellion in the north, the MPLA rebellion in the South had different reactions on the leaders, but in one voice people demanded Swarajya and got it.

We got freedom but have we got Swarajya - self reliance? We have not risen up to our own expectations and hopes. Why—No Unity? Greed, Jealousy, Corruption - Failure.

How will we get real Swarajya? By a second freedom struggle? People are fed up with our leaders - The Poverty, the Disease, the Disorderly behaviour even in Parliament House and Assemblies, the growing population, pollution, environmental deterioration are worrying all of us. It is a vicious circle. It we don't act people will not. If people do not cooperate can leaders do anything? (KIM - KARTIVYAM)

Surely a rebellion or another revolution will occur. This negative thinking of destroying trains, buses, cars, public property, encounters, fights and fire – make our minds numb. We have to take positive view like the Japanese - KYOSET - How is it other countries have progressed so well when we are going-down in every sphere. KYOSHI - in Japan means - something like our view of Dharma - "no harm to other - do your duty". We all know our duty and we know our faults. Our conscience tells us what is right and what is wrong. We have a glorious future in front of us. We have vast resources, our knowledge can make us a glorious country in the world. Infact it can rule the world - or rather lead the world.

Let me give you just one example - Health. To keep our people healthy is a big problem just now in our country - a heart operation or treatment can cost lakhs which the ordinary man on the road cannot afford. But our Vedas our Atharva Veda has given wonderful knowledge to treat people. A good system of alternate medicine can be established. Even Hospitals like Apollo and others are utilising this knowledge. It is now in circulation as pranic healing. Pancha Bhutamlu - energy from can be usefully utilised. Non-medical treatment is possible for many diseases.

Visible Aura - a safety armour covering our skin - is god's natural gift to us. KIRLIN Photography only can show this. We can cure all diseases. There should be no conflict with allopathic system of medicine. It should be complementary. It is cheap and available every where - in cities, towns and villages. We don't even have to touch the patient nor have big equipment.

What also does this country at this hour need.

1. We should stop all destruction by hooligans.
2. Punitive Punishment for Destruction of all public property.
3. Declaration of assets every year by politicians.
4. Moral education.
5. We do not need any reservations of any sort.

—Dr. (Ms.) K. Lakshmi Raghuramaiah
(founder and Projector of the sprawling building 'Sarojini House')

Gandhi On Woman and Society

"Woman will be unquestioned leader and having found her place in human evolution will shed her inferiority complex. Woman is the incarnation of Ahimsa. Ahimsa means infinite love, which again means infinite capacity for suffering. Let her translate that love to the whole of humanity."

— M.K. Gandhi

"When woman, whom we call *abala* becomes sabala. All those who are helpless will become powerful." Gandhi, addressing A.I.W.C. in 1936. Such empowering, may not be bestowed upon them by legislation or assistance offered by man — they must gather strength to stand up on their own, lift the self, by the self. — Truth alone wins."

—M.K. Gandhi

Do you know?

Freedom Struggle and its beginnings

1857 was not the first war of independence. Santhal Revolt of 1784 was the beginning of freedom struggle in its own way. Tilka Majhi, its great-leader, was ultimately defeated after many skirmishes and battles and was caught. He was tortured and hanged.

The Flouting of the Basis of Partition

It was clearly agreed at the time of partition and Pakistan signed an agreement to ensure the rights and safety of the minorities after partition in their respective countries. But after partition, a continuous trail of torture, persecution, armed attacks and forced conversion of minorities was in a planned and forceful way which resulted into a reduction of minorities from 20% in 1947 to 2% now. Even in the so called friendly Bangladesh for which India sacrificed a lot in the 70 even at the cost of its economic destabilisation, the number of minorities has scaled down to 14% from 30% in 1947.

About Subhash

The magnanimity and majesty of the man leading the nation in his respect for his political rival by christening the latter as the Father of the Nation is unmatched. He named one of his brigades after a man who debunked his voluntary organisation in India as a Bertram Mill's circus show and who maliciously denigrated his significant victory against his (Gandhiji's) nominee in Congress Presidential election. Of course, Mahatma ji tried to make amends, when it was too late, to call Subhash "a price among patriots".

The women in India fought for and earned their right to vote in 1931, a time when several European countries had not established any voting rights for women.

The first Provisional Government of Azad Hind by the India Independence of Azad Hind was formed and proclaimed on foreign soil. The task of the Provisional Government was to launch and conduct the struggle for the expulsion of the British from the soil of India and then to bring about the establishment of Permanent National Government of Azad Hind on Indian soil, till then the Provisional Government was to administer the affairs of the country in trust of the Indian People.

There is an interesting quality in the portrayal of the feminine. She is prakriti (nature), the undifferentiated matter of the universe. This is the prime reason that woman is compared to earth-like the earth, she gives sustenance, strength and like. The concept of the Divine Mother arises from the concept of Sakthi. She is the consort of Shiva and she is the mother of all existence."

— M.K. Gandhi

"Ours is a struggle not only against British Imperialism but against world imperialism as well, of which the former is the key—stone. We are, therefore, fighting not for the cause of India alone but of humanity as well. India freed means humanity saved.

—Subhash Chandra Bose

Freedom or Myth

Fifty years ago we were freed from the bonds of foreign rule. But are we really free? Have we been free from the shackles of customs, conventions, from the basest elements of human being, from the evil designs of internal enemies and above all, from the modern day politicians. Politics has always been the game of scoundrels but it is at its bay and an abode of devil and is promising a hell only to the common man who is suffocated not only by environmental hazards but by having no breather from all sided exploitations, tortures, injustices and gimmikeries. We are in the bonds of many isms - nepotism, favouritism, opportunism, groupism, separatism, anti-nationalism — communism and communalism are now old phrases. It's a herculean task to be free from all these bonds and establish a clean society where the common man can lead a dignified life.

The constitution of India embodies fundamental equality between men and women. But equality is a concept, an attitude, a way of life. Yet have we been able to ensure equality for all? The discrimination between two genders in Indian society is writ large. We shout from the housetops for the improvement of the status of Indian women. They still await independence - independence from injustices of male dominated society, independence ensuring equal share in policy and decision making processes in the highest echelons of administration and in the legislative bodies at the national, state and local levels and independence for equal status at home and in society. The hollow talks of women's emancipation and empowerment are redundant.

Women have to be free from the inferiority complexes of self-underestimation and self-pity. They will regain their ancient status by their own strength and determination. No one is going to shower petals on them. There is an inbuilt contradiction. Equality in the real sense means the relegation of men from their unbriddled power and position. Hence, no one is going to redeem the women.

Sometimes women are themselves their own enemies. They are ridden with the conventional beliefs that they are born as women with a low position due to their sins in the past life, that they will get 'Moksha' or a better life in rebirth, only if they are the epitome of sacrifice and obedience. The women alone draw a line of discrimination between a son and a daughter. They are mainly responsible for the indifferent sometimes inhumane treatment meted out to their daughters-in-law. They make their daughters meek and submissive to the extent that they suffer all kinds of atrocities and injustice at the hands of their mothers-in-law or husbands till they are burnt or die in desperatioon. Society also shuns them if they act otherwise. The status of women at home and outside is in peril.

Dismantle the myth of freedom. We should not be swayed by the misnomer of men and women being poles apart and of their distinct areas. The true spirit of partnership between men and women only can pave the way of universal peace and harmony. Progress, environmental safety and a new set of moral values would automatically emerge as both together can create the psychological climate for promoting the interests of humanity. The feeling of apathy towards women, hostile or antagonistic attitude for her have arisen due to the misconception that women are attacking and indulging in the fields of men — may be in the sphere of professions, policy and decision making arena or legislative bodies. This is sheer stupidity and incongruity. The view is not sustainable at all. On the contrary, the present plight of women is consequential of the denial of her due place as half of the section of society.

No nation can progress or strive forward unless the society as a whole participates in its evolution with a whole hearted commitment. The transformation is essential and urgent.

The potential virtues and abilities of women must find a proper avenue for their realization and utilization as well. The role of women in socio-economic development in nation building, running the administration and framing the legislation cannot be negated or ignored. The country can reach the heights of success and be foremost in the comity of nations when all of us co-operate with each other imbibed by the traits of honesty, integrity, impartiality and justice and design the destiny of our nation.

—Dr. Nirmala Dwarkadas

When bad men combine, the good men associate, else they will fall one by one, and unpitied sacrifice in a contemptible struggle.

—Edmund Burke (1756)

सूर्यो चका सर्वलोकस्य चक्षु - र्न लिप्यते चाक्षु पैर्वाह्यदोषैः।
एकस्तका सर्वभूतान्तरात्मा न लिप्यते लोकदुःखेन बाह्यः।।

–कथा उपनिषद

Just as the sun, which is the eye of the whole world, is not tainted by the ocular and external defects, similarly, the self, that is but one in all beings, is not tainted by the sorrows of the world. It being transcendental.

अग्ने नय सुपथा राये अस्मान् विश्वानि देव वयुनानि विद्वान।
युयोध्यस्मज्जुहुराणमैनो भूयिष्ठा ते नमउक्ति विधेम।।

–इसा उपनिषद

O Fire! O god! Knowing, as thou do, all our deeds, lead us by the good path for the enjoyment of the fruits of our deeds; remove from us all crooked sins. We offer thee many words of salutation.

"The definition of truth every person could find in his or her own conscience.

"True morality consists, not in following the beaten track, but in finding out the true path for ourselves and fearlessly following it"

"The first condition of non-violence is justice all round in every department of life.

—M. K. Gandhi

"Ends and means must be deemed convertible. Ahimsa is the means. Truth is the end. It we take care of the means, we are bound to reach the end sooner or later."

—M. K. Gandhi

A Nation Comes of Age India at 50 Some Remarkable Women of India in 50 years of Independence

Smt. Sarojini Naidu

She was the first outstanding administrator in Independent India and died as Governor of U.P. in 1949. She was a pioneer and leader in many fields. A renowned poet, orator, social reformer and patriot, she was the most reckoned leader of the Indian women's movement. She had neither to fight nor struggle for her position or status. In the galaxy of the prominent women of this epoch (50 years), she stands out not only in India but amongst the women of the world and displayed a harmonious and wide vision for humanity.

Dr. Muthulaksmi Reddy

A pioneer women legislator before independence, she was instrumental in getting abolished Devdasi system and was responsible for many laws being enacted like control of Immoral Traffic in women and children and prevention of cruelty to them and child marriage etc. She established First Cancer Research Institute and Hospital in South India in 1951.

She was the first lady recepient of 'Padma Bhusan' in 1956.

Raj Kumari Amrit Kaur

A princes by birth, she was noted for her statesmanship and established All India Women's Education Fund Association, and worked incessantly for the opening of the Lady Irwin College. Apart from initiating the schemes for the expansion of maternity homes child welfare centres, and control of Malaria. Leprosy, T.B., Cancer and measures for prevention of diseases and the improvement of the nation's health, she rendered distinguished services in the U.N. and allied U.N. International Assemblies and Associations in early years of our Independence.

Ms. Vijayalakshmi Pandit

She was the one who enhanced the prestige of the Indian Women in the world and fought for equal rights for all human beings irrespective of sex, race, colour or creed. She was the first woman to lead the country's delegation to the United Nations and was elected President of the U.N. Assembly in 1953, a unique honour for any woman. She was the first woman to have represented her country as Ambassador in three of the great world capitals.

Ms. Kamla Devi Chattopadhyaya

Smt Kamla Devi is one of the most dynamic women in India. A social rebel and pathfinder recepient of Watumull Foundation Award in 1962, Padma Bhushan and Magasaysay Award for community leadership in 1966—citation says she "has had the perception and courage to discover and develop solutions in contemporary needs of her society, founder of the Bhartiya Natya Sangh and the Asian Theatre Institute, a UNESCO aided institution.

Ms Hansa Mehta

Smt. Mehta made her mark as one of the foremost educationists in the country. She was associated with Bombay University Board of Studies Gujarat University, President Bombay Primary Education Board even in pre-independence era, and was senate Member SNDT University and its Vice-Chancellor (1946-48), member Secondary Education Commission (1952-53), Member All India Council for Secondary Education Commission (1952-53) and All India Council for Secondary Education (1955) and President Inter-University Board (1956), a founder member and vice-chancellor of Maharaj Sayaji Rao Univ. Board (1949-1958).

She represented the Govt. of India on many delegations abroad. The Nuclear Sub-Committee on the Status of Women of the U.N. (1946), Human Rights Commission of the U.N. (1947-52) and its Vice-Chairman (1960-52), member of Indian Delegation to UNESCO Conference (1956) and Deputy Leader of the Indian Delegation to UNESCO Conference in Paris (1958-1960).

Ms Dhanvanthi Rama Rau

She was instrumental in the formation of the International Planned Parenthood Federation and its Hon. President in 1953. In the fifties, she had been associated with social and moral Hygiene, Rehabilitation of crippled children and Blind school for the Rehabilitation of children needing special care. In 1965, she received the Albert and Mary Laskar Award for services to the cause of Planned Parenthood, Padma Bhushan in 1959, Laskar Award from the U.S., Watumull Award for Family Planning .Leadership in 1961 and thc Family of Man Award in 1969 from the U.S.

Indira Gandhi

At the age of 13 Indira Gandhi attended her first secret meeting of fighters, she represented the third generation of Nehrus in the freedom struggle since she joined Indian National Congress in 1938, she took an active part in India's movement for independence.

As Prime Minister of the country she was engulfed between autocratic and democratic tendencies. She was known as a "tigress among one hundred monkeys". During her tenure, India made tremendous strides in the areas of food production and an industrial base. In her times, she was regarded the world's most powerful political woman.

The ascension of a woman to the world's most populous democracy was especially significant for Indian women, who had traditionally been subservient to men. She was also an inspiration to people in other Third World Nations. Yet, inspite of her weilding unbriddled power and her being at the helm of affairs in India for 16 long years, negligible could be done for Indian women and hardly any women could come up to decision making levels, in legislatures or other political and social fields.

Ms Lata Mangeshkar

Melody queen Lata, a unique artist, commands a place in the hearts of the people of India. Through her art and her life, she has served and strengthened goodwill among the people of our land. Her golden voice has been compared to a shaft of pure light, and her music has given solace, strength and joy to millions. Her songs wafted on the waves her melody and her magic enthralls the hearts of people beyond the boundaries of our land in London and New York.

For decades she has achieved a preeminent position in the culture of India, recognised as star and, of course, as celebrated concert artist. Continously for three years, she was the winner of the coveted "Filmfare award" (equivalent to Oscar) Padmabhushan in' 1969 and Rajiv Gandhi National Sadbhavana Award for 1996 (in 1997).

M.S. Subbulakshmi

Sangita Kalanidhi Priyadarshini she has excelled in Karnatic Music Konark Samman, the Magsaysay Award for Public service, the Indira Gandhi award for National integration and the Spirit of the freedom have been conferred on her over the years. She has grace, dignity, beauty and a voice that is a great national asset.

Ms Sitara Devi

Fighting for her place as a dancer, ultimately she succeeded. Gurudev Tagore gave her the title 'Nritya Samrajani' or 'The Queen of Kathak'. She received Kalidas Sammelan and the Padmashri, Nritya Vilas and the Sangeet Natak Akadami Award. She set up a school for dancing in London.

Mother Teresa – A Legand

"God has not called me to be successful, he has called me faithful. Her mission was to bring succour to the lives of the poorest of the poor." Bharat Ratna, Templeton Prize, The Nobel Peace Prize, the U.S. Medal of freedom, Sadbhavana Award were themselves honoured when they were conferred on her. The First Citizen of the World and the founder of the Missionaries of Charity, she will always be remembered as one longing for humanity and the one above all religions. She selflessly and ceaselessly dedicated herself to the slums of India, the sick and hungry and the destitutes. Dignity and worth of the individual, peace and communal harmony were dear to her. Her life-long contributions will be cherished by Indian people for ever.

Quotes From Mother Teresa

"The begger, the leper, the victims of AIDS, do not need discussions and theories they need love."

"Dealing with the poor is a divine encounter."

"The good news is that God loves us. Let us be grateful for that love by loving others."

"The other day I dreamed that I was at the gates of heaven. And St. Peter said, Go back to Earth, there no slums up here.

On a woman she found on a Calcutta street

I knew she was dying. After I did what I could, she took my hand, gave me a beautiful smile and thanked me. She gave me more than I gave her.

On happiness

Happiness is the sign of a generous person. It is often the mantle of self-sacrifice.

On forgiveness

Forgiveness offers us a clean heart, and people will be 100 times better after it.

On the poor

(They) don't need pity; they need love and compassion. If you don't know them, you don't love them and don't serve them.

On service to God

Give yourself fully to God. He will use you to accomplish great things on the condition that you believe much more in His love than in your own weakness.

On her order

If the rich people can have the full service and devotion of so many nuns and priests, surely the poorest of the poor and the lowest of the low can have the love and devotion of us few. 'The Slum Sister' they call me, and I am glad to be just that for His love and glory.

On the family

The family is a precious and beautiful gift of God, and let us make sure that we never destroy this beautiful gift but keep the family united through prayer, love and sacrifice.

"She said the poor people are great people. They can teach us many beautiful things. The greatest injustice we have done to our poor people is that we think they are good for nothing. We have forgotten to treat them with respect, with dignity as a child of God. Often I think they are the ones to whom we own are greatest gratitude. They teach us.

On sacrifice

A sacrifice to be real must cost, must hurt, must empty ourselves. The fruit of silence is prayer, the fruit of prayer is faith, the fruith of faith is love, the fruit of love is service, the fruit of service is peace.

A prayer she composed

Make us worthy, Lord,

To serve our fellow men

Throughout the world who live and die

In poverty or hunger.

Give them, through our hands

This day their daily bread,

And by our understanding love,

Give peace and joy.

At her Funeral, a message from Pope John Paul II "From the cold bier, the unforgettable and dear mother continues to speak to us and seems to repeat the Lord's words it is more blessed to give than to receive .... At the close of the century which has known terrible extremes of darkness, the light of conscious has not been altogether extinguished. Holiness, goodness, kindness, love are still recognized when they appear on history's stage.

The Archbishop of Calcutta Henry D' Souza:—

"Perhaps the greatest message she has given to the world is the value and dignity of human life. All human life is precious, in whatever condition we find it."

Begum Akhtar

An awardee of Padmshri and posthumously of Padmabhushan, Begum Akhtar has excelled in classical music known as Faizabadi Akhtari known for her sweetness and fragrance. A singer of great promise she was hypnotizing her audience and reached the heights of fame and popularity. A noted ghazal singer selected easily understable lyrics with meaningful verses and poetic imagination. Her emotional style captivated the hearts of audience. Her contribution to Urdu poetry and ghazals will always be cherished.

Aruna Asaf Ali

Posthumouly awarded Bharat Ratna in 1997, Aruna Asaf Ali, nee Ganguli, was a brave and revolutionary patriot. Her dauntless deeds in the Quit India movement of 1942 had given her imperishable reputation. When Congress leaders were arrested, on 9th Aug., she was enraged and rushed forward and unfurled the tricolour, signalling the beginning of Quit India Movement. By this one brave act, she had inspired a whole generation of young men and women. Then, she functioned underground, adopted violent means to drive away the British. In 1958 she became the first Mayor of Delhi but was soon disillusioned, and never sought public office. She won the Lenin Peace Prize and the Indira Gandhi Award for National Integration.

Madhuri Ben Shah

Ms Madhuri Ben Shah had an illustrious educational career. She was granted British Council Scholarship and Smith Mundt Grant and Fullbright Fellowship by U.S. Educational Foundation not only for the pursuit of knowledge but also for spreading it as a Professor in U.S. Univ. As the vice-chancellor of S.N.D.T. Women's univ, she for the first time experimented the 'open university' system when more than 4000 persons including some septuagenarians took advantage of this and continued their education from the point they had left off earlier. Firmly believing in equality between men and women in every respect, she was elevated to the coveted post of Chairperson of University Grants Commission - the first woman to be entrusted with such responsible and prestigeous chair. She is a great educational luminary of immense repute.

P.T. Usha

Asia's greatest woman athlete P.T. Usha became India's great hope for Olympic metal, after she won five medals of the Asian games. The bronze slipped through her fingers by a quarter of a second, but still will always be a role model to female athletes in India.

Kiran Bedi

Kiran Bedi is the quintessential supercop, India's first woman IPS officer. As DCP (Traffic) in Delhi she was dubbed 'Crane Bedi' because of her relentless zeal in towing away illegally parked vehicles - including those of the CBI director and his sister-in-law.

She famously clashed with Delhi's lawyers, which resulted in the Wadhwa Commission finding her guilty of having instigated a mob attack. Yet, in one of her first postings, armed with a baton, she took on a sword-wielding Sikh crowd and prevented a riot. She seems to have made a habit of direct action and being indiscriminate about it. In Delhi she had a Congress

MP arrested and ordered a lathi charge on a BJP rally at the Red Fort.

No matter where she has been posted, she has left a stamp of her own.

Navjyoti was the brain child of Dr. (Ms) Kiran Bedi. She realized during her tenure as DCP North Delhi that more than half of the criminals apprehended were drug and substance abusers. Drug demand reduction as a crime preventive strategy was therefore envisaged by her with the ultimate aim of social development. In the process her idea was to redefine the role of the average policeman and mould him as a change agent. Navjyoti—'New Light' was thus founded in 1987 with the aim of guiding those lost in the last alleys of deadly addiction and crime from darkness into light. And, despite her other assignments, she continues to supervise its work as its general secretary. From drug deaddiction centre in nine Police Stations, it initiated a stitching centre for crime affected women in Yamuna Pushta, one of the largest slums in Delhi. Now Navjyoti's drug treatment cum rehabilitation center, programmes for street and working children, women development programmes welfare work among women in India's largest Tihar Jail and rural development.

The first lady police officer to lead the Republic Day parade, Kiran Bedi expressed her feeling, immense pride and a love for my country. This country which bestowed upon this honour, which made me capable of donning the police uniform. There is something in an uniform which evokes the feelings of patriotism and natural pride, and a true mind. If you love justice, this uniform will get justice out of you.

In this male dominated society, inspite of controversies, she has risen to heights. This year, in 1997 she has been conferred Joseph Bouys Award for creativity in Germany by an institution of German -Swiss - Collaboration.

This Magsaysay award-winning cop has come out on top, whatever the punishment posting.

Arundhati Roy Could Become First Indian Citizen to Win Booker

Arundhati Roy, author of the celebrated *The God of Small Things* could well become the first Indian citizen to win the Booker Prize for English fiction.

Princess of Prose Arundhati Roy

She brings recognition to and opens a global market for Anglo Indian writing.

"Roy stretches the Englsh language in all directions. With extraordinary linguistic inventiveness Roy funnels the history of South India through the eyes of seven-year-old twins". Booker Committee.

The sense of moral uprightness of a Christian Community seeps through in her book "The God of Small things".

A Kottayam gi'rl, Roy triumphed because she had the guts and the overwhelming 'talent to invent a new idiom and vocabulary to tell the story of a seemingly remote people. She has become now a Deity of Prose. Her achievement is never to forget the small things in life: insects, flowers, wind and water. She took Indian writing in English to a new height. She proved nothing is beyond Indian women's Reach.

Since its release in India on April 5, the book has created waves in international literacy circles, selling more than 350,000 copies. It has been or is being translated into 22 different languages, including all the European languages, besides Japanese and Korean.

Dr. Ms. Kalpana Chawla - First Indian Woman Astronaut

The first Indian American space astronaut has a doctorate in aerospace engineering from the University of Colorado. A mission specialist has been a member of six member crew and she is in space at present at a successful mission. This promising young girl has put new feather in India's fame.

Daredevil Kalpana from Haryana earned a unique place for Indian Women going into the orbit "dream journey".

Wing Commander (Mrs.) P. Bandopadhyay

Wing Commander (Mrs.) P. Bandopadhyay, VSM (11528) Med, was commissioned in Army Medical Corps (AMC) as a Lieutenant in Jan 68. As a Medical Officer she has held high stress portfolios.

She is presently posted at the Defence Institute of Physiology and Allied Sciences, New Delhi. She has been carrying out pioneer research work in High Altitude Physiology, Clinical Cardio Respiratory Physiology, Biofeed-back breathing exercises on improving muscular efficiency and chemoreceptor sensitivity to name a few.

She had been awarded numerous honours including Gold Medal in Medicine, Silver Medal in Physiology and Pathology and numerous other awards. During these sorties she has also been experiencing the combat stresses and monitoring the physiological changes in the aircrew.

First lady doctor to be awarded "Vishist Seva Medal" in 1973.

She was the first and the only Armed Forces Officer and the first lady medical officer cum scientist, ever to have undertaken a unique and remarkable "Arctic Mission" in the Indo-Soviet Project "HIMDOM".

Mahasweta Devi wins Magsaysay award

Mahasweta Devi, the Bengali novelist and champion of tribal communities, is a noted journalist, writer of unquestionable power and consumate artistry, she has been conferred Ramon Magsaysay Award for journalism, literature and creative communication arts in 1997. She lives her causes, often sacrificing her writing to do what she feels she must do. South Africa president Nelson Mandela gave the pestigious Jnanpith award for the year 1996 for her "outstanding contribution to the enrichment of the Indian literature" and donated the prize money to a tribal welfare society.

Her compassionate crusade through art and activism to claim for tribal peoples a just and honorable place in India's national life is widely acclaimed.

Indian Women Still Await Independence Women and Freedom Movement

In the first organized war of Independence in 1857, a woman, Lakshmi Bai, queen of Jhansi was in the forefront. In 1930, Tens of thousands of women joined the salt satyagraha of Gandhi. In the South, the Salt March that culminated in Madras was led by a woman Rukmini Lakshmipati. In Quit

India movement, when most of the menfolk were in prison, women came to the forefront and took charge of the struggle. It was not only a display of courage and daring but they showed a tremendous organizational power.

Although men have accepted the fact that a woman can work, that she can be another source of income in a poor family, the average Indian women is by no means independent.

The rural women has remained within the confines of her home. Structures are still patriarchal. The decision-making process has been dominated by men.

Women are becoming a party to the destruction of their own species as they are unable to break out of the vicious circle of undervaluation by others and by themselves.

What we really have to do is to start a movement and change the attitudes of people toward women. That can actually change the crime rate, the infant mortality rate and the status of a woman at home.

"Everything associated with divinity is referred to as 'Mata' when we are all born, we have no cognizance of our existence. Yet, we cling to our mothers instinctively. She gives a sense of protection, a feeling of security. That innate faith makes her our First God."

In Rig Vedic Society women were equal, if not superior, to men.

यस्तु सर्वाणि भूतान्यात्मन्येवा नुपश्यति, सर्वभूतेषु चात्मानं ततो न विजुगुप्सते।

He who sees all beings in the self itself, and the self in all beings, feels no hatred by virtue of that realisation.

ISA Upnishad

"It is better to be the widow of a hero than the wife of a coward."

—Dolores Ibarrun (1937)

World Religions and Equality - Hindu Tradition - Copenhagen – UN Forum

There have been many religions in the world since creation some have disappeared, some have survived and some are just existing. Whatever may be the reasons for this one can never argue that one religion is better than another religion. All religions seek the same. Actually what is religion? Etymologically religion is one which devotes the human beings ties to divinity but then the question comes what is divinity? What is Divine? Is there a god? If so where? How is he/she/it who has seen god. We shall not go into those hair splitting problems. Let us not call the Divine as God - Jesus Christ, Rama or Krishna or Buddha or Mohammed.

We will call that power which controls this world which controls the sun and moon and earth, that controls the seas and skies, the destinies of man, women, animals and kingdoms that controls the working system of the world as Divine. This miraculous undiscovered power, we call it Divine. You can call this Divine in whatever way you like just as you call your child as baby, darling and duckling - call this divine power by any name you like Jesus, Mohammed or Rama. These gods talk in the same language and all the religious tenets explained by them are also same. Fundamentally there are no differences between the religious tenets. What I say religion I am saying religion as a religion deviod of customs, beliefs and superstitions. Somehow when you look back at the history of Religions we discover the decline of religion in this century since the world. Why? Let us ask ourselves? The answer is not simple. May be it is a vicious circle that we cannot answer, today. If there was no decline of religion there might not have been wars and if there were not wars there might not have been the decline of religion.

Practically today all religions are really dead or about to die. Their graves are ready. But suddenly people have woken up to the gravity of the situation and there is a great show of resurgence of religion all over the world. It is evident every where latently and blatently. Will a new religion evolve from the death of old religions? Will a new world religion evolve to save the world? Let us think about it leisurely when we get back home. But now let us think and discuss if this new resurgence of religion likely to effect the status of women. The resurgence of religion and religiousity - now evident world wide introduces a new and unrespected element in the way of influences with which the women's movement has to cope with. Therefore it is very likely that the new element will effect in some unknown fashion the status of women. In olden days have the religions affected the status of women? May be they did. May be they did not. I am standing here before you today to tell you how my religion - Hinduism had affected and what influence it had on the status of women.

On this matter there are two conflicting and contradictory theories among the people of the world. There are some who believe that Hindu religion is very strict, conservative and turned Hindu women into slaves. There is another traditional belief that Hindu women were kept on a pedestal as Godesses and ardhanariswari and were divinified. Both these beliefs are extreme. If both the beliefs are true then Hindu women are slaves or divinified lost all humanity.

A Hindu woman is a very difficult woman to understand. She is an enigma - the byproduct of Hindu religion, Indian culture which has embraced multifarious cultures.

Newspaper Clippings Courtsey MCM Library (Post — Beijing)

Chinese Women Fall Prey to Western Ways

V Radhika, Beijing

Women Groups in China are voicing concern over the growing commercialisation of Chinese society, and consider it an insidious trend that does not augur well for Chinese women.

The advent of the 'Pepsi-Madonna' culture as a consequence of the opening up of China's economy will, in their opinion, have adverse repercussions on the role and status of Chinese women.

Representatives of various groups participating in the NGO forum meeting at Huairou feel that many girls in China have "fallen prey to the lure of designer clothes and Western culture, a .culture which is extremely biased against women and views them merely as commodities to be used by men." What disturbs the participants at the forum the most is that dress sense among the young girls is China's metropolises are guided by what in fashionable circles is *haute coutre* rather than by what they are more comfortable in.

"Just a couple of years ago, young girls in Beijing were concerned with their studies and career. But increasingly it is found that an increasing number of girls are more pre- occupied with the latest dress in the market, which hair-do they should sport and finally whether their boyfriend or boyfriends will like it or not," said a professor from the University of Beijing.

The activists said that while they were not opposed to girls wearing good clothes and mixing freely with the boys, they were concerned about the emergence of a culture which lays too much emphasis on physical appearance and turns women "into commodities to be used by others."

Some university teachers who spoke to this reporter said that many girls experience a feeling of insecurity and rejection as they are not able to fit into this culture. The phenomenon is more pronounced in the case of students who migrate from the rural provinces.

"It is a common sight to see girls discussing their lipsticks, clothes, hair-do and so on.

What upsets me is that most of the time they are not doing it for themselves but to please their boyfriends," said a member of the All-China Women's Federation.

Incidentally, it is only in the last two years that women's issues have emerged as a separate area of concern in China. There have been speculations about whether it is a consequence of China playing host to the UN Conference on Women or if many women genuinely feel the need for a gender sensitivity.

Nonetheless, there is a widespread appreciation among women's organisation from other parts of the world that finally Chinese women are willing to talk about issues and problems faced by them.

Some of the issues that several women's organisations in China are going to take up in this meeting are human rights domestic violence, molestation and sexual harassment in public places like subways, public transport, female foeticide which is widely prevalent in rural areas and also the problem of girl-children dropping out of school.

Many women feel that with the advent of multinational corporations the issue of sexual harrasment in offices is also going to become important.

China has a very adverse sex-ratio of 85 girls for every 100 boys.

One of the main contributory factors is the preference for a male-child which is due to customs and traditions which are in men's favour. The Government policy of one child in urban aeas and two children in rural areas has also contributed to the adverse ratio. According to a member of the China Women Prosecutors Association, despite a Government ban, ultra-sound scanning to disclose the sex of a child and abortions continue.

The Pioneer

5 September, 1995

The Beijing Carnival

It needs more than a lion's heart not to take a Women's congregation anywhere with dead seriousness. And a conference under the United Nations auspices must usually be beyond reproach. It is thus that the great conference about to conclude at China's capital, Beijing, will go down in history as a platform where action for women's uplift was dreamed, and left to be fulfilled. The UN conference in Beijing-both the official one and the other at the level of non-governmental organisations—proved yet again that to talk of women's rights and equal opportunities for them is still a fashion in which females noisily assert themselves and males mockingly surrender, both with full knowledge that at the end of the day things would remain unchanged demanding no adjustments from either side. The Beijing meet held a great promise for publicity bonanza for the Chinese government, which had an opportunity to show (through BBC and other outlets) how this ancient Asian society has left behind its legacy of female torture in the form of cramping a woman's feet just to satisfy male fantasy. What publicity, and of what kind, China will derive finally is still to be assessed. Mrs Hillary Rodham Clinton did her bit to paint China in dark hues, in furtherance of her husband's US policy to shoot down Beijing's human rights record. There was an assortment of so-called rights' activists, including those championing the lesbians' rights, clamouring for social acceptance by governments across the world.

Beyond the cardinal fact that women must be treated as equals of men—a tragic social lag in this nobody realises more acutely than one in a poor country - Beijing had no other message to get across. But this message got enmeshed in all kinds of irrelevances. Nothing proved more pointedly how sharply does the world stand divided between women in the poor part of the globe and those in its richer districts, and how ready is the UN to endorse the unrealities or rights and abuses for the females. Even the Vatican's withdrawal of opposition to women's sexual freedom and the Islamic governments' compromise on women's rights are unlikely to change the world greatly. In a male-dominated world where an overwhelming number of men themselves remain without basic rights, equal rights for women are at best a dream and, at worst, the first task of development in a poor society. UN jamborees with 23,000 females overwhelming a city, as they did to Beijing, will remain international carnivals with little resolve to achieve a strong social objective. Women's uplift, through ruthless moral, legal and social action, must continue to be the prime objective of the poor world for the basic task of development. The sooner the world realises this fact, the better would it succeed in getting down to its task, leaving the fashionable picnics of the Beijing type for the rich women to enjoy.

The Hindustan Times
6 September, 1995

Women divided over 'family values'

Beijing, Sept. 5. After an opening-day display of unity in the struggle for women's equality debate flared today at the UN women's conference on the hot topic of family values, reports AP.

The gathering was energised by the appearance of one of the world's most famous women: Mrs Hillary Rodham Clinton, who won a standing ovation when she appealed for better access to health care for women and girls.

As the Fourth World Conference on Women moved into a second day, the nearly 5,000 official delegates were splitting into working groups to begin debating the conference's proposed platform, which calls for steps to alleviate women's poverty and improve health care, education and job opportunities for women.

In the opening salvo of what is expected to be a major battle, the Vatican today complained that the draft document gives short shrift to the family.

Vatican spokesman Joaquin Navarro told reporters in Beijing that the word 'family' appears only four times in the 120-page document. Because the overwhelming majority of the world a women marry and have children, he said, that amounts to "imbalance".

Pakistan Prime Minister Benazir Bhutto, too, said she hoped to see more in the document about the traditional family.

"The more close-knit the family is, the more close-knit society itself will be" she said.

However, she said it was important for the conference to focus on areas of agreement such as the need for, more job and educational opportunities for women.

Women's health was the main theme of Mrs Clinton's conference debut, a speech to a panel on that subject.

"In too many places, the status of women's health is a picture of human suffering and pain," she told an audience of about 500 that included actress Jane Fonda.

The First Lady, making a two-day visit, was expected to push for improved human rights worldwide without, specifically singling out conference host China, which is tokchy about its running dispute with the Clinton administration on human rights.

Huairou: Women activists at the grassroot forum on women here today staged a mass protest against the French decision to resume nuclear tests in the Pacific calling for a global boycott of French goods, an AFP report said.

About 200 women from various NGO's protesting outside the Peace tent on the forum site, also condemned the forum host nation China for conducting its second nuclear test in August.

They rammed their anti-nuclear message home by brandishing banners demanding a stop to all nuclear tests. The women NGO representatives said they would officially present letters to the governments of China and France, demanding that they abandon all nuclear testing and nuclear weapons.

Indian Express

6 September, 1995

Delegates differ, but not on 'gender'

Aditi Kapoor

Beijing, Sept. 5. The United Nations is being accused of "turning into a one language organisation" as French delegates in the main committee today disputed the language of the platform of action when translated from English to French in what may become an extended debate on the language of the various documents before the committee. The honourable delegates also disagreed on how to incorporate formerly agreed language of UN conferences on key terms-verbatim or changed to suit the new document. The group, however, agreed upon the commonly accepted meaning of the threatened term 'gender'.

***

The Pakistan NGOs were taken aback when their prime minister Benazir Bhutto announced to the world yesterday that her country had agreed to sign the UN Convention on the Elimination of Discrimination Against Women (CEDAW). "The issue was being debated but obviously this has been a last minute decision," Pakistan NGO delegate Nilfoer Bakhtair fold a conference newspaper. "I did not know of it when I boarded the plane."

***

South African president's estranged wife Winnie Mandela faced the Chinese love for security and systems in its full glory at the welcome ceremony at Beijing yesterday. She came late to the function and was stopped at the gates of the Great Hallkof the People from entering the auditorium. Reports say there was almost a fist -fight between her group and the Chinese security guards when as the delegates inside spoke of peace and love for mankind. The lady left the city this morning to meet some of her country women at the more informal NGO venue in Hauirou.

***

With over 350 discussion groups being held at Huairou every day and 60 parallel events at the UN conference in Beijing besides cultural programmes, press conferences and rendezvous with old and new friends, the hosts have offered the delegate a way to relax their aching bodies. In the last six days, an estimated 10,000 delegates have tried their feet on *Photo,* a magic instrument on which one can rest their feet and slowly ease the pain out. "It's new and intriguing but a great gift," says Hogan from New Zealand.

The Times of India

6 September, 1995

No more violence please, say women

Mona Eltahawy

Beijing, (WFS) Sept. 7. Their names did matter. Hundreds of women in black came from all walks of life to stand in candlelit silence for an hour to mourn violence against women and to share stories of their pain.

The fact the Chinese police would not let the women take their march a few steps out of the NGO Forum area made their pleas all the more poignant.

While they kept their silence, their banners spoke to condemn the violence they had gathered to expose.

"Don't sell women's bodies to sell your products" "Real men don't rape". "Fight poverty, not the poor."

After their hour's silence ended, the women spoke of their experiences.

"We wear black to protest violence against women. This candle symbolises bringing light to those women who are in darkness. There are millions of women at homes still in darkness so we speak for them," said one women from India.

"I am a comfort woman from the Philippines. I was a victim of rape and sexual slavery during World War II and I appeal to you to stop wars because we had a very painful experience at the hands of the Japanese army and American soildiers," said another.

"I come from Cyprus. In my country we have been divided for 21 years. We have 200,00 refugees, we have missing people. I am a refugee in a divided island. We want the human right issues to be a primary issue of this conference and we demand solidarity and peace," said another.

It is estimated that in many countries, one quarter to more than one half of women have been physically abused by a present or former partner.

According to a United Nations fact sheet, a quarter of female gynaecological patients in Norway have been sexually abused by their partners, one in five women in the United States has been raped, in the biggest slum in Bangkok, half of all married women are beaten regularly and in Peru 70 per cent of all crimes reported to police are of women beaten by their husbands.

During wars, women and children make up the bulk of refugees and invading armies have for centuries raped the enemies' women.

Several years ago, Palestinian and Israeli women began wearing black and demonstrating against the violence of the Arab-Israeli conflict.

Their protests became the inspiration for women all over the world, many of whom now march every Thursday and on International Human Rights Day on December 10.

"I am from the islands of the Pacific. Whatever violence you face in your own country from the army or from your own men, we have the same problem. When you are crying we are crying also because we identify with all your misery as women," one woman emotionally told the gathering.

For the next two weeks, delegates will focus on violence against women as one of 12 areas of concern that governments around the world must address.

One protestor from New Zealand sent an urgent appeal to the official conference. "Let the media and all those present portray to those sitting at the conference that their conscience, their moral values and all those things they hold dear with their families be the guidelines to the decisions they make."

The women, singing "we shall overcome," marched along the main road of the NGO Forum and then stood face-to face for almost an hour with Chinese police who told them that marching outside the area was in violation of Chinese law.

Not everyone at the march was in black. A Kenyan woman wearing a dress splashed with bright yellow explained her choice of attire, "I decided not to wear black because I am black and I wanted to wear a dress to show that the sun shall rise. There is hope no matter how subjugated or hopeless we feel," she told the marchers. "We cannot lose hope, here in Beijing. "In the midst of all of you, we feel that the sun shall rise."

The Hindustan Times

8 September, 1995

Indians urge comprehensive health care for women

V. Radhika

The activists demanded that women's right to comprehensive health care should be included in paragraph 94 of the document which talks about the right of women to control their fertility. The final prep-corn meeting in New York in March could not achieve a consensus on the term "control their fertility" and hence it was bracketed. And when the paragraph came up for discussion, the working group not only removed the bracket but also agreed to the activiss demand pertaining to all aspects of health care.

The demand for comprehensive health care has also been voiced by the African delegates and they welcomed its conclusion as "a step in the right direction". The activists have scored another victory of sorts on the issue of clinical trails involving women. While the draft document had restricted itself to clinical trials of contraceptives, the working group has decided to include all drugs, including contraceptives.

The other areas on which Indian activists are actively lobbying now at various levels are transparency, commitment from developed countries for seven per cent of GNP as development aid, debt reduction and cancellation.

Agencies add: "WE ARE determined, we will achieve", the world's largest women's gathering, the non-governmental organisations (NGO) form meet—closed here on Friday on these words amid music, dance and speeches-all on a solemn note.

Sans the festivity of the opening ceremony, the crowd that stood braving the rains at the outdoor Kuumba stage area only capsuled the experiences of resolution and friendship-strengthened and developed over the past eight days.

The Pioneer,
9 September, 1995

NGOs meet closes with call for equality

A raucous grass-roots women's forum with a spectacular pageant and one final spat over security, leaving the stage to the United Nations conference where religious conservatives and feminists were locked in a battle for the future of sexual equality, report agencies.

Meanwhile, simmering tensions over freedom of expressionane threatening to boil over at the Fourth World Women conference, as tightly policed China shows increasing impatience with the debate and dissent the meet has brought.

Chinese authorities breathed a sigh of relief at the end of the 10-day grassroots meeting where thousands of delegates from non-governmental organisations posed a constant security threat with their freewheeling ways.

The forum was deliberately isolated in a rural suburb, one hour from central Beijing so that Capital residents were not exposed to demonstrations, discussions and issues rarely raised in Communist China's tightly controlled society.

There were hugs, tears and vows to meet again as women activists from more than 150 nations said farewell. But an Australian dance troupe was blocked by security men from performing because it is affiliated with Amnesty International and includes in its story an account of a Tibetan nun jailed for opposing Chinese rule in Tibet.

Many women said they had endured harassment, heavy-handed security and police surveillance throughout the meeting.

But at a news conference organised on the last morning, several women complained that western press reports only picked up "negative factors" and failed to see "productive things" from the forum.

At the main conference site, tight security regained the spotlight when police detained briefly a Hong Kong television crew after a scuffle during presentation of a human rights petition.

Xinhua said the incident erupted when cameraman Au-Yeung Cham hit a guard who was trying to stop a protest march from obstructing traffic.

Inside the hall where the biggest event UN meeting is taking place, battles of a different kind were under way.

They involved decisions on whether to keep phrases enclosed in so-called "holy brackets" in a declaration be issued at the end of the conference and which is meant to set the agenda for women's right in the next 10 years.

The battles primarily involved disputes about whether modern views of women's rights should take precedence over traditional religious and other practices.

With one week to go before the declaration is issued, only about 10 per cent of 430 bracketed items have been solved, a UN spokeman told the media.

In a protest on the conference grounds, about 10 women carried a petition with more than a million signatures, urging the UN to implement a 1993 human rights declaration. Plainclothsmen stepped in, trying to get the women to fold up posters showing a woman with her mouth gagged.

Indian Express

9 September 1995

China profits by meet

The Chinese made the most of the opportunity by selling their handicrafts, says

Promilla Kalhan

There appears to have been a good deal of entertainment for the delegates at the NGO get-together at Huairou, China, as well as at Beijing a week later. Shrewd business-persons as they are, the Chinese made the most of the opportunity to display and sell not only Chinese food but their famous silks and watches to the world's women. Special shops for these items came up in both the towns.

The only English language daily brought out in China entitled *China Daily* thoughtfully published *Worlds Women,* a mini-sized daily covering all aspects of the United Nations Fourth World Conference on Women and the NGO forum. It carried prominent ads of Chinese silk, sold at a China Silk fair which did not restrict itself to silk but had on sale ready-made garments, knitted underwear, bed linen, embroidered table linen and clothes, cosmetics and hand-painted textiles.

From all accounts, the nearly 40,000 women gathered for the conference lapped it all up. They returned to their respective countries loaded with bundles. The more serious among them, a fraction of the lot, did also indulge in women's favourite pastime, shopping, but they fulfilled their duty of attending workshops and discussions on women's equality, still a dream, which was the purpose of the World Conference.

While talking to some of the Indian delegates on their return from the conference in China, it was evident that there were some differences in perceptions concerning their goals even among the Asian women. According to Aparna Basu, secretary general, of the All India Women Conference and those from South-East Asia.

To the latter solidarity among the family is important, therefore, women in those countries do not wish to stand up against male dominance. "It is different with us," says Basu, adding "We are stressing that the dominance of man must end. There are differences between the current status of women in South East Asia and India. In China, there is almost 80 to 90 per cent literacy among the women there. Elsewhere, in the region it is around 80 to 85 per cent and of the women are literate. Moreover, women here are drowned in poverty."

Pious intentions expressed at world women's conferences about improving Women's position is one thing but getting their suggestions' implemented is another. Where are the funds to come from? According to one delegate, all the countries in the world should restructure their existing budget priorities to earmark 20 per cent of their budgets, as has been recommended by the UN, to five priority areas, namely universal basic education, universal primary health care, safe drinking water, adequate nutrition for the malnourished and essential family planning services for all willing couples.

Donor countries from the ad advanced world should help the developing countries with funds saved from reducing military spending and other high profile expenditure to the extent of one third of poor countries' needs she added.

Special administrative provision must be made for violence against women and special police and family courts should be set up for the quick disposal of such cases. India has a law whereby a rape culprit can be locked up in jail for seven years. If it is a custodial rape, the punishment to the offender is 10 years in jail. But laws on paper alone are not sufficient. It is doubtful if many culprits are punished. They either disappear or are not proceeded against by poverty-stricken victims.

The Beijing conference has done one thing if little else, it has spread awareness of the fact that of the 1.3 billion people living in poverty more than 70 per cent are women which is the tragic consequence of women's unequal access to economic opportunities.

Inhuman customs like sati have largely been curbed in India. But there seems to be an increase in rape cases. Issues specific to the developing world were not of very great importance to the developed countries at Beijing. This is proved by the fact that debt relief and poverty elimination still remain in brackets in the Platform of Action of the UN.

While some delegates felt that if nothing else, the Beijing Conference brought about awareness of the problems of women, there are others like Suhasini Ali of the Democratic Women's Association who feels that both India's country paper and the UN's Platform of Action document left much to be desired. "India's country paper did not even mention religious fundamentalism as an obstacle to womens progress, she said and added that "what we need is structural transformation, not structural adjustment."

Others felt that the new economic policy had only added to women's woes by raising the prices of food and other items of daily use. This matter was raised at the NGO meet.

But advanced countries looking for new markets in India were not enthusiastic about the matter. Indian delegates like

Ali emphasised that in India the rich may be getting richer but the poor were never so badly off as they are today.

This is proved by the fact that in cities like Delhi not only rag pickers but others as well can be seen rummaging for left-over food at garbage dumps.

Both Ali and Hamida Habibullah, president of the Indian Council of Child Welfare felt that more funds should be directed towards welfare activities, that family planning methods should be properly tested before being offered for mass distribution.

Shobhana Ranadey president of the All India Women's Conference hits out at the plans for privatisation of education which "turns this human right into a profit-making industry". She also criticised increasing military spending, one of the main constraints in economic growth and empowerment of women.

Tough battle ahead for women

Ela Dutt

Beijing, Sept 11- Even as women are overjoyed by some major strides made in the field of sexual rights, their implementation is going to be one of the toughest battles they will have to fight in the coming days.

Governments hammering out the 'Beijing declaration, and the 'Platform for Action' have agreed over the weekend to some radical language specially in the section on health.

It reads, "The human rights of women include their rights to have control over and to decide freely and responsibly on the matters related to discrimination, and violence."

Originally, Governments of many Islamic and Catholic countries and others had difficulty considering any language that indicated sexual freedom for women. Their understanding of sexual rights was limited by a perception that it was meant to engender promiscuity and license. But years of hard work by women delegates and Non-Governmental Organizations has succeeded in conveying the broad-based meaning of sexuality and the total health status of women and their right to protect their health and well-being.

The victory over the weekend signifies a significant change in the understanding of most Governments of the world. Saudi Arabia, however, known for some of the most prohibitive regulations on women behavior, is not attending the conference.

"Equal relationships between women and men in matters of sexual relations and reproduction, including full respect for their integrity of the person, require mutual respect, consent and shared responsibility, for sexual behaviour and its consequences," the lines of para 97 read on.

"For those of us who've been through Cairo and Copenhagen (Women's Conferences held in 1980 and 1985 respectively), this really is a great step forward," asserted Ms. Gita Sen, who reported to the NGOs attending the briefing yesterday. The section on sexual language was reached because of the general accomodating approach adopted by countries on both the right and the left of the issue.

In fact, the conference has been largely characterised by this consensus approach because 1995 is regarded as the eve of the 21 Century, by which time countries appear to believe they must advance the status of their women and empower them. The most insurmountable aspect is the part where countries must put their money where their mouth is. Extra resources are going to be very hard to come by to translate some of the objectives of the conference into action. Meanwhile, NGOs have set up a scoreboard on the commitments made by various Governments. From the 23 speeches they have so far analysed. India has committed itself to new initiatives in education, health, advancement of women, women's human rights, and the rights of the girl child.

The sexual rights agreed to in the document, are however, going to prove the hardest to implement because they require the greatest intrusion either by Governments or other entities into the lives of individual families. In a country like the United States, for instance, it could provoke lawsuits where ironically, organizations like the American Civil Liberties Union might have to protect individual rights or the right to privacy. And in countries like India, forcing compliance at the family level will be most difficult just as any legislation, for instance dowry, has not seen the result intended even after a decade.

Women's groups are already planning strategies in Beijing for the oncoming years after they get back home from here.

The Statemen

12 September, 1995

In Beijing - a Cry from the heart

By Shilu Ranganathan

Beijing, Sept 11. "Equality, Development and Peace" are the words emblazoned on every available space, on posters, on banners, on arches, on flags, on bundings, on doors, on windows, in restaurants, in bars, theatres, in department stores, all over Haiurou and Beijing. They are not merely words, but a cry from the heart of each one of the 31,000 women from 2000 organisations in 200 countries who converged on the suburfs of Haiurou 60 kms from one of the world's most modern city, Beijing, the capital of the Peoples' Republic of China. They came with hope in their hearts to voice their views on major global issues and problems facing women. The full impact of the mammoth gathering has yet to be felt in the rest of the world, but in Haiurou the feeling of accomplishment and resolve are expressed all round and delegations are leaving for home with optimism and hope for the future of mankind.

The Beijing NGO Forum was the most successful, and the alternate days of hot sunshine and monsoon rain failed to put a damper on the spirits of this massive gathering of Women, unprecedented in post War history. The first NGO forum in Mexico City in 1975, was attended by a mere 3,000, the second in Copenhagen drew 8,000 and the third at Nairobi attracted 13,000. As a preparatory to the Fourth World Conference on Women convened by the United Nations at Beijing from 4-15 Sept. 1995, the NGO Forum programme covered almost 5,000 events, starting the day with plenaries, going on to workshops, training, lectures, exhibitions, with cultural shows at the end of the day.

The tone of the conference was set on the very first day, the highlight of the plenary being a video-recording of an hour-long message from Aung Suu Kyui, heard in pindrop silence by a crowd of 4,000 women, standing shoulder to shoulder in the hall of the Haiurou International Conference Centre built to comfortably accommodate 2,000 people. Each morning after an early beakfast, women assembled at the bus-stops alongside their place of stay, around 9 a.m. They were taken to the NGO Forum site, from where they proceeded on foot to the Global Tent, the hub of conference activities, housing a desk for every need. This tent, was sea of colour and hummed with activity till late in the night. These women converged on the Global Tent from 32 hotels and 60 apartment houses to attend 200 daily workshops held in 75 meeting rooms and 86 tents. Most women walked around holding maps aloft or looking for volunteers, specially those clad in yellow T-shirts, special to the interpreters.

Workshops were on women's participation in political affairs, economic development, human ecology, poverty, women's rights, racial and ethnic issues, health care, violence against women, media representation of women, science and technology and helping women to reach their potential. The plenary session every morning at the Haiurou International Conference Centre saw Supatro Masdit, forum convener, introducing speakers ranging from women ministers, leaders of various NGO groups and expert U.N. policy makers. They analysed global factors with impact on society and proposed strategies for social transformation.

Women participants from grass-root organisations were among the most active at the forum. The Arab tent focussed on denial of human rights to Bosnia. Burqa-clad women from the most fundamentalist society in the world marched arm in arm with women clad in salwars, jeans, and skirts.

Serious discussions, lectures and workshops were not the only was to express ideas. Plays, pantomimes, processions, music, dance and singing were a common means of expression. "We don't want war" was a cry heard every-where. "Give up nuclear testing — have you forgotten the horror of Hiroshima?" The consensus of the Forum was "Without peace, there is no equality and without peace, development is only a house of cards."

The Hindu

12 September, 1995

Beijing and Beyond

The final platform of action hammered out after days of intense acrimony at the UN conference on women at Beijing unfortunately contains nothing that could be considered path-breaking on the very crucial issues that confront women. So engrossed were the thousands of delegates with ensuring that sections of the draft which did not meet with their opproval do not get passed that much of what should have been stated was overlooked. Many issues of tremendous complexity were but touched upon in passing, with delegates wrangling bitterly on topics like sexual freedom at the cost of discussing literacy, political participation, economic equality and health care which are denied to millions of women all over the world. It was obvious from the start that the enshriing of sexual freedom in the final declaration would be opposed by the Islamic nations, the Catholic West and other developing nations since this is not a priority area for them and, is, infact, against their cultural norms. However, the point which was reiterated and correctly so was that the abuse of women in any form cannot be concrete plan of action which will realise the UN goals articulated at the Nairobi conference ten years ago, the Beijing meet has not helped unwilling governments to tackle the problems which concern women. If the target of equality by 2000 put forward at the Nairobi meet was unrealistic, it is so all the more now.

In many issues concerning women, it would be no exaggeration to say that there has been a move backward with fundamentalists and conservatives gaining ground in many parts of the world. However, though the indicators of disadvantage in employment, earning, inheritance and violence are dramatic, it is obvious that there is also a growing acceptance of the role of women in all fields. And this was the track on which the grassroots workers who attended the meeting, though at a different venue, focussed on. If there is one positive gain from the conference, it is that it provided grassroots workers from all over the world a great opportunity to network and develop new ideas and campaigns. However, if their activism and dynamism have not come across very clearly, it is perhaps because the spotlight has dwelt disproportionately on issues like Ms Hillary Clinton's attack on human rights in

China and the views of powerful women's lobbies pushing their own narrow interests. The gulf between the Third World and the privileged western societies was less obvious at the NGOs meet as was the divide between the fundamentalist opinion and mainstream views. Official delegations, it is now clear at conference after conference, are often hostage to the powerful lobbies that use such meetings to further their own agendas whether relating to opposing-abortion or to the promotion of sexual freedom. If the voices of those at the grassroots who daily confront the problems that afflict the world's dispossessed women get greater prominence at future meets, it will service to eliminate some of the biases that hold women back.

The Hindustan Times,
16 September, 1995

Beijing meet adopts documents

Beijing, Sept. 15 (PTI) India today stole the show at the concluding session of the Fourth World Women Conference which adopted the two final documents through consensus, despite reservations expressed by Islamic countries and the Vatican over sexual reproductive rights.

India received a thunderous applause as its leader, Mrs Sarla Gopalan, said that the country had no reservation in the adoption of the three-page Beijing declaration and the bulky 145-page "Platform for Action".

The Indian Secretary for Women and Child Development, Mrs. Gopalan was the first speaker at the concluding session to say it had no reservation towards the adoption of the document listing a plan of action for development of women.

Before Mrs. Gopalan, representations of 27 Islamic and Catholic countries, particularly those from Latin America, expressed reservations but aqreed on the adoption by consensus of the political document listing a plan of action for development of women.

Shyamala Shiveshwakar adds

The main committee which concluded its final meeting at 4.45 a.m. has cleared the remaining contentious portions in the draft Platform for Action and the Beijing Declaration that will be adopted at the final plenary session later today.

While resolving such difficult issues as financial resources and macro-economic measures for eradication of poverty, the committee also tried to sort out the differences relating to the sovereign responsibilities of nations in implementing the draft platform which makes references to full respect for all religious and ethical values, cultural back-ground and political convictions.

A footnote on this was put up for consideration to the drafts global framework. Several delegations had said that if the footnote was not included in the section on health they would have to express their reservations at the plenary session. Meanwhile several others had called for its deletion. Since no consensus could be reached, even after an hour-and-a-half of discussions, the chairman ruled that it should be delated.

The other contentious issues concerning Sexual orientation was finally removed from the draft. However, the committee approved the text which reaffirmed that reproductive right rests on the recognition of the basic right of all couples and individuals to decide freely and responsibly the number, spacing and timing of their children and to have the information and means to do so. It also approved the text calling for the elimination of gender-based violence and all forms of sexual harassment, prostitution, pornography, sexual slavery and exploitation in eluding violations resulting from cultural prejudice, racism, xenophobic ethnic cleansing, religious and anti-religious extremism and international trafficking in women and children.

The draft Beijing Declaration that has been approved by the committee also expresses the determination of Governments to assure peace for women and recognise the role that women have played in the peace movement, work towards peace and complete disarmament under strict and effective international control, support negotiations on the conclusion of a universal and multilaterally and effectively veriable nuclear test ban treaty and intensify efforts and action to achieve the goals laid down at the Nairobi meet.

Alternative Declaration

Dissatisfied with the 'weak' language and the backsliding in the Declaration being negotiated by the government representatives, the NGOs, late lastnight, released an "interim version" of an alternate Beijing "Declaration".

Contending that the "declaration" represents what millions women around the world wasnt out of this conference, they called on all Governments to recognise and ensure women's equal rights to a decent standard of iving as agreed in the Internal Government of Economic, Social and Cultural Rights.

Differences may weaken Beijing document

No sooner has delegates approved an ambitious UN blueprint for achieving women's equality than governments began opting out of its obligations.

"No duplicity or hypocrisy here. It's part of a UN-ordained method, known as expressing reservations," for achieving consensus while allowing disagreement with policy guidelines.

The 189 governments at the UN women's conference adopted its platform for action and declaration of principles by consensus on Friday. No vote was taken.

Many of the more than 40 countries that took exception to parts of document began their speeches by saluting that spirit of cooperation.

"My delegation submits to the consensus underpinning the declaration and 'platform' a representative from Ethiopia said in a typical prelude before voicing reservations. Speakers during the 12-day conference's final session were not identified by name, but by country.

Ethiopia objected to what it felt was the platform's emphasis on sexual freedom at the expense of health, education and other issues.

Predominantly Roman Catholic and Islamic countries made up most of the dissenters. Those governments previously said they disagreed with the references to sexual freedom because they felt it encouraged promiscuity, undermined the traditional family and condoned abortion.

In UN parlance, reservations allow governments to announce they will not abide by parts of the documents without rejecting it in whole. The platform is not binding but serves as a guide to governments and voluntary organizations.

While some delegations objected to specific sections, many Muslim countries, such as Kuwait, said they would reject all parts contrary to Islamic law and custom.

The Philippines and several other delegations noted that abortion was illegal in their countries and would continue to be so, despite the platform's call for adequate reproductive health care.

"During earlier sessions, when countries stated their intention to reserve," some delegations said the large number of objections would weaken the final document.

Angered by the lack of access and the extra fees they had to pay, disabled women at the world conference on women demanded a refund on Friday from the United Nations.

"We feel very bitter because our exclusion has been so blatant."

Several dozen disabled people attended the UN Women's conference. — AP

—The Pioneer,

17 September '95

Time to Speak out

"GO to China and stand up for American values."

An American veteran to World War II said these words to me as I was leaving the V-J Day observances in Hawaii last weekend to go to Beijing for the United Nations Fourth World Conference on Women.

A few days later, as I stood before the conference delegates preparing to give a keynote address, the veteran's words came back to me, Looking out at the sea of faces representing nearly every country in the world, I appreciated even more the privilege of living in a free society As an American, life, liberty and the pursuit of happiness are my birth rights and they are birth rights of all Americans, the rights we take for granted are fought for and died for around the world.

If some countries, citizens are not allowed to vote, speak their minds, assemble freely or exercise their faith without fear of persecution, arrest or even torture. These are what we commonly think of as violations of human rights. But, as the women's conference taught us, it is also a violation of human rights when, in countries, around the world, women and girl are valued less, fed less, fed last, overworked, underpaid, not schooled and beaten up.

If one message rang clear from the conference, it is that women's rights are human rights. And human rights are women rights when babies are denied food, or drowned, or suffocated, or their spines broken simply because they are born girls. It is a violation of human rights when women and girls are sold into the slavery of prostitution, sometimes by their own brothers and fathers.

It is violation of human rights when a leading cause of death worldwide among women ages 14 to 44 is the violence they are subjected to in their own homes. It is a violation of human rights when young girls are brutalised by the painful and degrading practice of genital mutilation, which happens to millions of women in Africa.

It is a violation of human rights when women are denied the right to plan their own families, and that includes being forced to have abortions or being sterilised against their will.

Today, women bear the brunt of human rights violations around the world. As long as those violations persist - and discrimination and inequities remain commonplace - a peaceful and prosperous life is sadly beyond our reach.

One reason we have not progressed further is that so many women have been afraid to speak up and speak out. As I said to the conference delegates, it is time to break the silence so that women every where have a greater say in the future we share. As different as we may be, there is more that unites then divides us. The conference proved that.

I am grateful that on behalf of our country I had the opportunity to attend this conference with men and women from all over the world who are committed to speaking out and taking action against abuses and injustices that fly in the face of human rights.

If we take bold steps to better the lives of women, we will be taking bold steps to better the lives of children and families too. Families rely on mothers and wives for emotional support and care. Families rely on women for labour in the home. And increasingly, families rely on women or income needed to raise healthy children and care for other relatives.

The women's conference by itself won't change any lives. But I hope that, by encouraging people to take notice of these issues, it will help lead us to a world in which every women and girl is given the respect and dignity she deserves.

The Hindu
17 September, 1995

Women's meet hailed

Beijing, Sept. 16 — The United Nation's conference on women, which ended here last night was a jump-start for the 21st century, Bella Abzug, the former American Congress woman, said. Women would be the leaders of the next century.

Betty Friedan, the author of "The Feminine Mystique", published in the 1960s, said she believed that the U.N.'s Fourth World Conference on Women and the Non-Governmental Organizations' Forum on Women that preceded it in Hauirou, 35 miles northeast of Beijing, could give rise to a woman's "movement in China, or at least to a further expression of democracy.

"I had to climb over a wail to get into our conference site at Huairou in order to give a workshop," said Ms Friedan, who is in her 70s. Two veteran feminist firebrands were optimistic that the conferences would have a lasting effect on China.

"I think the Chinese who came here benefited a great deal and by word of mouth I would expect many more will, said Ms. Albzug, who is wheel chair-bound.

The conference ended with the approval of a document designed to advance the status of women worldwide. Some delegations disapproved of parts of the paper however, illustrating a divide between liberal Western nations and an unusual coalition of more conservative states, including Catholic and Islamic countries.

In the end, the dispute became a battle between the secular and the spiritual, with President Fujimori of Peru, in a seemingly direct challenge to the Vatican, saying "The Catholic Church is trying to prevent the Peruvian state from carrying out a modern and rational policy of family planning."

The Peruvian President, who said he had come to address the final session on the conference against the advice of my advisers, insisted that he was not making a call to create blocs of nations or States to rise against the Vatican."

There were signs of a wider conflict, however at least in Latin America, where countries like Ecuador, Argentina and El Salvador stood firmly by the Vatican.

The 150-page Platform for Action document that was finally agreed seemed to satisfy both the Catholic and Islamic world on the one side, and the permissive West on the other, by combining an acknowledgement.

The Chinese Government had moved the NGO forum to Huairou because it feared that the virus of free discussion might be uncontrollable if it took place in Beijing.

Since the Tiananmen Square massacre of June 1989, the Government has stamped at any sign of a demonstration.

The Times, London

17

RESERVATION FOR WOMEN IN PANCHAYAT BODIES

We hear about it in Mahabharata and Sukraneti Sara and also in Buddhist and Jain texts of 5th and 6th centuries. Krishna Deva Raya, the great Emperor of Vijayanagara mentions about his "Dharma Reethi" in his Amuckta Malyada and Madhava, one of the builders of Vijayanagara empire wrote a great treatise on Dharma Sastra called "Parasara Madhaveeyam".

Panchayats played a major role in the implementation of administration and also justice in ancient India, and our history tells us that Grama Panchayats were the bed-rocks for any developmental activity.

Panchayat class where highly respectable people elected by the villagers. Mahatma Gandhi speaking about Grama Swaraj and Panchayat Raj said.

"Our native ancient Institutions like Grama Panchayats should be revived. India is really a country of Republics. Ours is a country of self-ruled institutions."

Huyan-Tsang of China, the famous traveller of 18th century, wrote, highly appreciating our Panchayat Raj system and several historians have written books analysing this ancient system.

But, with the coming of Britishers into India, this system of decentralisation had been rooted out, with selfish motives.

After a certain lapse of time, it was difficult even for them to rule the country with the help of their English collectors. So, again the process of decentralisation had to be adopted for forming Municipalities, District Boards and Panchayat Boards. Nationalist movement sought democratic decentralisation "True democracy can not be run by 20 people sitting at the centre. It will be possible only when every village, from the bottoms is run by themselves" said Gandhiji in his "Future India".

After the exit of Britishers, our National Government was formed and our constitution clearly laid down certain ideology guaranteeing certain constitutional rights like equal opportunities, and social and economic and political justice for all.

For achieving these goals and ideals, some more effort is needed. As per the recommendations of Balwant Rai Mehta Committee, village level Panchayats, Taluq Development Smithies, district level Parishads have been formed and they are functioning well.

Women's Participations

Women are not to be treated as weaker segment of society or as passive beneficiaries, of the development process. Priorities and pace of development must have direct relevance to women's development. Every dimension of development has to assist their future. So as to improve the status of women and for all round development of society, it is necessary so as to improve the status of women and for all round development of society, of villages and also women as producers and providers and also as individuals with a right to live with human dignity. In a society, where caste, class and culture tend to discriminate people, renewal of effort would be meaningful only when the full potential of the silent half is harnessed.

For effective participation of women, more opportunities should be created, to realise their potentiality, which will enable them to build a bright tomorrow.

Women should be involved at all levels, in planning decision-making, policy-making and in implementations of all programmes. Awareness of their rights and responsibilities should be created among women, to assert themselves. A national action-plan should be prepared to bring about a change and it should be a meaningful change.

Rajiv Gandhi tried to bring about a major change in the mind set of people and encouraged $33\frac{1}{3}$ reservation of women in all Panchayat Raj bodies. He felt that time has come to put our commitment to certain ideals into action. For that sake, he made a beginning for a movement, a powerful movement.

Women in Governance

Reservation for women in public services was made by Govt. of Andhra Pradesh in exercise of the powers conferred by the provision to Article 309, read with clause (4) of Article 16 and Article 335 of the Constitution of India. Amendment to the AP state and subordinate service rules was made accordingly.

Government of Andhra Pradesh Abstract

Public services—Reservation for women in public services—Amendment to General Rule 22—A—orders issued.

General Administration (Services) Dept. Go Ms MO 928

dated 6.10.1995

Read the following

Notification

In exercise of the powers conferred by the provision to Article 309, read with clause (4) of Article 16 and Article 335 of the constitution of India. The Governor of Andhra Pradesh hereby makes the following amendment to the Andhra Pradesh state and subordinate service rules.

(2) the amendment hereby made shall be deemed to have come into force in so far as it relates to the reservations to the extent of 30% of pasts.

(*a*) with effect from the 2nd January 1984 to each category of OC, SC, ST and to the unclassified BCs and

(*b*) with effect from the 17th October 1990, to the categories of BCs and classified into groups, the physically handicapped are ex-servicemen quota.

Amendment

In the Andhra Pradesh state and subordiante services rules for sub-rule (2) of rule 22(A) the following shall be substituted namely.

2. in the matter of direct recruitment to parts for which women and men are equally suited there shall be reservation to women, to an extent of 30% of the parts in each category of OC, BC—A, BC—B, BC—C, BC—D, S.C., ST and physically handicapped and ex-servicemen quota.

Provided that if sufficient number of women condidates are not available, the vacancies shall be filled in by men".

Explanation

It is hereby clarified that all selection made in accordance with sub rule (2) prior its amendment shall be, deemed always to have been made in accordance with this rule : and shall not entitle any person to enforce 30% reservation merely on the ground that this amendment is made with retrospective effect".

(By order and in the name of Governor of Andhra Pradesh)

M.S. Rajajee

Chief Sec. to Government

Govt. of Andhra Pradesh Abstract

Public services—state and subordinate services—$33\frac{1}{3}\%$ Reservation for women in direct recruitment to public services—Fixation of Roster points reserved for women—orders—issued.

Women's Development and child welfare (Estt-I) Parliament GO, MS No. 41.

Dated 1.8.1996

Read the following

1. GO MS. No. 99 (ser. D) Dept dated 8.3.1996
2. GO MS No. 237, GA (ser. D) Dept dated 28.5.1996.

Order

In the GO first read above, orders were issued that in the matter of direct recruitment for posts for which women and men are equally suited, these shall be reservation to women to the extent of $33\frac{1}{3}\%$ of the posts in each category of OC, BC—A, BC-B, BC-C, B.C.D, SC, ST and physically handicapped and ex-service women quota and that if sufficient number of women candidates are not available, the vacancies shall be filled by men. In the G.O second read above an amendment to the rule 22—A of the Andhra Pradesh state and subordinate service rules has been issued to this effect.

2. The Government considered that for implementation of reservation for women in public services, it is imperative to fix roster points for women in the existing point roster provided for each category of scheduled castes, scheduled tribes backward class, in terms of General rule 22 of the Andhra Pradesh state and Subordinate Service rules. The reservation for women is in the nature of "compartmentalised horizontal reservation". To ensure this objective after careful consideration, it is decided to earmark the first vacancy in each vertical reservation category, including the general category *i.e.*, SC, ST, BC and OC categories and every subsequent third vacancy shall be filled in by women. Accordingly 5 point in SC, 2 points in STs, 2 points in BC group—A, 4 points, in B.C group—B, 2 points in BC group—D and 18 point in OCs are earmarked for women. It is also decided that BC—group C with only one point in 100 vacancies, the vacancy reserved in every third 100 points roster shall be given to women.

3. In pursuance of the above decision, a statement showing the existing roster points in each of the said categories, and the roster points fixed for women is annexed to this order.

4. All the recruitment agencies, under the Government and the Government undertakings, Quasi Government institutions included Government aided institutions and Local Bodies, whose services are governed by the Andhra Pradesh, state and subordinate service rules are directed to observe the roster points fixed for women. They should ensure that the reservation for women is reason for not filling the vacancy earmarked for women candidates before the vacancy is filled up by the men candidates. Any deviation or lapse in this regard will be viewed seriously.

5. Necessary amendments to the Andhra Pradesh and subordinate service rules will be issued separately.

(By order and in the name of Governor of Andhra Pradesh)

Rachel Chatterjee

Secretary to Government

Government of Andhra Pradesh Abstract

Public services—state and subordinate services $33\frac{1}{3}\%$ reservation for women—introduction of principles of carry forward implementing the reservation in a Government jobs for women on par with Scheduled Castes, Scheduled Tribes and backward classes—orders—issued.

Women's Development and Child Welfare (ESTT)

Department

GO MS No. 56 Dated 28.10.1996

1. GO MS. No. 99 G.A. (ser. D) Dept date 8.3.96
2. GO MS. No. 237 G.A. (ser. D) Dept date 28.5.96
3. GO MS. No. 41, W.D. & C.W. Dept date 1.8.96
4. From the commissioner, W.D. & C.W. Hyderabad Do Lr. No. 90 72/C1/96 date 22.6.96

Order

At present, the carry forward principles as incorporated in Rule 22 of the Andhra Pradesh state and subordinate service Rules are applicable in favour of Scheduled Castes, Scheduled Tribes and Backward Classes in respect of Government jobs.

Due Commissioners, Women's Development and Child Welfare, Hyderabad vide her. D.O. Lv. 4th read above has recommended for the carry forward in Government Jobs in favour of women on par with Scheduled Castes, Scheduled Tribes and Backward Classes.

Government, after careful consideration of the matter hereby decided to introduce the carry forward principles in favour of women in respect of reservations to the Government Jobs on par with Scheduled Castes, Scheduled Tribes and Backward Classes and other castes, with immediate effect.

(By order and in the name of the Governor of Andhra Pradesh)

Rachel Chatterjee

Secretary to Government

Govt of Andhra Pradesh Abstract

Public services—introduction of principle of carry forward system in respect of vacancies of Backward Classes (all) groups and women in implementing the reservation in Govt. Jobs on par with the Scheduled Castes and Scheduled Tribes in the matter of direct recruitment-amendment to rule 22nd and 22—A of the Andhra Pradesh state and subordinate service rules, 1996—orders—issued.

General Administration (ser—D) Department Go(P) no 65.
Dates 15th October 1997 read the following

Order

The followng notification will be published in AP Gazette.

Notification

In exercise of the papers confered by the proviso to Article 309 of the constitution of India and of all other powers here unto enabling the Governor of Andhra Pradesh hereby makes the following amendments of the Andhra Pradesh state and subordinate service rules.

Amendments

In the Andhra Pradesh State and Subordinate Service, Rules for rule 22 and rule 22(A), the following shall be substituted respectively.

Rule 22, Special Representation (Reservation)

1. Reservation may be made for appointments to a service class or category in favour of scheduled castes, women, physically handicapped meritorious sportsman, ex-servicemen and such other categories as may be prescribed by the Government from time to time to the extent and in the manner specified herein after in these rules or as the case may be in the special rules. The principle of reservation as herein after provided shall apply to all appointments to a service class or category.

(*i*) by direct recruitment, except where the Government by a General or special order made in the behalf exempt such service, class or category.

(*ii*) otherwise than by direct recruitment whose the special rules lay down specifically that the principle of reservation in so far as it relates to Scheduled Castes and Scheduled Tribes only shall apply to such service class or category to the extent specified therein.

2. (*a*) The unit of appointments for the purpose of this rule shall be one hundred vacancies of which fifteen shall be reserved for Scheduled Castes, six shall be reserved for Scheduled Tribes, twenty five shall be reserved for Backward Classes and the remaining fifty four appointments shall be made on the basis of open competition and subject to rule 22 A of these rules.

(*b*) Out of fifty four appointments to be made on the basis open competitions, three appointments shall be reserved for direct recruitment of the physically handicapped persons.

(*c*) in the case of appointments to clerical posts including the posts of typists *i.e.*, in group-II and group-IV Services and in the case of posts in the Andhra Pradesh Police Subordinate Service, to which the principle of reservation of appointments applies out of 54, as the case may be, 51 appointments to be made on the basis of often competition, two appointments shall be reserved for direct recruitment of ex-servicemen.

(*d*) in the case of appointments to the posts of senior Assistants. Jr. Assts, junior stenographers, typists and record Assistants in the offices of Heads of Departments, Assistants, Section Officers, Typists cum Assistants, Junior stenographers and record assistants in the secretariat to which the principle of reservation of appointments applies. Out of fifty four, as the case may be, Forty nine appointments to be made on the basis of open competition, one appointment shall be reserved for direct recruitment of meritorious sportsmen.

Provided that the claims of members of the Scheduled Castes, Scheduled Tribes, Backward Classes, Women and the physically handicapped persons, or ex-servicemen as the case may be, shall also be considered for the remaining appointments which shall be filled on the basis of open competition, the number of appointments reserved for that category, shall in no way be affected during the period of reservation for that category is in force.

(*e*) Appointments under the rule shall be made in the order of rotations in a hint of notation.

Note : 1. The principle of reservation for women candidates to the extent of 30% in the matter of direct recruitment shall be from 02.1. 1984 to 27.05. 1996.

2. The principle of reservation for women candidates to the extent of $33\frac{1}{3}\%$ in the matter of direct recruitment shall be with effect from 28.5. 1996.

(By order and in the name of Governor of Andhra Pradesh)

M.S. Rajajee

Chief Secretary to Government

Priority for Women in IAS, IPs Planned

Reiterating its commitment to ensuring the participation of women in governance through the smooth passage of the much-delayed Women's Reservation Bill, Govt. intends to make the Indian women and child development ministry, the nodal point for creating and maintaining a comprehensive disaggregated data base for quantitative and qualitative data.

According to the Eleventh Five Year Plan, Proactive efforts will be made to provide competitive exam training and prioritise recruitment of women to All India services, especially IAS and IPS services.

The purpose of maintaining a gender data would be to base new initiatives on facts and figures, assess the gender impact of programmes and assess the level of women's participation in planning and implementing programmes.

These will be simultaneous training and inputs for women in Panchayat Raj institutions, to enable them to influence gender-sensitive local planning and implemention. Gender disagregated data on the participation of women, especially in SCs/STs and minority women, in elected constitutional bodies, council of ministers and in over-all government sector will be collected and made available in the public domain. To tackle, the double discrimination faced by Muslim women, women and child dist ministry will formulate and implement a pilot scheme for "Leadership development for life, livelihood, and civic empowerment of minority women.

In the first phase, the scheme would be launched in five states with large minority population and is expected to reach

35,000 to 50,000 women directly and hundreds of thousands indirectly. One of the important tasks is to curtail the evil effects of television on women's lives through a gender-informed media policy.

Passage of the Women's Bill—Why Still a Distant Dream

Lack of political will is the main reason for the delay in passing the women's Bili. Another important factor is the financial status of the people wantering to be elected to the parliament, because only rich people are getting elected.

On top of everything, some of the MPs, a quarter, have either criminal charges against them and pending cases in courts. A study by the Public Affairs Centre, Bangalore on the 14th Lok Sabha (Times of India—23rd July 2008) throws a good deal of light on the actual composition of parliament. The interesting bit of the study is an analysis of the wealth of the MPs. This has become possible after the Supreme Court in 2002 ruling made it, mandatory for all the candidates who contest Lok Sabha to declare their assets.

The study says that on an average, an MP is worth 1.64 crores. If the Schedule Castes and Scheduled Tribes members are taken out, the figure rises to 2 crore. These is, of course, great variation in the wealth of individual members. Put the average assets of MPs of all major political parties are 1 crore and upward. Only the members of communist parties have assets well under one crore. This shows that by and large, only sich people are getting elected to Parliament.

We vote for our legislators into parliament but unfortunately we know very little about them. There is no process to cell them back. Parliament is a great levellor, where farmers, teachers, business tycoons, and scions of political dynasties sit next to each other. Behaviour of some is questionable, sometimes. Under these circustances, How can a woman, though well educated and intellectually competent can enter the parliament and participate in the deliberations feely and effectively, without great financial support behind. It is a costly affir to get elected to legislatures and more so for parliament.

When we want to judge Indian democracy and parliament, there is no comparison with the other developing countries.

Women's MPs in Lok Sabha

The number of women MPs in our Lok Sabha is as per this table enclosed.

No. of Women MPs

1952-57	⟶	22
1957-62	⟶	27
1962-67	⟶	34
1967-71	⟶	31
1971-77	⟶	22
1977-79	⟶	19
1980-84	⟶	28
1985-89	⟶	44
1989-91	⟶	27
1991-96	⟶	39
1996-98	⟶	39
1998-99	⟶	43
1999-2004	⟶	49
2004-2008	⟶	44

Ten years before, the member of women parliamentarians all over the world was only 13 percent.

Ruvanda stands first in the whole world. In the lower house, women elected were 56.3 percent there. Sweden stands second in the rank, with 47 per cent women representations. Revolutionary Cuba has 43.2 representation of women holding 3rd rank in the whole world. Finland, Holland, Argentina, Denmark, Angola, Costarica, Spain, Norway, Belgium, Mozambique, Newzealand, Iceland, Nepal and South Africa stand in Serial order. In Asia, among the top 20, Nepal only could find place as 16th member. In Latin American countries, representation of women in Assemblies is 26.5%.

The position of women in the great rich countries is alarming. Mother of all democracies, England has only 19.3%. In America, it is only 16.3% whereas in Italy, it is 16.1%. In Ireland, the percentage of women is 14.2% and in France, it is only 13.9%.

Indian women 'got right to vote' in 1920. But, it was confined to only women with economic level. In 1930, Smt. Malhutahshem Reddy entered into the assembly for the first time in the year 1930. In 1935, all women of India got right to vote as per the Indian Act. Later on, British provinces had 56 womens, only who entered Assemblies.

After serious discussions, constitution Amendments, No. 73 and 74, 33% reservation was made available to women in Gram Panchayats, Mandals, Zilla Parishads and Municipalities and other local institutions. Out of this number, 1/3 was reserved for SC and ST women. This came into practice after 1993. But, reservation for women in Lok Sabha and Assemblies has not obtained consent till now. Indicating a renewed effort at evolving consensus on the stalled Women's Reservation Bill Prime Minister, Manmohan Singh informed Rajya Sabha that he would convene an All Party meeting after the March 20 Parliament break.

Sri Somnath Chatterjee, Speaker of the 14th Parliament, bidding good bye to Parliament said "For him a great regret was the House not having been able to pass the Women's Reservation Bill, which would have gone a long way towards genuine and effective empowerment of 50 percent of the population". He also expressed the hope that all Parties would reach unanimity to evolve a clear consensus on the issue in the next Lok Sabha.

Many sittings and reports have spoken about the necessary of reservation of women and a great amount of awareness had been brought about in all sections of the people. This is a congenial atmosphere created by one and all consciously or unconsciously.

So, let us hope that a day would come when all women can feel proud and joyful for their achieving a forum for articulating their urges and aspirations and concerns.

"If women are allowed to be enlightened the world will appear in all its glory" says Markandey Katju, a judge of the Supreme Court of India.

"I would like to boycott such an assembly which has no proper representation for women" said Mahatma Gandhi.

Women Voters More in Number

In 6 states—Andhra Pradesh, Kerala, Manipur, Meghalaya, Mizoram and Puduchery, women voters are more in number. If political parties can select women for contesting for the elective bodies, it would be good for them and the political set up also. This will prove to be an experiment.

In 2004, women voters were 32.19 crores but by 2009, their number increased to 3406 crores. Women who are half of the population, must have the same number of women representatives. If democracies have to flourish well, this will be a major issue.

Though there are less number of women elected for the legislative bodies, there is considerable progress in education for women. In every Mandal Headquarter we are able of see schools and colleges for girls and scholarships and free education is offered. So, girds and their parents are feeling happy for achieving this progress.

In Arab countries, only 9 per cent of women on an average could go to Parliament. But in a country like ours, the same level of representation is these on par with Arabs, which is a serious matter. In Pacific countries, only 4 per cent of representation is these for women, which is to be taken seriously.

Fighting Gender Equality

As the manager of the Home and our culture, a woman is on ceaseless quest for giving a meaning to life. So, what a needed is not an agitation. Demands of our times are such that women should rise above petty differences and stand against inequality. Hindu date 15th December has pointed out in the Editorial that "The Bill will not and cannot do to achieve goal of gender equity it can only help in breaking new ground in this directions".

After 1960, there has emerged a group of strong women's views; those writers have started writing in terms of complex culture; a search for real self has created transforming values and rewriting about new ideology and values.

Conclusion

Our main purpose is to empower women to fight all social injustices and make her sufficiently competent to bring about social change in the near future.

18

SUMMING UP

We have to go a Long way

Indicating a renewed effort at evolving consensus on the stalled Women's Reservation Bill, Prime Minister Sri Man Mohan Singh said in Rajya Sabha that he would convene an all party meeting.

Responding to a strong plea by Ms Brinda Karat and Sri Seetharam Yachury CPI(M) Dr. Man Mohan Singh said "I will go back to the political parties and seek a consensus".

Ms Karat pointed out that unless the Bill was passed, there was no chance of women getting reservations in the next elections to the Parliament and the State Assemblies. In her own words, her statement is as follows. "The Government will be held solely responsible for the Bill not setting through". Giving support to her statement, Mr. Yechury urged the Prime Minister to give a categorical assurance of the Govts. interest on the issue."

Days rolled on. To achieve consensus, a parliamentary committee was formed with Sir EM Sudarsan, Nachiapparn, a Senior Congress MP from Rajasthan as Chairman and was intrusted with the responsibility of studying pros and cons of the women's Bill. Its term was completed and so Nachiappan requested in writing Sri Hamid Ansari, Chairman of Rajya Sabha, to extend the term of the committee, saying that the committee members were wanting more time to study the bill because several political parties were opposing the Bill in its present form. They are proposing to introduce the Bill and bring out its constitutional amendment. They are suggesting to give power to decide about the quota to the states women and to give place to women of the backward and oppressed communities in the women's quota. They brought about this compromise formula after discussing with several political parties and voluntary organisations.

The committee members toured all the states and met the concerned people to gather their opinion.

They Visited Hyderabad also and met women's organisations in the matter and women gave their opinion about the Bill.

Representatives of 22 women's organisations met the Vice-President and Rajya Sabha Chairman Hamad Ansari on 12.2.09 and he assured women's organisations that the Central Government would take note of the grounds well of opinion in favour of requiring one third reservation for women in Parliament and state legislatures.

The delegation of women's groups met Sri Somnath Chatterjee and asked him to intervene to ensure the passage of the bill; without further delay. The respresentatives also met parliamentary standing committee Chairman Sri Nachiappan and requested him to preserve the bill and to immediately table its recommendations before Parliament. They asked him to ensure proper debate on the 108th Constitutional Amendment Bill and its passage without any dilution of its provisions during the 12th session of Parliament. 500 women gathered assembled for the domonstration at Parliament street. The delegation criticised both the National democratic alliance and the United Progressive Alliance for keeping the Bill pending in the name of "consensus".

The groups included the All India Democratic Women's Associations, the Badhuwa Mukti Morcha, the Samata. The Centre for Women's Development Studies, the Guild of Services, The joint Women's programme, Mata Sundari college, the Muslim Women's Forum, the National Federation of Indian Women, Nirmala Niketan, Prayatan, Swasthik Mahila, Wada Na Todo, World Council, Arya Samaj, the Young Women's Christian Association.

I think all this past history and chronology of events would provide a base for us from which we can face new challenges of 21st century and work for changes from time to time. I am not one of those who believes that we, coming out from an old era, simply to welcome new novel ideas of course, we keep changing but we have to maintain continuity to suit to the changing conditions.

Talking about the ideal of women's emencipation, justice Markandeya Katju, judge of the Supreme Court of India, says "If women are allowed to be enlightened the world will appear in all its glory". He feels that "Indian Society is still largely male-dominated and most women do not have real freedom. A cultural struggle is needed to sweep away the feudal and medieval mentality from which such a situation arises". Birth of a female child's regarded as a disaster. From the day of her birth, a girl is viewed as a burden and a liability. The desire for having sons determines both the quality and quantity of investment that parents make in their female children. This social acceptance of the girl's neglect is understandable when we consider the demand of the basic rights begins within the four walls of her own home. This discimination is born out of certain cultural and religious values. So a movement is to be built up.

In spite of so much of discrimination a girl is proving her metle and praying multiple roles in family as a mother, as a wife and as a maker of a new generation very successfully. Girls are stinning in every walk of life on account of her brilliance, and we hear of chaos of large companies, judges, rulers and some in top positions. We have heard of Mandana Misra's wife, who mediated between Misra and Sankaracharya very, efficiently and impartially. Such intelligence can be effectively used for the welfare of society, when once our rulers recognise women's power of participation and judgement our ancestors said that a women should discharge her duties as "Karyeshu Dasi, Karaneshu Mantri that "Sayaneshu Rambha, Kshamaya Dharithri." They felt with her tact, tolerance and sixth sense, a woman would be able to play her role by herself.

Greatmen like Raja Ram Mohan Ray our Veereshalingam Pantulu, Maharshi Karve and others have worked for the emancipation of women in India and it has been accepted that their attempts did not go waste, and they had influenced the lives and thinking of people in India to a great extent.

Gandhians concept of development and women's equality, has changed the focus from "women's development" to "women in development". Society has to be sensitised on gender and not on sex. We need a redefination of our ethos and approach for women's development.

An overview of society leads us to the conclusion that a women's role is very unusual, in the present context of modernism when compared to the past times change is inevitable. It is entering in, as a gush of wind, though some are not willing to invite it. Even before, human minds are ready to receive change, it is coming as a necessity. We cannot throw away certain ideas that it is a feminist argument. It is in the interest of the family that a women is given recognition and it is also in the larger interest and development of society that a women is made economically and socially free to play her role.

There are no problems concerning women only. They are all social problems.

There must be the will to take up the great deal of changing ideals into positive attitudes.

Anthropologists have indicated how the value of women is often determined by their economic roles in society. Miller's study (1978) shows a marked difference in the value placed on female children in both western and southern India. Miller correlates the low mortality rate of female children in the wet price aggriculture of the region. If should be noted that in the wheat growing area of the north, there is little need for female labour and female babies are considered a lialility.

Though the working woman is able to adjust within the family fold social values are not able to give her, her due place in the affairs of the society or the family.

Freedom does not mean conpetition with men. It is a state of mind, where in a women can work with ease and confidence and without any exploitation.

"Blessed the God, who made me a man and not a woman". Thus runs a Hebrew prayer. A time has comes when we have to prove that blessed the God, who created women, to make man's life fuller and richer."

INDEX

G

H

I

N

O

P